Returning to the Gospel

The Message of Jude for the African Church

Emmanuel Kwasi Amoafo

© 2025 Emmanuel Kwasi Amoafo

Published 2025 by Langham Academic
An imprint of Langham Publishing
www.langhampublishing.org

Langham Publishing and its imprints are a ministry of Langham Partnership

Langham Partnership
PO Box 296, Carlisle, Cumbria, CA3 9WZ, UK
www.langham.org

ISBNs:
978-1-78641-046-7 Print
978-1-78641-305-5 ePub
978-1-78641-306-2 PDF
DOI: https://doi.org/10.69811/9781786410467

Emmanuel Kwasi Amoafo has asserted his right under the Copyright, Designs and Patents Act, 1988 to be identified as the Author of this work.

All rights reserved. No part of this publication may be reproduced, stored in a retrieval system or transmitted, in any form or by any means, electronic, mechanical, photocopying, recording or otherwise, without the prior written permission of the publisher or the Copyright Licensing Agency.

Requests to reuse content from Langham Publishing are processed through PLSclear. Please visit www.plsclear.com to complete your request.

All Scripture quotations, unless otherwise indicated, are taken from the Holy Bible, New International Version®, NIV®. Copyright ©1973, 1978, 1984, 2011 by Biblica, Inc.™ Used by permission of Zondervan.

Scripture quotations marked (ESV) are from The Holy Bible, English Standard Version® (ESV®), copyright © 2001 by Crossway, a publishing ministry of Good News Publishers. Used by permission. All rights reserved.

British Library Cataloguing-in-Publication Data
A catalogue record for this book is available from the British Library

ISBN: 978-1-78641-046-7

Cover & Book Design: projectluz.com

Langham Partnership actively supports theological dialogue and an author's right to publish but does not necessarily endorse the views and opinions set forth here or in works referenced within this publication, nor can we guarantee technical and grammatical correctness. Langham Partnership does not accept any responsibility or liability to persons or property as a consequence of the reading, use or interpretation of its published content.

The call of Jude to "contend for the faith" is one of those eternal imperatives in Scripture that cannot be ignored. It is as legitimate for us today as it was back then. Amoafo's dissertation is a timely work of contemporary relevance. We must be grateful for this prophetic and timely study.

J. Kwabena Asamoah-Gyadu, PhD
Presiding Bishop, Methodist Church Ghana
Immediate Past President,
Trinity Theological Seminary, Legon, Ghana

African Christianity, and indeed all of global Christianity, needs the penetrating insights from Dr. Emmanuel Kwasi Amoafo. His reading of the epistle of Jude redirects us to look at the fundamentals of the faith, and to examine ways in which we need major reformation. Scholars, pastors, and all followers of Jesus Christ are indebted to him for the diligence and pastoral heart that went into this dissertation.

Casely Baiden Essamuah, DTh
Secretary, Global Christian Forum

Dr. Amoafo offers in this book not only an excellent exegesis of the book of Jude, but also a careful application to African problems. This book offers a stellar model of how to hear Scripture transformatively today, useful to both church leaders and scholars.

Craig S. Keener, PhD
F. M. and Ada Thompson Professor of Biblical Studies,
Asbury Theological Seminary, Kentucky, USA

Across the face of the earth today, there is a hunger for spiritual reality that supersedes one's physical limitations. This is not a new quest but one that has motivated people's exploration for millennia. There have been individuals and institutions ready to offer attractive philosophies and unlimited experiences to gratify the pursuit. The problem is that these encounters can capture and destroy one's mind, emotions, and spirit. Amoafo examines a biblical scenario that mirrors this present-day craving, exposes the potential traps, and proposes the way to encounter the God of the Bible and experience supernatural gifts while remaining grounded in and safeguarded by biblical truth.

Douglas P. Lowenberg, PhD
Executive Director,
Association for Pentecostal Theological Education in Africa, Ethiopia

For over twenty years, I have had the privilege of engaging with Dr. Amoafo, a dedicated Bible scholar and gifted educator committed to biblical authenticity. His thesis highlights the often-overlooked message in the book of Jude. In a world where people pursue material success at all cost, and many are misled by the unfulfilled promises of various "gospels," Jude's call to defend the faith once delivered to the saints is more crucial today than ever. This message is significant for believers in Africa and beyond, especially as modern secular ideologies erode core Christian principles. Understanding the essence of the gospel is essential for followers of Jesus to be fruitful in today's complex world with multiple voices speaking to us daily.

Dennis Tongoi, DTh
Director Emeritus, CMS-Africa

This dissertation is dedicated to the memory of Dr. Byang Kato, the outstanding and inspiring African Christian leader of an earlier generation, who blazed the trail of contending in Africa for the faith once for all delivered to the saints. In his brief years in this world, Dr. Kato fought tirelessly and bravely for the cause of biblical Christianity in Africa to ensure that African Christians become, first and foremost, Christian Africans. May the Lord continue to use Dr. Kato's work to restore to the church in Africa today the apostolic faith of the early New Testament church that turned its world upside down (Acts 17:6).

Contents

Abstract xiii

Acknowledgements xv

Abbreviations xix

Chapter 1 1
   Introduction and Statement of Problem
      Introduction 1
      Background to the Study 1
      Purpose of the Study 5
      Statement of the Problem 5
      Methodology 5
      Research Questions 6
      Research Question 1 6
      Research Question 2 6
      Research Question 3 7
      Significance of the Study 7
      Delimitations and Limitations 7
      Key Terms 8
          Biblical Christianity 8
          Pentecostals/Pentecostalism 8
          Charismatics/Charismatic Beliefs 9
          Syncretism 9
          Contextualization 9
          Worldview 10
          Christo-Paganism 10
          Over-Realized Eschatology 10

Chapter 2 11
   Biblical-Theological Review of Jude
      Introduction 11
      Historical Context 11
          Author 11
          Date 12
          Recipients 12
          Social and Religious Background 13

Literary Context	14
Genre	14
Language	14
Use of Apocryphal Books	15
Similarity with 2 Peter	16
Canonicity	17
Importance	17
Form and Structure	18
Theological Context	18
The Trinity	18
Christology	19
Ecclesiology	19
Eschatology	20
Exegesis	20
Methodology	20
The Seven Biblical Principles Drawn from the Text	21
Greeting (Jude 1–2)	22
Reason for Writing (Jude 3–4)	23
The Apostates and Their Judgment by God (Jude 5–16)	27
Contending for the Faith (Jude 17–23)	35
Doxology (Jude 24–25)	40
Hermeneutics	41
Methodology	41
Jude's Meaning	41
Principles of Biblical Christianity	43
Implicit Principles of Biblical Christianity	43
Explicit Principles of Biblical Christianity	44
Summary	45
Chapter 3	**47**
Social Science Literature	
Introduction	47
GPCC Development and Growth	48
Religious Factors	48
Socio-Economic and Political Factors	56
GPCC Profile	59
Action Faith Ministries International	59
International Central Gospel Church	60
Lighthouse Chapel International	61
Perez Chapel International	62
Global Revival Ministries	63

    GPCC Theology and Praxis 64
        Theology 65
    Praxis 70
        GPCC Ecclesiology 70
    Summary 76

Chapter 4 77
    Methodology
    Introduction 77
    Overview of Exegetical Study 77
    The Nature of this Study 78
    Research Questions 1, 1A, and 1B 79
    Exegetical Study 79
    Research Questions 2, 2A, and 2B 80
    Integrative Critical Analysis 80
    Research Questions 3, 3A, and 3B 81
    Q Methodology 81
    Validity and Reliability 83
    Research Ethics and Informed Consent Protocol 84
    Summary 85

Chapter 5 87
    Results and Analysis
    Introduction 87
    Findings 88
        Research Questions 1, 1A, and 1B 88
        RQ2, RQ2A, and RQ2B 88
        RQ3, RQ3A, and RQ3B 91
        Q-Sort Data for Addressing Research Question 3B 91
    Analysis: GPCC Theology and Praxis 111
        The Prosperity Doctrine 112
        Deliverance from Witchcraft 116
        The Man of God 118
    Summary 119

Chapter 6 119
    Conclusions and Recommendations
    Introduction 119
    Addressing the Research Questions 119
        Research Questions 1, 1A, and 1B 119
        Research Questions 2, 2A, and 2B 120
        Research Questions 3, 3A, and 3B 120

Answering the Problem Statement 120
Implications: GPCC Theology and Praxis 121
    GPCC Syncretism 121
    GPCC Christo-Paganism..122
    Implications of GPCC Syncretism and Christo-Paganism 124
    Religious Implications..124
    Socio-Economic Implications 126
    Political Implications..126
Recommendations for Change: Applying Jude's Principles of
    Biblical Christianity..127
    Principle No. 1..127
    Principle No. 2..128
    Principle No. 3..131
    Principle No. 4..132
    Principle No. 5..134
    Principle No. 6..134
    Principle No. 7..135
Recommendations for Further Study 137
    Restoring Pentecostal Imperatives in the GPCC 138
    Addressing Syncretism and Christo-Paganism in the GPCC 139
    Establishing Contextual Biblical Training for GPCC Leaders.....141
Summary..144

Appendix A 145
    Q Methodology Data of the GPCC Sorts

Appendix B.. 175
    Q Methodology Data of the Jude Sort

Bibliography 203

List of Tables

Table 1. Implicit principles of biblical Christianity suggested by the text 44

Table 2. Explicit principles of biblical Christianity suggested by the text 45

Table 3. Similarities and differences between GPCC theology and praxis and Jude's principles of biblical Christianity 90

Table 4. The thirty-five statements sorted by the GPCC leaders 97

Table 5. The two ends of Factor 1: Assent to Jude's principles and NT orthodoxy 98

Table 6. Further demonstration of assent to Jude's principles and NT orthodoxy 100

Table 7. Subfactor A 101

Table 8. Subfactor B 102

Table 9. Eigenvalues and percentage of variation with the Jude sort added 105

Table 10. The two ends of the Jude sort 106

Table 11. The different ranking of statements by the GPCC and Jude sorts 107

Table 12. Further evidence of differences between the GPCC and Jude sorts 109

List of Figures

Figure 1. The scatterplot 94

Figure 2. Grid showing the composite GPCC sort 96

Figure 3. The scatterplot without the Jude sort 105

Figure 4. Grid showing the Jude sort 106

Abstract

The purpose of this study is to identify principles of biblical Christianity from an exegetical study of Jude's epistle that can act as guidelines for advocating contextualized biblical Christianity in the five leading autonomous Pentecostal-Charismatic churches in Ghana.

In the introductory first chapter, a submission is made of the background and purpose of the study, the statement of the problem, the study's research questions, and the significance of the study. In the second chapter, the study's exegetical study of Jude's message concludes that Jude's call to his readers "to contend for the faith once for all delivered to the saints" (Jude 3) meant upholding, preserving, and persevering in seven principles of biblical Christianity, identified by the study's analysis of the text. The third chapter examines what the social science literature reveals about the religious, socio-economic, and political factors that led to the establishment and growth of the five Ghanaian churches. It also examines the current theology and practices of these five churches. The fourth chapter submits the study's methodological framework, the fifth chapter presents and analyses the results obtained from the research data, and the sixth chapter submits the study's conclusions and recommendations for praxis change and additional research.

By relating the essence of Jude's message to the current theology and praxis of these five Ghanaian churches, the overriding aim of this study is to see the churches spiritually strengthened as they apply the principles of biblical Christianity the study has identified from Jude's epistle in their various contexts.

Acknowledgements

This study must have first been conceived in the heart of God and implanted in my mind by his Holy Spirit because of the palpable sense of his continuous grace and mercy that have guided and provided all the resources that have been required for every step of researching and writing the study. It is to almighty God, therefore, that overall credit must be given for this study.

Without the blessing, love, support, and encouragement of my dear wife Esther, completing this study would have been an uphill battle. My children—Kwame Anthony, Kwame Nkrumah, Yaa Henrika, Abena, and Kofi—did not begrudge me the time I had to be away from them both physically and emotionally on this study journey. I thank the Lord for their prayers, love, encouragement, and understanding.

The prayers and financial support of my local church community have been indispensable in bringing this study this far. The ACK Christ Church leadership and congregation, my fellow Fenesi Directors, the Fenesi Men's Bible Study Fellowship, the leadership of the Butere Diocese, the congregation of the Muthaiga Christian Fellowship, and many others still, all gave willingly of their resources to provide all the financial support that was required on this journey. I particularly thank David Gatende for his committed financial support over many years, and Terry Davidson for his generous and ready financial support.

My brother William, his wife Melvina, and their children opened to me both their hearts and their home with great affection on the various occasions I traveled through Accra en route to Lomé to attend the PAThS classroom sessions. I am also very thankful to my sister Monica who contributed her prayer support and her culinary skills to ensure that my every visit to Ghana was a memorable one. I thank them sincerely for their very warm and genuine hospitality.

Rev. Dr. Lt. Col. Vincent Setsoafia and his wife Akosua hosted me with an unforgettable demonstration of the love of God during my research data collection trip to Ghana in October 2017. Without Dr. Setsoafia's guidance, exemplary encouragement, and inspiring support with using the dedicated software PQMethod to collect and analyse my empirical research data, it is no exaggeration to say that I would probably not have been able to use that research tool and methodology at all. I owe them a real debt of gratitude for their heartfelt love and assistance.

I am very grateful to Rev. Dr. Robert Ampiah-Kwofi of GRM and the other leaders of the five churches highlighted in this study who provided me with access to their churches, their pastors, and their congregations to enable me to carry out this study's empirical research. May the Lord use the insights in this study to help them all to contend for the faith once for all delivered to the saints.

My deepest appreciation goes to the entire PAThS faculty for their prayers, their dedication, their godly mentoring, their unwavering encouragement, and their very genuine commitment to shepherding me through this dissertation journey. My dissertation supervisor, Dr. Douglas Lowenberg; the provost, Dr. Bill Kirsch; the dissertation coordinator, Dr. Chuck Wilson; the institutional editor, Rev. Beth Lord; and all the lecturers who taught the various PAThS courses have all played indispensable superintending roles in the writing and completion of this dissertation.

I particularly thank Dr. Bob Braswell, the PAThS Dean of Research, a world-renowned expert in Q Methodology, who went beyond the call of duty, even during a bout of serious illness, to work patiently, perseveringly, and gently with me over several months through the intricacies of Q Methodology. Dr. Braswell's mentoring aimed to ensure that my Q-Sort report would be of doctoral quality to stand up to scrutiny anywhere. Only the Lord himself can sufficiently reward him for this.

Without the IT expertise of Fredrick Awinyo, who committed himself to helping me with the distressing and perplexing formatting challenges that frequently cropped up during the writing, this dissertation would certainly not have passed the test of the PAThS form and style guidelines. I am indebted to Fred without measure for all his ready assistance throughout the duration of my writing.

The friendship, support, and prayers of the 2013 PAThS cohort, of which I am a fortunate member, cannot go unmentioned. My dear fellow cohort members have been faithful travel companions on this dissertation journey. The Lord did not put us together in vain. I especially thank Rev. Abraham Obeng-Amoako who faithfully and kindly drove us to and from Lomé and Accra to attend the PAThS Lomé classroom sessions.

The whole village raises the African child, as the old saying goes. Everyone mentioned above, and many others not mentioned, have been part of the village that has nurtured, raised, and supported this dissertation to bring it to its current completed form. May the Lord richly bless you all!

Abbreviations

ATR	African Traditional Religion
EAR	East Africa Revival
ESV	English Standard Version
GDP	Gross Domestic Product
GNB	Good News Bible
GPCC	Ghana Pentecostal-Charismatic Churches
KJV	King James Version
TLB	The Living Bible
NIV	New International Version
NKJV	New King James Version
NLT	New Living Translation
NT	New Testament
OT	Old Testament

CHAPTER 1

Introduction and Statement of Problem

Introduction

The full title of this study is *Contending for the Faith in the African Context: An Exegesis of Jude in Relation to Theology and Praxis in Ghana*. The study presents an exegesis of the Greek text of the Epistle of Jude. In this epistle, written to a Christian congregation in the first century, Jude addresses departures from biblical Christianity that are a result of the influence of false teachers who had infiltrated the congregation. Jude exhorts this congregation to contend for, and to persevere in biblical Christianity, which he describes as "the faith that was once for all entrusted to the saints" (Jude 3 NET Bible).

The aim of this study is to identify principles of biblical Christianity from Jude's epistle that can act as guidelines for advocating contextualized biblical Christianity in the five leading autonomous Pentecostal-Charismatic churches in Ghana that are identified below in the background to this study.

Background to the Study

The reality of the phenomenal growth of Christianity in Africa in the last few decades has been well chronicled by both scholars and social scientists. The African scholar Lamin Sanneh, for example, has used convincing statistics on the growth of Christianity in Africa to support his assertion that the facts about the expansion of Christianity in Africa are little in dispute.[1] Social

---

1. Sanneh, *Whose Religion Is Christianity?*, 14.

scientist Philip Jenkins has offered equally compelling statistical and demographic evidence to support his claim that "over the last century the center of gravity in the Christian world has and will continue to shift inexorably southward, particularly to Africa."[2]

A notable characteristic of this expansion of Christianity in Africa is that most of this growth has been in the Pentecostal and Charismatic denominations of the faith as distinct from the various forms of missions Christianity introduced into Africa by Western missionaries in the nineteenth and early twentieth centuries. Ogbu Kalu has described this phenomenon as "the explosion of Pentecostalism in Africa."[3] Sanneh remarked that the dramatic growth in Pentecostal and Charismatic Christianity is "largely responsible for the current shift in Christianity's center of gravity from the North to the South."[4]

Allan Anderson has defined Pentecostalism as a form of Christianity that is characterized by "an ecstatic *experience of the Spirit* and a tangible *practice of spiritual gifts*."[5] He notes that in its growth around the world, Pentecostalism has adapted itself to different cultural contexts.[6] Jenkins concurs with this view, noting that Pentecostalism frequently adapts "Christian belief to local custom."[7] Birgit Meyer has observed that "by its very nature, Pentecostalism lends itself to being recast over and over in new forms; at the same time, however, these forms are similar enough to present themselves as Pentecostal or as Charismatic."[8] These observations are particularly true of the Pentecostal movement in Africa where most Pentecostal and Charismatic churches have indigenous origins and are decidedly African in nature and expression. Anderson notes that "the largest Pentecostal churches in the world today are found in sub-Saharan Africa, Latin America, and on the eastern rim of Asia from Indonesia to Korea."[9] In his foreword to Kwabena Asamoah-Gyadu's book, *Sighs and Signs of the Spirit*, Martin Lindhardt observes that "Pentecostalism is first and foremost a religious and spirit-centered movement

---

2. Jenkins, *Next Christendom*, 3.
3. Kalu, *African Pentecostalism*, 169.
4. Sanneh, *Disciples of All Nations*, 275.
5. Anderson, *To the Ends of the Earth*, 8. Emphasis original.
6. Anderson, 2.
7. Jenkins, *Next Christendom*, 8.
8. Meyer, "Praise the Lord," 96.
9. Anderson, *To the Ends of the Earth*, 2.

that appeals to Africans because it offers a particular kind of religiosity, most notably the experience of the power of the Holy Spirit."[10]

Ghana is one of the sub-Saharan African countries in which some of these large Pentecostal churches have taken firm root. With almost 65 percent of the Ghanaian population estimated to be Christian,[11] a disproportionate number of these Christians identify themselves as Pentecostals.[12]

Kwabena Asamoah-Gyadu has defined Ghanaian Pentecostals as:

> Christian groups which emphasize salvation in Christ as a transformative experience wrought by the Holy Spirit and in which pneumatic phenomena including speaking in tongues, prophecies, visions, healing and miracles in general, perceived as standing in historic continuity with the experiences of the early church as found especially in the Acts of the Apostles, are sought, accepted, valued, and consciously encouraged among members as signifying the presence of God and experiences of his Spirit.[13]

Asamoah-Gyadu notes that the largest and best-known Pentecostal churches in Ghana today are African independent churches that belong to the neo-Pentecostal and neo-Charismatic movement that emerged in the late 1970s. Stanley Burgess has explained that the terms neo-Pentecostal and neo-Charismatic have been used by scholars in recent years to denote Christian groups "with Pentecostal-like experiences that have no traditional Pentecostal or charismatic denominational connections" and whose greatest concentrations of strength today are in "the prophetic African independent churches, in Asia—especially the house-church movement in China—and in Latin American countries, especially Brazil."[14] Paul Gifford has noted that one of the most striking features of the development of Ghanaian Christianity in the last three decades "has been the proliferation of [these] new autonomous Pentecostal churches."[15] He observes that "the word 'charismatic' is used

---

10. Lindhardt, *Sighs and Signs*, xv.
11. "Ghana," *Joshua Project*, https://joshuaproject.net/countries/GH.
12. Larbi, "Nature of Continuity and Discontinuity."
13. Asamoah-Gyadu, *African Charismatics*, 12.
14. Burgess, "Neo-Charismatics," 928.
15. Gifford, "Ghana's Charismatic Churches," *Journal of Religion in Africa* 24 (1994): 241.

of these, to distinguish them from the churches of established Pentecostal denominations like the Assemblies of God."[16]

The five pioneering and leading Pentecostal-Charismatic churches in this movement in Ghana are: Action Faith Ministries International, International Central Gospel Church, Lighthouse Chapel International, Perez Chapel International, and Global Revival Ministries. Gifford argues that these Pentecostal churches "are an increasingly important sector of Ghanaian Christianity."[17] Birgit Meyer agrees that these churches "have become central factors in the country's public culture."[18] She describes these churches as being multi-ethnic, transnational, and mostly located in the urban areas of the country, where they mainly seek to attract upwardly mobile younger men and women.[19] Asamoah-Gyadu observes that, since their ascendancy, the theology and practices of these new autonomous and fast-growing Pentecostal-Charismatic churches have had far-ranging effects on Christianity as a whole in Ghana.[20]

In his seminal study of Pentecostal churches in Ghana, Gifford concluded that these new autonomous Pentecostal and Charismatic congregations and their leaders are far more focused on material success, health, wealth, and deliverance from witchcraft than on Christian spiritual formation and discipleship.[21] He has described this deviation from Christian spiritual formation and discipleship as being "perhaps Ghanaian Christianity's most pressing issue."[22] Asamoah-Gyadu, in his more recent study of these churches, has confirmed that this is still the case by noting that their "spirituality and teachings fall short of biblical and theological standards."[23]

These observations by scholars who have dedicated considerable time and effort to studying these new autonomous Ghanaian Pentecostal and Charismatic churches imply troubling departures from biblical Christianity

---

16. Gifford, 241.
17. Gifford, 241.
18. Meyer, "Pentecostalism and Neo-Liberal Capitalism," *Journal for the Study of Religion* 20 (2007): 13.
19. Meyer, 13.
20. Asamoah-Gyadu, *African Charismatics*, 60–63.
21. Gifford, *Ghana's New Christianity*, 60–62.
22. Gifford, *African Christianity*, 108.
23. Asamoah-Gyadu, *Sighs and Signs*, xi.

on the part of these churches. It is in this regard that the theology and practices of the five leading Ghanaian Pentecostal-Charismatic churches identified above have been highlighted and examined in this study. In this study these churches will henceforth be collectively referred to as the Ghana Pentecostal-Charismatic Church or with the acronym GPCC – not to be confused with the acronym of the Ghana Pentecostal Charismatic Council.

Purpose of the Study

The purpose of this study is to identify principles of biblical Christianity from an exegetical study of Jude's epistle that acts as a guideline for advocating contextualized biblical Christianity in the GPCC. This research seeks to discover what the Spirit is saying through Jude's text that can speak today to the context of the GPCC as they confront theological challenges that may very well be similar to those faced by the church in Jude's day.

Statement of the Problem

The problem statement of this study, therefore, is this: From an evangelical and Pentecostal understanding of Jude's epistle, how should Ghanaian Pentecostal-Charismatic Christians, in demonstrating biblical Christianity in their theology and praxis, "contend for the faith that was once for all delivered to the saints" (Jude 3 ESV)?

Methodology

This study is primarily exegetical in nature, supplemented by social science literature and field research pertaining to the views and teaching of GPCC leaders. The exegesis of Jude's epistle has taken note of the epistle's historical context and examined its textual critical issues with a view to relating the essence of Jude's inspired message to the current context of the GPCC. The research's exegetical analysis has interacted with the insights of various scholars in order to identify how the church has historically interpreted this text and elicit from the text clear principles of biblical Christianity in line with Jude's meaning. The exegetical work has drawn heavily on the work of Richard Bauckham, whose scholarly yet readable commentary on Jude presents a widely respected and much-referenced detailed analysis of textual, linguistic, structural, and theological issues related to the epistle.[24]

Research findings from a Q-Sort analysis have been used to identify and understand the shared perceptions of GPCC leaders as concerns their theology and practices. These shared perceptions have then been reviewed in the light of Jude's principles of biblical Christianity.

Research Questions

The following three research questions arose out of the statement of the problem.

Research Question 1

1. What principles of biblical Christianity emerge from an exegetical study of the Greek text of the epistle of Jude?
    - A: What is Jude's meaning of the key phrase, "contending for the faith once for all delivered to the saints" in relation to the teaching of the false teachers?
    - B: What accepted evangelical interpretations have arisen from various scholars' exegesis of Jude?

Research Question 2

2. What does the social science literature reveal about the origins, the development, the theology, and the practices of the five leading autonomous Pentecostal-Charismatic churches in Ghana?
    - A: What does the social science literature reveal about the religious, socio-economic, and political factors that led to the establishment of the GPCC?
    - B: What does the social science literature reveal about the theology and practices of the GPCC?

---

24. Bauckham, *Jude–2 Peter*, 1.

Research Question 3

3. What does GPCC leaders' own output reveal about their theology and practices?
   - A: What does the content of GPCC leaders' teachings and writings reveal about their theology and practices?
   - B: What do GPCC leaders' own points of view reveal about their theology and practices?

Significance of the Study

One significance of this study is that its identification of Jude's principles of biblical Christianity can encourage and empower Ghanaian Pentecostal-Charismatic ministers to exemplify and more vigorously defend in their ministries "the faith that was once for all delivered to the saints" (Jude 3). Another significance of this study is that it can spur the GPCC to conform its faith and practices to the *missio Dei* imperatives of biblical Christianity and motivate these churches to engage more actively in the mission of God in Ghana, where there are still a number of unreached people groups.

Delimitations and Limitations

This study has focused primarily on the five Pentecostal-Charismatic churches in Ghana identified above because of limited time and limited financial resources. Also, as has been observed from this study's subsequent review of the social science literature, the theology and practices of these five churches have had a defining influence on the Pentecostal-Charismatic movement in Ghana as a whole.

The purpose of the exegetical study of Jude was not to offer a new or innovative interpretation of Jude. It was, instead, to present a convincing interaction with the text that satisfactorily addresses research questions 1, 1A, and 1B. This study has therefore referred minimally to textual variants, grammatical forms, syntactical constructions, extended meanings of Greek words, and problems of translation in the text except where Jude's essential meaning was affected. It has also not included a detailed discussion of redaction, genre, sources, and Jude's extra-biblical contexts because this study limited itself to what is considered to be the final form of the text as traditionally accepted by the Christian church throughout the centuries.

This study has discussed Jude's meaning and intention within the context of the book itself and its theological relevance to this study's research questions. It has adopted a mirror reading of the text, investigating in broad terms the teaching and behaviour of the false teachers who contradicted what Jude refers to as "the faith." It has considered what the false teachers were teaching and doing that was of such great concern to Jude and how this, in Jude's understanding, posed such a danger to the church then and now.

The first reason for these delimitations is that detailed and technical examinations of Jude's composition, interpretive issues, and idiomatic use of Greek words, phrases, and tenses have already been undertaken by accomplished scholars. This study has thus reviewed how the church has interpreted this book historically and what accepted evangelical views have arisen from the exegesis of recognized scholars. The second reason is that this study's primary emphasis was to identify clear principles of biblical Christianity from the epistle that can act as guidelines for advocating contextualized biblical Christianity in the five leading autonomous Pentecostal-Charismatic churches in Ghana that are the subject of this study.

Key Terms

Biblical Christianity

The term *biblical Christianity* refers to the understanding that a Christian is a person who has entered into a vital personal and living relationship with God through repentance from sin and faith in Jesus Christ that has resulted in spiritual rebirth and regeneration by the Holy Spirit (John 1:12–13; John 3:3; John 17:3; Titus 3:5–6). This spiritual regeneration is evidenced in a transformed lifestyle characterized by the fruit of the Holy Spirit (Gal 5:22–23) and submission to the lordship of Jesus Christ in every area of one's life (Luke 9:23) as taught in the New Testament (NT).

Pentecostals/Pentecostalism

The term *Pentecostal* refers to Christians who hold to the doctrines of spiritual regeneration through repentance and faith in Jesus Christ, the baptism in the

Holy Spirit evidenced by speaking in tongues,[25] the gifts of the Holy Spirit (1 Cor 12), holy living, and the absolute and final authority of the Bible. The term *Pentecostalism*, in turn, refers to the movement of Christians who hold to these doctrines.

Charismatics/Charismatic Beliefs

The term *Charismatic* is derived from the Greek word *charisma*. Paul uses this word in 1 Corinthians 12 to refer to various gifts of the Holy Spirit that include, among others, the word of wisdom, the word of knowledge, faith, healing, miraculous powers, prophecy, distinguishing between spirits, speaking in different kinds of tongues, and the interpretation of tongues. The exercise of these gifts in the GPCC is a matter of some controversy, as will be discussed below.

Syncretism

The term *syncretism* refers to the mixing of Christian worldview assumptions with non-Christian worldview assumptions that are incompatible with biblical Christianity.

Contextualization

The term *contextualization* refers to the process by which the gospel is presented and expressed in ways that are appropriate and relevant in a given cultural context through the use of an indigenous language and indigenous cultural concepts. Charles Kraft argues that contextualization is essential for engendering a Christian expression that is appropriate both to a given sociocultural context and to the truths of the Bible.[26]

---

25. The Pentecostal perspective of the baptism in the Holy Spirit is that this is a Christian experience separate from and subsequent to the Christian's salvation experience that is always accompanied by the "initial physical evidence" of speaking in other tongues as the Spirit gives utterance. This Pentecostal perspective is derived from the five narratives in the book of Acts where believers were baptized in the Holy Spirit (Acts 2:1–13, 8:14–19, 9:17–18, 10:44–46, and 19:1–7). Pentecostals hold that the baptism in the Holy Spirit provides essential power for Christian witness and mission.

26. Kraft, *Appropriate Christianity*, 4.

Worldview

The term *worldview* refers to the way a person or a group of people perceive, understand, and explain reality. These understandings are learned indirectly from birth onward and assumed to be true and accurate.

Christo-Paganism

The term *Christo-paganism* refers to attaching essentially pagan worldview assumptions and beliefs to ostensibly Christian practices.[27]

Over-Realized Eschatology

The term *over-realized eschatology* refers to expecting the eternal blessings of the "not-yet" eschatological period in the "already" of today.[28] Scholars also describe this phenomenon as "premature triumphalism."[29]

---

27. Kraft, "Culture, Worldview and Contextualization," 405.

28. Vander Pol, "An Over-Realized What?," Gig Harbor Reformed, https://gigharborreformed.wordpress.com/2009/09/30/an-over-realized-what/.

29. Malcolm, "Premature Triumphalism in Corinth," *The Expository Times* 128 (2016): 115.

CHAPTER 2

Biblical-Theological Review of Jude

Introduction

This chapter addresses Research Questions 1, 1A, and 1B through an exegetical study of the Greek text of Jude. This exegetical study will first present the historical, literary, and theological contexts of the epistle. It will then offer an exegesis of Jude aimed at identifying the meaning of the text that is consistent with the author's original intent for his original audience. This will be followed by a hermeneutical effort to establish principles of biblical Christianity drawn from Jude's meaning found in the text that are relevant to believers today, especially to the GPCC.

Historical Context

Author

The author of the epistle identifies himself as Ἰούδας (Ioudas, Judas; English translators have generally used the name Jude), "a servant of Jesus Christ and a brother of James" (Jude 1). In seeking to identify the Jude who authored this epistle, scholars generally agree that of the five men in the New Testament named Jude, the most plausible choice is the brother of James and the half-brother of the Lord Jesus Christ.[1] Of the five men named Jude in the NT, first, Judas Iscariot can be eliminated for obvious reasons. Second, Judas of

---

1. Bauckham, *Jude-2 Peter*, 21–23; Kelly, *Epistles of Peter and Jude*, 231–34; and Green, *Second Epistle of Peter*, 155.

Damascus (Acts 9:11) and Judas Barsabbas (Acts 15:22–32) had no obvious familial relationship with James. Third, Judas, probably also called Thaddaeus (Luke 6:16; John 14:22; Acts 1:13; Matt 10:3; Mark 3:18), is not described as a brother of James but instead, as a son of James; the genitive Ἰακώβου is better translated "of James" which clearly implies a family name.[2] The remaining Jude, the brother of James and son of Joseph and Mary, therefore, seems to be the most appropriate choice for the author of the epistle (Matt 13:55–56).[3] Michael Green notes that the early church fathers Tertullian, Clement of Alexandria, and Origen all attributed the authorship of this epistle to this Jude.[4]

Bauckham notes that, like Jesus' other half-brothers, Jude was not a follower of Jesus during his earthly ministry (Mark 3:21, 31; John 7:5). He suggests that Jude became a believer in Christ after the resurrection (Acts 1:14)[5] and includes Jude among the brothers of the Lord mentioned in 1 Corinthians 9:5, who all became traveling missionaries in the era of the early NT church.[6]

Date

Bauckham places the date of the epistle's writing around AD 65. He notes that the antinomian heresy attacked by Jude, which is similar to that in 2 Peter, was widespread in the early days of the church – that is, the first century.[7] He also notes that the references to the *parousia* in the epistle (Jude 1, 14, 21, 24) reflect the expectations of the first century church.[8] Particularly convincing, he adds, is verse 18, where Jude implies that some, if not all, of the original apostles were still living when he wrote the epistle.[9]

Recipients

The identity of the church or churches to whom Jude writes has been a subject of much debate among scholars. Norman Hillyer has suggested that

---

2. Kelly, *Epistles of Peter and Jude*, 231–33.
3. Hillyer, *1 & 2 Peter, Jude*, 16.
4. Green, *Second Epistle of Peter*, 42.
5. Bauckham, 14.
6. Bauckham, 14.
7. Bauckham, 14.
8. Bauckham, *Jude–2 Peter*, 11.
9. Hillyer, *1 & 2 Peter, Jude*, 16.

the general atmosphere of the letter and its reference in verses 17–18 to the recipients having heard some apostles firsthand could suggest that the church or churches were located in Syrian Antioch.[10] Jerome Neyrey has expressed the view that the church or churches could have been located in Asia Minor, or even in Egypt.[11] Bauckham's view is that Jude wrote to a predominantly Jewish Christian community in a Gentile society who were familiar with the biblical texts that included the apocryphal writings to which Jude refers in his letter.[12] The scholarly speculation about the recipients of Jude makes it difficult to hazard a guess about who the recipients really were. For this reason this study takes the view that the *content* of Jude's epistle, now at our disposal, is of greater importance than the exact identification of the epistle's recipients and their location.

In verse 17, Jude reminds his unidentified readers of the teaching that, at their conversion, they originally received from the apostles. He does not mention his own instruction to this company of Christians. This suggests that, although Jude himself was not one of the original missionaries who planted the church or churches to whom he is writing, he was personally known to them.[13]

Social and Religious Background

The social and religious background of Jude is similar to that of other early Christian literature written in the middle to latter part of the first Christian century.[14] Various NT passages (2 Cor 10–11; 1 John 4:1; 2 John 10) give the impression that during this period certain itinerant Christian teachers spread false teaching that became a frequent source of trouble in the early NT churches. It appears that the false teachers in Jude belonged to this category, as will be indicated in this study.[15]

In the Epistle of Jude, the false teachers' spurious claims of inspired visions (Jude 8) and the elitist implications of these claims seem to parallel the claims of other false teachers in 1 Corinthians attacked by Paul. The false teachers'

---

10. Hillyer, 16–17.
11. Neyrey, *2 Peter, Jude*, 29–30.
12. Bauckham, *Jude–2 Peter*, 16.
13. Neyrey, *2 Peter, Jude*, 41.
14. Fee and Stuart, *Bible Book by Book*, 423.
15. Fee and Stuart, 424.

appeal to the authority of private and exclusive visionary experience is also found in 2 Peter 2:3; Colossians 2:18; and Revelation 2:24. Jude's false teachers demonstrated an antinomianism that resembles that found in Corinth (1 Cor 5:1–6; 6:12–20; 10:23) and the prophetic teaching of "Jezebel" and her followers in Revelation 2:14, 20–22.[16] The false teachers' antinomianism was evinced by their changing "the grace of our God into a license for immorality" (Jude 4 NIV). The early church taught that although Christians are under the law of grace and the Spirit, they were not free from the moral imperatives of the Law (1 Cor 9:20–21; Gal 5:22–24).

Literary Context

Genre

Bauckham argues convincingly that, contrary to the opinion of many scholars, Jude is not a "catholic letter" addressed to all Christians, but rather a genuine "epistolary sermon" written to a specific, localized audience to address a specific situation of concern.[17] He explains that an epistolary sermon, in contrast to an ordinary NT epistle, is characterized by the sermonic nature of the epistle. A sermonic epistle, in contrast to an ordinary epistle, is characterized by its essential nature as a homily or sermon the writer would have delivered to his readers if he had been physically present with them. Other NT epistles that are considered to be epistolary sermons or homilies include James, Hebrews, and 1 John.[18]

Language

Bauckham has commented on Jude's impressive command of NT Greek. Jude uses the Greek vocabulary widely and effectively, employing perhaps the highest number of *hapax legomena* found in the NT.[19] Although Jude's sentence construction is simple, he uses it with admirable rhetorical effect. His images and phrases seem to have been carefully chosen to give his work the

---

16. Bauckham, *Jude–2 Peter*, 12.
17. Bauckham, *Jude–2 Peter*, 3.
18. Klein, Blomberg, and Hubbard, *Introduction to Biblical Interpretation*, 433–34.
19. Bauckham, *Jude–2 Peter*, 3.

urgent impact he sought.[20] Jerome Neyrey describes the epistle as being "carefully crafted, with a skill and intent that commands attention and respect."[21] However, considering Jude's Jewish and Galilean background, Neyrey has expressed doubts about Jude's authorship of the epistle because of his effective and impressive use of Hellenistic Greek.[22] Neyrey's view is countered effectively by Kelly, who notes that Jude's command of NT Greek demonstrates the kind of rhetorical skills that a Jewish preacher in Greek would have acquired in first century Palestine through a familiarity with Hellenistic Jewish literature and listening to Jewish and Christian sermons.[23]

Use of Apocryphal Books

A notable literary feature of the epistle is Jude's use of apocryphal books. The apocryphal passages Jude quotes are from *1 Enoch* (circa 170 BC) and the *Assumption of Moses* (circa 4 BC - AD 30).[24] Green has observed that these apocryphal works were popular among both Christians and Jews during the first century and that Jude's citations from these works were common among first century Christian writers.[25] He supports this view by citing the instrumentality of angels giving the law in Galatians 3:19 and Hebrews 2:2, and the statements in Acts 7:22; and James 5:17, as all alluding to apocryphal material.[26] Jude's use of these books, Hillyer suggests, should therefore not be taken as an endorsement of their inspiration, but should instead be seen like a present-day preacher making a citation from a well-known secular novel to illustrate a biblical point.[27] Paul did this in Acts 17:28 when he quoted pagan poets to make his teaching clearer to his audience in Athens.

---

20. Barker and Kohlenberger, *Expositor's Bible Commentary*, 1118.
21. Neyrey, *2 Peter, Jude*, 24.
22. Neyrey, 31.
23. Kelly, *Epistles of Peter and Jude*, 233.
24. Fee and Stuart, *Bible Book by Book*, 425.
25. Green, *Second Epistle of Peter*, 48–49.
26. Green, 48–49.
27. Hillyer, *1 & 2 Peter, Jude*, 18.

Similarity with 2 Peter

A significant literary feature of Jude is its marked similarity with 2 Peter.[28] Some scholars argue that Jude borrowed from 2 Peter.[29] Others have asserted that 2 Peter borrowed from Jude.[30] A third and more widely accepted view among scholars is that the many parallels in subject matter between Jude and 2 Peter can probably be attributed to the two authors' use of an unknown and unidentified third document that both writers independently adopted for the purpose of their own letters.[31] Green notes that the variation in vocabulary in the two epistles is considerable, with only a single clause (Jude 13 and 2 Pet 2:17) being virtually identical. He observes of the parallel passages in both epistles that, of the 256 words in Jude's version and 297 in 2 Peter's, only 78 are common to both letters. This means that 70 percent of the vocabulary is different and, in his view, supports the idea that the two authors used the unknown and unidentified third document rather than borrowing from each other.[32]

Contrary to the various scholars' assumptions that the similarity between Jude and 2 Peter depended on another redacted source, this study considers it to be quite feasible that under the inspiration of the Holy Spirit, both Jude and Peter could very well have addressed similar issues around the same time period without relying on a third written source. The two apostles might also have interacted at some point and discussed their mutual concerns about false teaching in the NT churches and thus the content of their two separate epistles show similarities.

Bauckham calls attention to the fact that there are differences between the false teachers that Jude and Peter address respectively in their epistles. He notes that, although both sets of false teachers demonstrate marked antinomian characteristics, those in 2 Peter, unlike those in Jude, are motivated more in their behaviour by an eschatological skepticism that held the view

---

28. For example, see Joseph R. Mayor, *The Epistle of St. John and the Second Epistle of St. Peter* (Grand Rapids: Baker Book House, 1965), i–civ.
29. Bigg, *Critical and Exegetical Commentary*, 216–24.
30. For example, see Bauckham, *Jude–2 Peter*, 141–43.
31. For example, see Hillyer, *1 & 2 Peter, Jude*, 18.
32. Green, *Second Epistle of Peter*, 50–55.

that, since there would be no *parousia*, there was equally no need to fear a future judgment against godless behaviour.[33]

Canonicity

Hillyer has noted that Jude's use of apocryphal material delayed the epistle's acceptance into the canon.[34] It is quite possible that the early church balked at accepting the letter as inspired because of the controversy that has, throughout the Christian centuries, surrounded the use of apocryphal literature. Bauckham observes, however, that by the end of the second century Jude was widely accepted as canonical by Tertullian in North Africa, Clement and Origen in Alexandria, and the Muratorian Canon in Italy.[35]

Importance

The Epistle of Jude is one of the shortest books in the Bible; it contains only twenty-five verses and considerably fewer than a thousand words in the original Greek text.[36] Green has decried the general neglect of the epistle in both the church and academy. He observes that Jude was written to address theological and behavioural problems very much like those faced by the church today. He writes that "so long as sin needs to be exposed, so long as man needs to be reminded that persistent wrongdoing ends in ruin, that lust is self-defeating . . . and that Christian theology has no right to outrun the faith once for all delivered to the saints, Jude will remain burningly relevant."[37]

Tokunboh Adeyemo rightly observes that the Epistle of Jude contains an urgent message for the church in Africa today. Adeyemo cites several reasons for his view. Among these are Africa's growing Christo-paganism and its widespread syncretism that denies the deity of Christ.[38] He notes that there is "an urgent need for people who are ready to defend the Christian message in Africa today."[39] Jude shared this urgent need to defend the faith

---

33. Bauckham, *Jude–2 Peter*, 154–56.
34. Hillyer, *1 & 2 Peter, Jude*, 18.
35. Bauckham, *Jude–2 Peter*, 17.
36. Fee and Stuart, *Bible Book by Book*, 425.
37. Green, *Second Epistle of Peter*, 11.
38. Adeyemo, "Jude," 1539.
39. Adeyemo, 1539.

in his day – hence the writing of his epistle and its relevance for the church in Africa today.

Form and Structure

Jude's epistle matches the form and structure of most NT epistles. He begins with a greeting (Jude 1–2), notes the purpose for writing (Jude 3–4), develops his main theme in the body (Jude 5–23), and concludes with a final doxology (Jude 24–25).[40] Some scholars have drawn attention to the chiastic structure of the epistle.[41]

Theological Context

The Trinity

Jude affirms a Trinitarian theology throughout his epistle. God is the eternal Father (Jude 1) and Saviour (Jude 5, 9, 14, 25) to whom glory, majesty, might, and authority belong forever and ever (Jude 24–25). He is also the Judge who judges the world of sinners and evil angels (Jude 5, 9, 14–15), and the King before whom his people will appear one day (Jude 24).[42] The second person of the Trinity is "our Lord Jesus Christ" (Jude 4, 17, 21, 25). Jude assumes Christ's messianic office and emphasizes his lordship by the use of two nouns; δεσπότης, "Master," and κύριος, "Lord" (Jude 4, 17, 21).[43] The Holy Spirit is mentioned twice in Jude. Jude asserts that those who are faithful to apostolic doctrine, unlike the false teachers, have the πνεῦμα, Spirit (Jude 19). He affirms that it is in the power and under the inspiration of the Spirit (πνεῦμα) that Christians worship, pray, and practice their spiritual disciplines (Jude 20–21).[44] Jude presents the salvation of Christians as being entirely Trinitarian; it is motivated by the love of God (Jude 1), implemented by the Spirit (Jude 19), and completed by the mercy of Jesus Christ (Jude 21, 25).

---

40. Fee and Stuart, *Bible for All Its Worth*, 56–57.

41. Edwards, "The Literary Structure Of Jude and How it Affects the Interpretation of 'The Faith' In Jude 3" (Dissertation, Baptist Bible Seminary, 2012), 1–10; and Coder, *Jude*, 6.

42. Ericson, "The Theology of Jude," 4.

43. Ericson, 4.

44. Ericson, 4.

Christology

Jude displays a high Christology. Jesus Christ is presented in the epistle as the Lord of the Church (Jude 4) and the mediator between God and the faithful, since it is through him that praise is offered to God (Jude 25). Jude holds that it is by him that God will grant to Christians the final expression of mercy in the gift of eternal life (Jude 21) and it is for him and his *parousia* that God is keeping the faithful (Jude 1). Jude also presents Jesus Christ as the sovereign Lord over the church whose authority is extended through his apostles and their teaching (Jude 17). It is in this regard that Jude addresses himself as a servant of Jesus Christ (Jude 1).[45]

Ecclesiology

Even though the word *church* is not used, the church and the preservation of its apostolic faith is a central concern of Jude's letter (Jude 3, 17–18). Jude defines the church as "God's holy people" and the "called" people of God (Jude 1, 3, 21). This implies that Jude sees the church as the special people of God who share in the communality of their love feasts (Jude 12),[46] and in their reverence for God (Jude 17–23).

Jude sees the church as being required to be faithful through its adherence to the apostolic faith by living under the authority of the Lord Jesus Christ (Jude 17, 25) and by engaging in various spiritual disciplines that will keep her in God's love (Jude 1, 20–21). Jude implies that it is by engaging in these spiritual disciplines that the church will remain blessed with God's abundant mercy, peace, and love (ἔλεος ὑμῖν καὶ εἰρήνη καὶ ἀγάπη πληθυνθείη – Jude 2). In contrast, the unfaithful, like faithless Israel in the wilderness (Jude 5), place themselves under the judgment of God by presuming on his grace, repudiating Jesus Christ in godless word and deed (Jude 4) and neglecting spiritual disciplines (Jude 17–23).[47]

---

45. Ericson, 3.

46. Hillyer, *1 & 2 Peter, Jude*, 254. Hillyer explains that the love feasts were meals of fellowship shared by all the members of the church on the Lord's Day.

47. Douglas and Tenney, *New International Bible Dictionary*, 554–55.

Eschatology

Bauckham rightly argues that the overarching theological perspective in Jude is eschatology.[48] He justifies this view by referring to the active hope of the *parousia* that pervades the entire letter (Jude 1, 14, 21, 24). He also points out that in verses 14–15, an eschatological perspective underlies Jude's argument that the false teachers are to be judged by the Lord at his return.[49] He further notes that Jude's eschatological theology expresses itself through his use of apocalyptic literature,[50] which had a considerable influence on the NT church.[51] Bauckham also observes, in agreement with Robert Harvey and Philip Towner,[52] that Jude's use of Jewish apocalypses reveals the extent to which the eschatological perspective was dominant in the NT church of his day.[53]

Exegesis

Methodology

The following methodological strategy will inform this study's exegetical analysis of Jude's text. First, for each portion of the text to be exegeted, the Greek text of Jude[54] will be presented first. Second, this will be followed by my own translation of Jude's Greek text, unless otherwise indicated. This translation is done with the meaning of Greek words derived from *The Shorter Lexicon of the Greek New Testament*.[55] Gerald L. Stevens' intermediate Greek text has been consulted for grammar and syntax.[56]

---

48. Bauckham, *Jude–2 Peter*, 9.
49. Bauckham, 10.
50. The word *apocalyptic*, derived from the Greek word *apokalypsis*, means revelation or unveiling. It refers to a type of Jewish and Christian religious writing with roots in OT prophecy that developed between the two Testaments, and in the first century. This is the same Greek word that is translated as "revelation" in Revelation 1:1. Jude's Epistle appears to be have been influenced by apocalyptic concepts such as the revelation of the end-time purposes of God and the ultimate establishment of God's kingdom on earth (see Douglas and Tenney, *New International Bible Dictionary*, 67).
51. Bauckham, *Jude–2 Peter*, 10.
52. Harvey and Towner, *2 Peter and Jude*, 151–52.
53. Harvey and Towner, 11.
54. Aland et al., "Epistle of Jude."
55. Gingrich et al., *Shorter Lexicon*.
56. Stevens, *New Testament Greek Intermediate*, 1.

This study's translation is undertaken with due reference to three English translations in the formal equivalence tradition (KJV, NKJV, and ESV), three English translations in the functional equivalence tradition (NIV, GNB, and NLT), and two English translations in the free tradition (TLB, and The Message). Third, following the presentation of the Greek text and its translation, textual observations that impact the meaning of the text will be presented, especially where the Greek grammar and syntax reveal significant insights. Fourth, the general exegetical analysis that will be offered after this will interact with various commentaries and the insights of various scholars, reflecting how the church has traditionally interpreted Jude.

The Seven Biblical Principles Drawn from the Text

The seven principles of biblical Christianity gleaned from Jude's epistle in this study have been obtained with reference to the apostolic witness preserved in the NT corpus as a whole, because Jude did not write in a theological vacuum. Although Jude does not clearly specify the content of the faith "once for all delivered to the saints" (Jude 3), it is evident that there was an extant body of apostolic teaching at the time he wrote that he refers to in verse 17 as the words spoken to his readers by the apostles of the Lord. These principles, therefore, are suggested by the text and have been obtained in conversation with Jude's overall meaning as he addresses departures from biblical orthodoxy throughout his epistle. This study therefore anchors its interpretation of Jude on a Pentecostal reading of the text with reference to the writings of other NT writers. This provides a theological framework to reflect and represent the spirit and content of Jude's "faith."

In drawing these seven principles of biblical Christianity from Jude, therefore, it is important to note that the study does not seek to misrepresent the epistle by making it say more than it does, nor does it seek a level of precision that Jude does not offer. The study has therefore been circumspect by emphasizing that these principles are suggested by the text, and that they are reflected in the NT corpus as a whole. Offering these principles as helpful guidelines for correcting theological errors in the GPCC is motivated by the fact that Jude wrote his epistle to confront and correct theological errors in his day that may very well be similar to those in evidence in the GPCC today.

Greeting (Jude 1-2)

In verses 1 and 2, Jude begins his epistolary homily by identifying himself and by using the first of his many triple expressions to describe and greet the believers to whom his letter is addressed.

Jude 1-2:

> Ἰούδας Ἰησοῦ Χριστοῦ δοῦλος, ἀδελφὸς δὲ Ἰακώβου, τοῖς ἐν Θεῷ Πατρὶ ἠγαπημένοις καὶ Ἰησοῦ Χριστῷ τετηρημένοις κλητοῖς. ἔλεος ὑμῖν καὶ εἰρήνη καὶ ἀγάπη πληθυνθείη.[57]

Translation:

> Jude, a servant of Jesus Christ and the brother of James, to those who have been called, who are loved in God the Father and kept for Jesus Christ. May mercy, peace, and love be multiplied to you.

Although Jude is the half-brother of Jesus (Gal 1:19) and the brother of James, who became the general overseer of the Jerusalem Church (Acts 15:13-21), in his greeting he humbly calls himself a slave (δοῦλος) of the Lord (Jude 1). The word δοῦλος here implies "a servant" in the sense of one called to serve the Lord. Jude's self-designation is significant because it demonstrates that he defined his identity not primarily on the basis of his family relationship with the Lord, but rather on his call to serve. The humility he displays by doing this is in sharp contrast to the presumptuous pride and arrogance of the false teachers whom he chastises throughout his epistle.

With the opening definite article (τοῖς), this adjectival phrase could serve as an *inclusio*. In other words, it could mean "the ones called" or "called ones"; the called ones who are loved by God the Father and kept by Jesus Christ. These two participles, ἠγαπημένοις and τετηρημένοις, are perfect passives – completed actions that have ongoing effects. This means that those who are called are loved and continue to be loved by God the Father. It means that they are kept and will continue to be kept by Jesus Christ.

With this in mind Bauckham refers to Jeremiah 31:3 and Romans 8:39 to argue that because this perfect participle implies that God's love, once bestowed on his people, remains, Jude uses his triple expression in verse 1 to describe the church to whom he writes as the eschatological people of God by

---

57. Aland et al., "Epistle of Jude," 827.

drawing from the Servant Songs of Isaiah, where Israel is described as called by God (Isa 41:9; 42:6; 48:12, 15; 49:1; 54:6), loved by God (Isa 42:1; 43:4; cf. 44:2), and kept by God (Isa 42:6; 49:8).[58] Also worthy of note is the word, τετηρημένοις, *kept*, in the perfect tense, which occurs five times in the epistle (Jude 1; twice in Jude 6; Jude 13, 21). This key word, to be examined more fully later in this chapter, points to Jude's emphasis on God's commitment to preserving his people from sin and Satan.

Bauckham argues that Jude's triadic benediction to the church, "May mercy, peace, and love be multiplied to you," is a Jewish greeting that is a comprehensive expression of God's blessing.[59] He explains that in Jewish thinking "mercy" denotes God's response of loving-kindness to his covenant people, with "peace" as the sense of well-being which results from this. By adding the NT word *love* to his benediction, Jude was expecting his readers to "read the Jewish greeting with Christian overtones: God's mercy shown in Christ, and Christian salvation in Christ."[60] Jude's opening benediction reminds his readers that Christians are those whom God has *called* into his kingdom, who are embraced and enfolded by God's *love*, and whom God is *keeping* safe through such dangers as the apostasy Jude addresses in this epistle, until Jesus Christ returns at his *parousia* to claim them for himself.[61]

Reason for Writing (Jude 3–4)

Jude 3–4:

> Ἀγαπητοί, πᾶσαν σπουδὴν ποιούμενος γράφειν ὑμῖν περὶ τῆς κοινῆς ἡμῶν σωτηρίας, ἀνάγκην ἔσχον γράψαι ὑμῖν παρακαλῶν ἐπαγωνίζεσθαι τῇ ἅπαξ παραδοθείσῃ τοῖς ἁγίοις πίστει. παρεισεδύησαν γάρ τινες ἄνθρωποι, οἱ πάλαι προγεγραμμένοι εἰς τοῦτο τὸ κρίμα, ἀσεβεῖς, τὴν τοῦ Θεοῦ ἡμῶν χάριτα μετατιθέντες εἰς ἀσέλγειαν καὶ τὸν μόνον Δεσπότην καὶ Κύριον ἡμῶν Ἰησοῦν Χριστὸν ἀρνούμενοι.

---

58. Bauckham, *Jude–2 Peter*, 25.
59. Bauckham, 27.
60. Bauckham, 27.
61. Adeyemo, "Jude," 1539.

Translation:

> Dearly beloved, although I was initially very keen to write to you about our common salvation, I was compelled instead to write to appeal to you to earnestly contend for the faith that was once for all delivered to the saints because certain people, who long ago were designated for condemnation, have crept in stealthily among you. These are ungodly people who pervert the grace of our God into sensuality and deny the authority of our only Master and Lord, Jesus Christ.

Ἀγαπητοί, "dearly beloved," denotes a warm relationship. Kelly argues that the meaning of κοινῆς ἡμῶν σωτηρίας, "our common salvation," refers to the corporate nature of salvation as understood by Jude and his readers, who saw themselves as being the people of God who enjoy real spiritual fellowship in and with Christ.[62] Neyrey argues that Jude's understanding of "our common salvation" includes the gift of the Holy Spirit (Jude 20), God's favour (Jude 4), righteousness (Jude 24), and a theology and conduct in keeping with the original tenets of the gospel.[63] "Delivered," παραδοθείσῃ, being a passive participle, implies that this faith, as oral or written tradition, was delivered by being handed down, passed on, or taught from one person to the next.[64] Although Jude does not specify who handed down this faith to his readers, a comparison with Jude 17 seems to indicate that it was the apostles of Jesus Christ.

Jude declares that this faith was once for all (ἅπαξ) delivered to his readers. This implies that this faith was delivered in a single time period and in a decisively unique way.[65] D. Edmond Hiebert notes that Jude assumes that his readers share his understanding that their divinely given faith allows for no subsequent additions nor alterations such as the false teachers were seeking to introduce.[66]

---

62. Kelly, *Epistles of Peter and Jude*, 246.
63. Neyrey, *2 Peter, Jude*, 54.
64. Arndt, Danker, and Bauer, *Greek-English Lexicon*, 762.
65. Arndt, Danker, and Bauer, 97.
66. Heibert, "Selected Studies from Jude," 147.

Jeffrey Edwards argues that Jude's understanding of the faith is that it must be accepted and understood as it was originally handed down.[67] He adds, "Over time the methods of communicating that faith may change, but the content of that faith must never change for it was once for all handed down from the apostles to the church."[68] Lucas and Green argue that Jude uses the word πίστις, "faith," to refer to those truths that his readers believe. They also note that Jude uses πίστις to mean the simple Christian truths that embody the basic teachings of the gospel. These truths, they further observe, are established permanently in their authorship and historical setting. They base this understanding on the meaning of the word, παραδοθείσῃ, "delivered" or "entrusted," which describes how God gave the gospel through the apostles, and ἅπαξ, "once and for all," which implies finality and definiteness.[69]

Concurring with this understanding, this study sees Jude's use of πίστις, "faith," as referring to the basic tenets of the gospel. In 1 Corinthians 15:1–4, Paul defines these in that first, Christ died for our sins; second, he was buried; and third, he was raised on the third day. Paul emphasized that in order to be saved Christians need to take a firm stand of faith on these basic elements of the gospel. This doctrinal foundation of the gospel is the first principle of biblical Christianity this study identifies as being suggested by Jude's epistle.

The word παρεισέδυσαν, "to lodge [or creep in] stealthily, secretly, unaware," is a verb in the aorist tense, implying that the false teachers are already present in the church. Bauckham notes that this word carries the meaning of "to infiltrate," and that Peter's use of the word in 2 Peter 2:1 and Paul's use in Galatians 2:4 both refer to heretical teachings that had infiltrated the churches to which they were writing.[70] Douglas Moo notes of these false teachers that "it is not that they are hidden from the readers, working in secret so the faithful are not even aware of them. Rather, they hide their real nature and purpose."[71]

The first *hapax legomenon* in the epistle is the word ἐπαγωνίζεσθαι. It carries the meaning of struggling and earnestly contending for something. This is an important word in Jude's epistle that was used in the context of the

---

67. Edwards, "Literary Structure of Jude," 43.
68. Edwards, 43.
69. Lucas and Green, *Message of 2 Peter and Jude*, 174.
70. Bauckham, *Jude–2 Peter*, 35.
71. Moo, *NIV Application Commentary*, 229.

athletic contests of the Greek Olympic Games.[72] Πίστει, faith, is another key word in Jude's epistle. Green argues that "the faith" here refers to "a body of belief... as opposed to the more usual meaning of 'trust'" and therefore Jude uses "the faith" as a way of identifying the known, verified, and recognizable body of teaching about faith in Christ.[73] With the expression "the faith once for all delivered," therefore, Jude means the apostolic teaching and preaching which was regulative upon the church.[74] Green further notes that Jude is referring to the normative gospel truths permanently delivered by God to his people through the apostles. Jude, Green further argues, is urging for the defense of a "vibrant, vital personal relationship with Jesus which inflames, invigorates and permeates every aspect of political, social and personal life."[75]

Daniel Harrington argues that the three elements in the qualifying phrase of verses 3 and 4 – ἅπαξ ("once for all"), παραδοθείσῃ ("having been delivered"), and ἅγιοι, ("the saints") – all serve to strengthen the impression that the author and his readers had a clear idea about the content of their Christian faith.[76] He adds that the faith of Jude and his readers is both traditional and objective and there had been no need to specify its contents further.[77] In Jude's perspective, the traditional Christian faith was in danger of being distorted by the false teachers who had intruded into the community he was addressing.[78]

Jude's main point in verses 3 and 4, then, is that he had originally intended to write a general treatise on various aspects of the gospel he and his readers share in common. He changed his mind, however, when he received disturbing news about a group of errant teachers who had surreptitiously come into the church to spread false teaching and to promote an antinomian worldview that "[perverted] the grace of our God into sensuality and deny our only Master and Lord, Jesus Christ" (Jude 4 ESV).

Jude describes the false teachers in three ways. First, they are ἀσεβεῖς, "godless," meaning they have no reverence for God. Second, they are ἀσέλγειαν; "licentious," "wanton," "antinomian"; they have no regard for the law of God.

---

72. Bauckham, *Jude–2 Peter*, 30–31.
73. Green, *Second Epistle of Peter*, 159.
74. Green, 159.
75. Green, 160.
76. Harrington, "Jude and 2 Peter," 193.
77. Harrington, 193.
78. Harrington, 193.

Third, the word, ἀρνούμενοι, "denying," a present participle, indicates that they are actively denying that Jesus Christ is their only Sovereign and Lord (δεσπότην καὶ κύριον); they refute the authority of God.[79]

In verse 4, Jude declares that both the character of these false teachers and their inevitable judgment by God were long ago described and predicted in biblical prophecy. These teachers, in Jude's view, therefore posed a grave threat both to the faith of his readers and to the gospel itself that the church had once for all received from the apostles. He was therefore writing to them this urgent warning, ἐπαγωνίζεσθαι τῇ ἅπαξ παραδοθείσῃ τοῖς ἁγίοις πίστει, to contend earnestly for their faith by rejecting and opposing the teaching and lifestyle of the false teachers.

Jude's purpose in writing his epistle, derived from verses 3 and 4, therefore, was not primarily to attack the false teachers, as scholars like Gerhard Krodel have argued.[80] Nor was it to present a general catholic letter of an ecclesiastical nature to all Christians everywhere, as others such as Daniel F. Watson have asserted.[81] It was, instead, as indicated in verse 3, an urgent appeal to his readers to contend earnestly for the faith.

From verses 5 to 16, Jude provides the background to this appeal – the false teachers, their false teaching, their ungodly character, and their inevitable judgment by God. From verses 17 to 23, Jude then spells out the practical details of how his readers are to contend for the faith.

The Apostates and Their Judgment by God (Jude 5–16)

In Jude 5-16, Jude's exposition on the background to his appeal in verse 3 is in the form of a Midrash (a kind of Jewish exegesis in which Scripture is applied to contemporary situations).[82] In this Midrash, Jude establishes that God's inevitable judgment of the false teachers' apostasy is prophesied both in OT types and in prophecy from the time of Enoch to the time of the apostles.[83] Jude's Midrash abounds with his usual triad of allusions and expressions. He begins from verses 5 to 7 by illustrating the prophesied doom

---

79. Hillyer, *1 & 2 Peter, Jude*, 238–239.
80. Krodel, *The General Letters*, 96.
81. Watson, *Invention, Arrangement and Style*, vii.
82. Klein, Blomberg, and Hubbard, *Introduction to Biblical Interpretation*, 30.
83. Bauckham, *Jude-2 Peter*, 4.

of the false teachers with three biblical narratives familiar to his readers – the wilderness experience of faithless Israel (verse 5), the experience of rebellious angels (verse 6), and the experience of Sodom and Gomorrah (verse 7). He then presents three characteristics of the false teachers: their abusive speech (verses 8–10), their unholy character (verse 11), and their godless behaviour (verses 12–16). One should first examine verses 5 to 7:

> Ὑπομνῆσαι δὲ ὑμᾶς βούλομαι εἰδότας ὑμᾶς πάντα ὅτι ὁ κύριος ἅπαξ λαὸν ἐκ γῆς Αἰγύπτου σώσας τὸ δεύτερον τοὺς μὴ πιστεύσαντας ἀπώλεσεν, ἀγγέλους τε τοὺς μὴ τηρήσαντας τὴν ἑαυτῶν ἀρχὴν ἀλλ' ἀπολιπόντας τὸ ἴδιον οἰκητήριον εἰς κρίσιν μεγάλης ἡμέρας δεσμοῖς ἀϊδίοις ὑπὸ ζόφον τετήρηκεν, ὡς Σόδομα καὶ Γόμορρα καὶ αἱ περὶ αὐτὰς πόλεις τὸν ὅμοιον τρόπον τούτοις ἐκπορνεύσασαι καὶ ἀπελθοῦσαι ὀπίσω σαρκὸς ἑτέρας, πρόκεινται δεῖγμα πυρὸς αἰωνίου δίκην ὑπέχουσαι.

Translation:

> Although you already know all this, I want to remind you that the Lord at one time delivered his people out of Egypt, but later destroyed those who did not believe. Also, those angels who did not keep their positions of authority but abandoned their proper dwelling, he has kept in darkness, bound with everlasting chains for judgment on the great Day. In the same way, Sodom and Gomorrah and the surrounding towns gave themselves up to sexual immorality and perversion. They serve as an example of those who suffer the punishment of eternal fire.

By beginning with the expression, Ὑπομνῆσαι δὲ ὑμᾶς βούλομαι εἰδότας ὑμᾶς πάντα ("although you already know all this"), Jude is implying that his readers, from the apostles' teaching they had once for all received (Jude 3), are already familiar with the three examples of OT types he is about to present to them concerning the character and behaviour of the false teachers. Of the word κύριος, Metzger notes that despite the weighty attestation in reliable manuscripts supporting Ἰησοῦς, the reading is difficult to the point of impossibility, and many scholars explain its origin in terms of transcriptional oversight.[84]

Jude's first example alludes to God's eventual destruction of the children of Israel who, in the wilderness, refused to believe that having miraculously brought them out of Egypt, God would surely bring them safely into the land flowing with milk and honey that he had promised them (Num 14). Jude's second warning example from the OT concerns the sin and fate of fallen angels. He implies that these angels, out of pride and lust, abandoned their God-appointed abodes to pursue godless activities. As a result God has sentenced them to be bound in chains in eternal darkness. Jude's third example is God's spectacular destruction of Sodom and Gomorrah and the surrounding towns because of their godlessness and gross sexual immorality (Gen 19:1–25).

With these three OT examples of God's sure judgment against godless backsliding, Jude reminds his readers that if Israel, God's chosen people, were later destroyed because of their unbelief and rebellion, so also would it be with the false teachers and those who abandoned their "faith" to join the misled community. Jude reiterates this point by citing the examples of the rebellious angels and the people of Sodom. These examples point to the deviant spirituality of the false teachers who were demonstrating unbelief in God (Jude 5), rebellious discontent (Jude 6), and gross sexual immorality (Jude 7).

These false teachers, in Jude's view, were physically immoral, intellectually arrogant, and spiritually disobedient to the Lord. For these reasons, as God had done in the three OT examples, he would certainly judge their apostasy very harshly.[85]

Jude 8–11:

> Ὁμοίως μέντοι καὶ οὗτοι ἐνυπνιαζόμενοι σάρκα μὲν μιαίνουσιν, κυριότητα δὲ ἀθετοῦσιν, δόξας δὲ βλασφημοῦσιν. ὁ δὲ Μιχαὴλ ὁ ἀρχάγγελος, ὅτε τῷ διαβόλῳ διακρινόμενος διελέγετο περὶ τοῦ Μωϋσέως σώματος, οὐκ ἐτόλμησεν κρίσιν ἐπενεγκεῖν βλασφημίας, ἀλλὰ εἶπεν Ἐπιτιμήσαι σοι κύριος. οὗτοι δὲ ὅσα μὲν οὐκ οἴδασιν βλασφημοῦσιν, ὅσα δὲ φυσικῶς ὡς τὰ ἄλογα ζῷα ἐπίστανται, ἐν τούτοις φθείρονται. οὐαὶ αὐτοῖς, ὅτι τῇ ὁδῷ τοῦ Κάϊν ἐπορεύθησαν

---

84. Metzger, *A Textual Commentary*, 657–658.
85. Green, *Second Epistle of Peter*, 170.

καὶ τῇ πλάνῃ τοῦ Βαλαὰμ μισθοῦ ἐξεχύθησαν καὶ τῇ ἀντιλογίᾳ τοῦ Κόρε ἀπώλοντο.

Translation:

> In this same way, these ungodly people too, relying on their dreams, pollute their own bodies, reject authority and insult celestial beings. But even the archangel Michael, when he was disputing with the devil about the body of Moses, did not himself dare to condemn him for slander but said, "The Lord rebuke you!" Yet these people blaspheme all that they do not understand, and the very things they do understand instinctively, like unreasoning animals, will destroy them. Woe to them! They have taken the way of Cain; they have rushed for profit into Balaam's error; they have been destroyed in Korah's rebellion.

In verse 8, with the words Ὁμοίως μέντοι, Jude implies that, in spite of the three examples he has set forth in verses 5–7, the false teachers persist in their godless conduct. Again, with the word, ἐνυπνιαζόμενοι, dreaming, Jude insinuates that the false teachers are offering up their dreams as visions to justify their godless teaching and behaviour.[86] Hillyer proposes that the expression, δόξας δὲ βλασφημοῦσιν, "blaspheme celestial or glorious ones (beings)," may be a reference to the false teachers' rejection of God's authority mediated through angels.[87] A detailed analysis of verses 9 and 10 is beyond the scope of this study. However, the gist of Bauckham's intriguing interpretation of these verses is that Jude used the OT and apocryphal references that are the subject of these verses to expose the spiritual conceit of the false teachers whose attitude to angels, as already noted in verse 8, revealed a rejection of all moral authority and submission to God.[88]

In verse 11, Jude again uses his stock triad of examples to present three prominent characteristics of the false teachers. First, Jude compares the false teachers to Cain who, out of sinful jealousy and unbelief, murdered his own brother (Gen 4:1–15; Heb 11:4). With this comparison, Jude was pointing out that the false teachers carry the potential of destroying the souls of his readers.

---

86. Kelly, *Epistles of Peter and Jude*, 260–61.
87. Hillyer, *1 & 2 Peter, Jude*, 248.
88. Bauckham, *Jude–2 Peter*, 64.

Second, Jude compares the apostates with Balaam, the prophet who, in his greed for financial gain, lured the Israelites into sexual immorality and disastrous idol worship (Num 25:1–2; 31:16; Deut 23:4) at Beth-Peor. By this comparison, Jude indicates that the false teachers are motivated by sheer greed for financial gain. This was contrary to the selfless piety of the true teachers of the gospel in NT times (1 Tim 6:3–5; Titus 1:11).

Third, Jude compares the false teachers to Korah and his confederates whose rebellion against the divinely appointed authority of Moses and Aaron in Numbers 16 resulted in their swift and dramatic divine punishment when the earth gave way beneath their feet and swallowed them alive.

With this third example, Jude is implying that the false teachers were certain of receiving from God this same kind of judgment; hence his lament, οὐαὶ αὐτοῖς, woe to them! As Bauckham has succinctly observed, Jude emphasizes throughout his epistle that "God's purpose in the gospel is to save sinners, not to promote sin."[89]

Jude 12–13:

> οὗτοί εἰσιν οἱ ἐν ταῖς ἀγάπαις ὑμῶν σπιλάδες συνευωχούμενοι, ἀφόβως ἑαυτοὺς ποιμαίνοντες, νεφέλαι ἄνυδροι ὑπὸ ἀνέμων παραφερόμεναι, δένδρα φθινοπωρινὰ ἄκαρπα δὶς ἀποθανόντα ἐκριζωθέντα, κύματα ἄγρια θαλάσσης ἐπαφρίζοντα τὰς ἑαυτῶν αἰσχύνας, ἀστέρες πλανῆται οἷς ὁ ζόφος τοῦ σκότους εἰς αἰῶνα τετήρηται.

Translation:

> These people are hidden reefs at your love feasts, eating with you without the slightest reservation; shepherds who feed only themselves. They are clouds without rain, blown along by the wind; late autumn trees without fruit, twice dead, uprooted. They are wild waves of the sea, casting up the foam of their own shame; wandering stars, for whom the gloom of utter darkness has been reserved forever.

In verses 12 and 13, Jude does not employ a triad of examples, but rather four metaphors drawn from nature to describe the false teachers: clouds in the

---

89. Bauckham, 41.

air, trees on the earth, waves of the sea, and stars in the heavens. Jude evidently uses the word οὗτοί ("these people") disparagingly here and in several other places in the epistle (Jude 8, 10, 14, 16, 19) to describe the false teachers.[90]

Rendered as "blemishes" in the NIV and some other translations, σπιλάδες is another *hapax legomenon*. Συνευωχούμενοι, "feasting together with you," refers to the early church's tradition of partaking in the Eucharist when they met.[91] "Shepherd," ποιμαίνοντες, is used here as a metaphor for pastors or ministers, as is frequently done in both the OT and NT (e.g. Num 27:16–17; Ezek 34:1–10; John 10:15–17; 1 Pet 2:25). In these verses, therefore, Jude is implying that the false teachers are dangerous hidden reefs who not only pose the danger of shipwrecking the faith of his readers, but also carry the danger of defiling their fellowship meals because they are like the shepherds of Ezekiel 34 who looked only after their own interests, not caring for the sheep entrusted to their care.

Jude's first example from nature, clouds without rain, implies that seeing clouds, one would expect life-giving rain, but that this expectation is not met. This portrays the false teachers as having nothing of value or benefit in their teaching to offer Jude's readers. As happens to all clouds without rain, Jude implies that the false teachers will eventually be blown away by the wind.[92] His second example is of autumn trees that are barren and without fruit. As with the clouds, in autumn one expects harvest, but this expectation is once again unmet. Jude's implication here is that the false teachers are devoid of spiritual fruit and will therefore fulfill no purpose of eternal value. In the NT, such fruitless trees are portrayed as only being worthy of being cut down (Matt 3:10; Luke 3:9). These first two examples point to the fact that clouds and fruit raise people's expectations of nourishment but from these false teachers nothing of any spiritual nourishment or value was to be expected.

Green sees Isaiah 57:20 behind Jude's third picture of the false teachers. "Foaming up," ἐπαφρίζοντα, is another *hapax legomenon*, and ἄγρια means "wild," or "untamed." He interprets Jude as likening the false teachers to restless waves of the sea that leave nothing but debris and destruction behind

---

90. Neyrey, *2 Peter, Jude*, 71.
91. Neyrey, 75.
92. Green, *Second Epistle of Peter*, 175.

in their wake.⁹³ Jude implies here that the leadership positions in the community for which the false teachers were clamoring would only result in an unruly churning without godly purposes or direction that would only point to themselves; they were only interested in themselves, not in the spiritual welfare of Jude's readers.⁹⁴ Jude's fourth example likens the false teachers to wandering stars (πλανῆται, "wandering stars," is evidently a play on the word, πλάνη, "error," from verse 11). Green argues that Jude borrows this metaphor from the Book of Enoch to refer to shooting stars that fall out of the sky and are engulfed in darkness.⁹⁵ Walter Wright observes that shooting stars, swallowed up in the darkness of the sky, capture well the shallow and temporary charisma of these false teachers who were not sincere leaders truly interested in the well-being of Jude's readers.⁹⁶

By thus portraying the false teachers as being as dangerous as reefs, as selfish as greedy shepherds, as deceptive as rainless clouds, as dead as barren trees, and as polluted as the foaming sea,⁹⁷ Jude warns his readers not to be so easily swayed and taken in by the false teachers' evidently smooth, impressive, and charismatic ways, their heretical theology, or their godless praxis.⁹⁸ A principle of biblical Christianity pointed out in these verses by Jude's scathing portrayal of the false teachers description is the need for selfless and humble servant leadership in the church.

Jude 14–16:

> Προεφήτευσεν δὲ καὶ τούτοις ἕβδομος ἀπὸ Ἀδὰμ Ἑνὼχ λέγων· ἰδοὺ ἦλθεν κύριος ἐν ἁγίαις μυριάσιν αὐτοῦ ποιῆσαι κρίσιν κατὰ πάντων καὶ ἐλέγξαι πᾶσαν ψυχὴν περὶ πάντων τῶν ἔργων ἀσεβείας αὐτῶν ὧν ἠσέβησαν καὶ περὶ πάντων τῶν σκληρῶν ὧν ἐλάλησαν κατ᾽ αὐτοῦ ἁμαρτωλοὶ ἀσεβεῖς. Οὗτοί εἰσιν γογγυσταὶ μεμψίμοιροι κατὰ τὰς ἐπιθυμίας ἑαυτῶν πορευόμενοι, καὶ τὸ στόμα αὐτῶν λαλεῖ ὑπέρογκα, θαυμάζοντες πρόσωπα ὠφελείας χάριν.

---

93. Green, 176.
94. Wright, *Relational Leadership*, 147.
95. Green, *Second Epistle of Peter*, 176.
96. Wright, *Relational Leadership*, 183.
97. Hillyer, *1 & 2 Peter, Jude*, 255.
98. Bauckham, *Jude–2 Peter*, 92.

Translation:

> It was also about these that Enoch, the seventh from Adam, prophesied, saying, "Behold, the Lord comes with ten thousands of his holy ones, to execute judgment on all and to convict all the ungodly of all their ungodly deeds that they have committed in such an ungodly way, and of all the harsh things that ungodly sinners have spoken against him." These people are grumblers and faultfinders who follow their own desires, boast about themselves, and flatter others for their own advantage.

In these three verses, Jude cites again from the Book of Enoch to stress his point. Hillyer observes that by quoting Enoch, Jude is contrasting the wicked angels of verse 6 with Enoch. He observes that although Scripture is not very explicit about this, the rebellious angels appear to have forfeited their heavenly home on account of their disobedience. Enoch, alternatively, gained his place in heaven by obeying God (Gen 5:22, 24).[99] Jude is therefore calling on his readers to emulate the rewarded faith of Enoch, rather than the punishable unbelief of the false teachers.

"Grumblers" and "faultfinders," γογγυσταὶ and μεμψίμοιροι, are both *hapax legomena*. Green notes that the onomatopoeic γογγυσταὶ is used in the Septuagint to describe the murmuring and bitter complaining of the Israelites against God in the wilderness (Exod 15:24; 17:3; Num 14:29).[100] Τὸ στόμα αὐτῶν λαλεῖ ὑπέρογκα literally means "their mouths speak big words." Jude described the false teachers with these words to point out their basic lack of reverence for God and their lack of faith in God's goodness and providential care of his people.

Jude's quote from Enoch 1:9 in Jude 15 uses the word ἀσεβεῖς, "ungodly," four times in various forms to emphasize his point that the ungodly conduct of the false teachers will certainly attract God's severe judgment. This judgment, Jude implies at the beginning of his quote, will be meted out when Christ returns at the *parousia* with thousands upon thousands of his holy angels, ἁγίαις μυριάσιν. In verse 16 Jude accuses the false teachers of using

---

99. Hillyer, *Jude*, 257.
100. Green, *Second Epistle of Peter*, 178.

loud and boastful words to flatter those among his readers on whom they depended financially for their prosperous living.

Contending for the Faith (Jude 17–23)

Having completed his stark descriptions and harsh denunciations of the false teachers' godless character and conduct from verses 5–16, now from verses 17–23, Jude arrives at the core and climax of his appeal to his readers to contend for the faith, which he had first announced in verse 3 as his purpose for writing the epistle. First, from verses 17–19, Jude urges his readers to persevere in the faith they had originally received from the apostles. He then follows this from verses 20–23 with two triads of exhortations on how his readers can practically contend for the faith.

Jude 17–19:

> Ὑμεῖς δέ, ἀγαπητοί, μνήσθητε τῶν ῥημάτων τῶν προειρημένων ὑπὸ τῶν ἀποστόλων τοῦ κυρίου ἡμῶν Ἰησοῦ Χριστοῦ ὅτι ἔλεγον ὑμῖν [ὅτι] ἐπ' ἐσχάτου [τοῦ] χρόνου ἔσονται ἐμπαῖκται κατὰ τὰς ἑαυτῶν ἐπιθυμίας πορευόμενοι τῶν ἀσεβειῶν. Οὗτοί εἰσιν οἱ ἀποδιορίζοντες, ψυχικοί, πνεῦμα μὴ ἔχοντες.

Translation:

> But you must remember, beloved friends, the predictions made to you by the apostles of our Lord Jesus Christ. They said to you, "In the last time there will be scoffers, following their own ungodly passions." These are the people who divide you, who follow mere natural instincts and do not have the Spirit.

Jude's beginning words, Ὑμεῖς δέ, "but you," in both verses 17 and 20, marks this important point of transition in his letter and implies a contrast between his readers and the false teachers. His command is made emphatic by using the pronoun *you*. The subject is built into the verb command so that this becomes very strong: "But you, yourselves, remember!" In verse 17, Jude uses the word, μνήσθητε, remember, in the imperative aorist tense to remind his readers of past instruction from the apostles they still needed to obey. In verse 18, Jude uses the word ἔλεγον ("they said") in the imperfect indicative tense to imply a continuous action that occurred in the past.[101] Jude uses these words to turn the ears of his readers from the voice of the OT prophets he has so far been using to the more contemporary voice of the apostles of the Lord Jesus Christ that still commanded the attention of Jude's readers. Jude implies with these words that some of his readers personally heard the apostles warn of false teachers such as those he was writing about who would almost certainly appear to haunt the church with heresies and divisions.

William Barclay notes that Jude's description of the false teachers in these verses implies that to the false teachers self-discipline and self-control were nothing; their one value was pleasure and their one dynamic was sensual desire.[102] These men, Jude concludes forcefully, do not even possess the Spirit of God (πνεῦμα μὴ ἔχοντες). Because ἔχοντες is a present participle, it implies that this is the current condition of the false teachers, further implying that they lived purely on the level of carnal, unredeemed life (ἐπιθυμίας, carnal desires).

Jude 20–21:

> Ὑμεῖς δέ, ἀγαπητοί, ἐποικοδομοῦντες ἑαυτοὺς τῇ ἁγιωτάτῃ ὑμῶν πίστει, ἐν πνεύματι ἁγίῳ προσευχόμενοι, ἑαυτοὺς ἐν ἀγάπῃ θεοῦ τηρήσατε προσδεχόμενοι τὸ ἔλεος τοῦ κυρίου ἡμῶν Ἰησοῦ Χριστοῦ εἰς ζωὴν αἰώνιον.

Translation:

> But you, beloved friends, building yourselves up in your most holy faith, praying in the Holy Spirit, keep yourselves in the love of God, waiting for the mercy of our Lord Jesus Christ that leads to eternal life.

In these two verses Jude uses three participles, ἐποικοδομοῦντες ("building yourselves up"), προσευχόμενοι ("praying"), and προσδεχόμενοι ("waiting"), and one imperative, τηρήσατε ("keep"), in a way that indicates that the participles are dependent on the imperative. His readers, in other words, are to keep themselves in the love of God by building each other up, by praying in the Holy Spirit, and by waiting for the mercy of our Lord. This is how they are to contend for the faith in contrast to the false teachers who were tearing

---

101. Mounce, *Basics of Biblical Greek*, 182.
102. Barclay, *Letters of John and Jude*, 198.

down the faith once for all delivered to them (Jude 4). These verses, in essence, represent one primary exhortation in three parts.

The first part of this exhortation is that Jude's readers are to hold firmly to the gospel truths, τῇ ἁγιωτάτῃ ὑμῶν πίστει, originally handed down to them once for all (Jude 3) by the apostles he has just mentioned in verse 17. Jude's use of the plural, ὑμῶν, implies that a communal, corporate, and committed study of the Word of God will bind them together. This is in contrast to the false teachers' divisive (ἀποδιορίζοντες) refusal to engage in such an active and sincere study of God's word in the assembly (Jude 19). Jude's exhortation here suggests two principles of biblical Christianity that echo Paul's thought in 2 Timothy 2:15–17: first, that sound biblical doctrine issues from disciplined Bible study; and second, that it results in godly living.

The second part of this exhortation is for Jude's readers to ἐν πνεύματι ἁγίῳ προσευχόμενοι (present, middle participle); "praying [or, you yourselves praying] in the Holy Spirit." James Dunn argues that Jude could be referring to various forms of Spirit-inspired prayer that include praying in tongues.[103] Pentecostals traditionally understand praying in tongues as a God-given capacity that is valuable because in the place of prayer it heightens a Christian's mood of praise, penitence, and petition.[104] Because Jude, like all the other NT authors, was "Pentecostal" by experience, he may very well have had in mind this capacity for enhanced prayer, enabled by the Holy Spirit as one of the means by which his readers should build themselves up in the faith. A principle of biblical Christianity suggested by this possibility, then, is that engaging in Spirit-inspired prayer is essential for the church, as echoed by Paul's thought in 1 Corinthians 14:4 that praying in tongues is a way by which Christians edify themselves.

The third part of this exhortation is that Jude's readers should ἑαυτοὺς ἐν ἀγάπῃ θεοῦ τηρήσατε, "keep themselves in the love of God." Jude has already referred to God's love for his people in verse 1. Jude implies here that, in contrast to the false teachers, his readers should remain in God's love by holding firmly to the gospel truths they have received from the apostles by

---

103. Dunn, *Jesus and the Spirit*, 245–46.
104. Packer, *Keep In Step*, 144.

nurturing godly unity in the assembly and by daily communing with God through Spirit-inspired prayer.[105]

As they obey this three-part exhortation to contend for the faith, Jude goes on to observe that his readers will be προσδεχόμενοι τὸ ἔλεος τοῦ κυρίου ἡμῶν Ἰησοῦ Χριστοῦ εἰς ζωὴν αἰώνιον, "waiting for the mercy of our Lord Jesus Christ that leads to eternal life." Jude is informing his readers that these three practical means of contending for the faith will demonstrate on their part a positive eschatological expectation of Christ's merciful salvation at the *parousia*. This is in contrast to the false teachers whose disobedience can only merit the Lord's severe judgment upon his second coming.[106] A principle of biblical Christianity suggested by this understanding is that a positive expectation of the *parousia* keeps the church faithful to Christ.

Jude 22–23:

> Καὶ οὓς μὲν ἐλεᾶτε διακρινομένους, οὓς δὲ σῴζετε ἐκ πυρὸς ἁρπάζοντες, οὓς δὲ ἐλεᾶτε ἐν φόβῳ μισοῦντες καὶ τὸν ἀπὸ τῆς σαρκὸς ἐσπιλωμένον χιτῶνα.

Translation:

> Have mercy on those who doubt; save others by snatching them out of the fire; to others show mercy mixed with fear, hating even the clothing stained by the flesh.

There are two schools of thought among scholars about the interpretation of these two verses. Some, like Neyrey, assert that it contains two clauses and refers to two classes of people.[107] Metzger has offered two reasons to explain why other scholars argue for three clauses and three classes of people.[108] His first reason is Jude's Jewish predilection for arranging his material in triads. His second reason is a concern to provide a main clause after three (or two) relative clauses. Metzger explains that these scholars regard the variants as aberrations that arose partly from scribal inattentiveness, and partly from indecision concerning διακρινομένους, which in verse 9 means, "to contend"

---

105. Bigg, *Critical and Exegetical Commentary*, 340.
106. Kelly, *Epistles of Peter and Jude*, 287.
107. Neyrey, *2 Peter, Jude*, 85.
108. Metzger, *Textual Commentary on the Greek*, 659.

but here in verse 22 means "to doubt."[109] Considering these to be adequately convincing reasons, the three-clause view provides the best explanation.

In these two verses, Jude explains to his readers that the fourth important way to contend for the faith is to engage in active discipleship and spiritual formation for the weaker members of the community. Jude considers this to be necessary because these weaker members may be wavering in their faith as a result of the influence of the false teachers. Jude also explains that his readers are to engage in active intercession for the salvation of the false teachers.

By the phrase Καὶ οὓς μὲν ἐλεᾶτε διακρινομένους, "have mercy on those who doubt," Jude seems to be appealing for the spiritual formation of those who, because of the influence of the false teachers, were exhibiting doubts about the apostolic faith.[110] "Save others by snatching them out of the fire," οὓς δὲ σῴζετε ἐκ πυρὸς ἁρπάζοντες, seems to be a reference to the active discipleship required by those who were seriously flirting with the heresies of the false teachers, and thereby courting the fires of hell.[111] This allusion is drawn from Zechariah 3:1–5, a passage that Jude has already used in Jude 9 where he quoted this OT passage from verse 9 of the apocryphal book, Assumption of Moses.[112]

Jude's third phrase, οὓς δὲ ἐλεᾶτε ἐν φόβῳ μισοῦντες καὶ τὸν ἀπὸ τῆς σαρκὸς ἐσπιλωμένον χιτῶνα, "to others show mercy mixed with fear, hating even the clothing stained by the flesh," appears to be directed at the incorrigible false teachers. By the expression "mixed with fear," Jude is implying that the false teachers are to be avoided because their fleshly behaviour and general godlessness posed a real danger of contaminating the faithful members of the community with both their antinomianism and their unavoidable judgment by God. Robert Harvey and Philip Towner note that Jude's words here also imply that, "as dangerous as these false teachers were for his audience, Jude nevertheless holds out for their repentance and salvation."[113]

Jude is also calling his readers' attention to the fact that, as the faithful members of their community seek to assist the compromised members, they

---

109. Metzger, 659.
110. Hillyer, *1 & 2 Peter, Jude*, 264.
111. Neyrey, *2 Peter, Jude*, 92.
112. Bauckham, *Jude–2 Peter*, 114–15.
113. Harvey and Towner, *2 Peter and Jude*, 159.

may themselves experience temptation through human carnality; while helping the fallen, Jude is therefore calling the faithful members to hate every aspect of sin, while not assuming that they are invulnerable to temptation and falling. Jude is urging his readers to exercise Christian mercy towards the false teachers. They are, however, to do so at arm's length, possibly through intercessory prayer guided by the Holy Spirit, as his earlier exhortation instructed in verse 20.[114] This suggests the principle of biblical Christianity that missions, evangelism, and discipleship are essential for the continuing spiritual health of the church.

Doxology (Jude 24–25)

Jude's epistle ends with his impressive, rousing doxology in verses 24–25:

> Τῷ δὲ δυναμένῳ φυλάξαι ὑμᾶς ἀπταίστους καὶ στῆσαι κατενώπιον τῆς δόξης αὐτοῦ ἀμώμους ἐν ἀγαλλιάσει, μόνῳ θεῷ σωτῆρι ἡμῶν διὰ Ἰησοῦ Χριστοῦ τοῦ κυρίου ἡμῶν δόξα μεγαλωσύνη κράτος καὶ ἐξουσία πρὸ παντὸς τοῦ αἰῶνος καὶ νῦν καὶ εἰς πάντας τοὺς αἰῶνας, ἀμήν.

Translation:

> Now to him who is able to keep you from falling and to present you without blemish in the presence of his glory with great rejoicing, to the only God, our Saviour, through Jesus Christ our Lord, be glory, majesty, power, and authority, before all time now and forever. Amen.

Jude's magisterial doxology functions as the formal closing of his letter.[115] The first part of Jude's great doxology is a confident prayer that God will preserve his readers from the heresies and spiritual dangers with which the false teaching are troubling their assembly and bring them to his intended eschatological destiny for them.[116] Jude assures his readers here that God is able to keep and guard them (φυλάσσω). Jude's implication is that, while it

---

114. Harvey and Towner, 117–18.
115. Neyrey, *2 Peter, Jude*, 94.
116. Bauckham, *Jude–2 Peter*, 124.

is God's responsibility to guard his people from the attacks of heretics and apostates, they have the responsibility of contending for the faith.[117]

Jude uses yet again another *hapax legomenon*, ἀπταίστους, to explain to his readers that ultimately it is only God himself who will preserve them from falling into heresy (implied by his use of the word ἀπταίστους, "stumbling").[118] Jude assures them that on account of Jesus Christ, they will, in the end, be a fit and joyful sacrificial offering to God (καὶ στῆσαι κατενώπιον τῆς δόξης αὐτοῦ ἀμώμους ἐν ἀγαλλιάσει).[119]

In the last verse of the epistle, Jude reminds his readers of four attributes of God: δόξα, "glory," refers to God's attribute of divine radiance; μεγαλωσύνη denotes God's kingly majesty; κράτος affirms God's absolute control over his world; and ἐξουσία, "authority," expresses God's sovereign power to do whatever he desires.[120]

Hermeneutics

Methodology

A two-pronged methodological strategy will guide the following hermeneutical effort to establish implications and patterns determined by Jude's meaning. First, the meaning of the text that is true to Jude's original intent for his original audience will be noted. Second, implicit and explicit principles of biblical Christianity drawn from Jude's meaning found in the text will be identified for the purpose of addressing research questions 1, 1A, and 1B.

Jude's Meaning

Jude's meaning can be discerned from the overall message that emerges from the three parts of his epistle. In the first part, from verses 1–16, Jude warns his readers about the infiltration into their midst of false teachers who, on the basis of their so-called visions, claimed the authority to teach. These false teachers demonstrated a godless and carnal lifestyle that had turned the grace of God into blatant antinomianism that denied the lordship of Jesus

---

117. Hillyer, *1 & 2 Peter, Jude*, 268.
118. Neyrey, *2 Peter, Jude*, 99.
119. Bauckham, *Jude–2 Peter*, 124.
120. Green, *Second Epistle of Peter*, 192.

Christ. Jude exhorts his readers to oppose these false teachers by defending the apostolic faith once for all delivered to them.

In this first part of the epistle, Jude impresses upon his readers the fact that the truths of the gospel and godly living are linked together and that contending for the gospel means affirming their faith and living the right way. Jude appeals to the OT, to apocryphal writings, and to the contemporary teaching of the apostles to confirm to his readers the certainty of God's judgment of the false teachers and any who follow them.

In the second part of the epistle, from verses 17–23, Jude reminds his readers of what they already know from the gospel truths imparted to them by the apostles. He reinforces this by presenting to them a series of practical steps they should take to contend for the faith. These steps include specific spiritual disciplines that will establish and strengthen their faith and help those who have compromised as they continue to anticipate the coming of Jesus Christ. In the third and final part of the epistle, in his matchless doxology in verses 24–25, Jude assures his readers that God is able to preserve those who faithfully contend for the faith and present them holy and blameless to himself at the second coming of Christ.

Erland Waltner and J. Daryl Charles have noted that Jude's use of key words throughout the epistle reflects a deliberate effort to emphasize important aspects of his message. They note that these key words also give unity and coherence to Jude's overall message.[121] Of particular note is the key word *keep* (τηρέω) in its various derivatives (vv. 1, 6, 21, 24). In verse 1, τετηρημένοις has an eschatological reference to Christians being kept safe by God for the *parousia* of Jesus Christ when they enter into their final salvation in his kingdom.[122] The word has a special appropriateness at the beginning of Jude's letter, with its concern that its readers be kept safe from the influence of the false teachers.[123] In verse 6, τηρήσαντας and τετήρηκεν are Jude's play on words to emphasize that, since the fallen angels had not *kept* their position, the Lord now *keeps* them in everlasting chains.[124] In verse 21, with the word τηρήσατε, Jude seems to be contrasting the apostate angels with faithful Christians who

---

121. Waltner and Charles, *Believers Church Bible Commentary*, 276.
122. Bauckham, *Jude–2 Peter*, 26.
123. Bauckham, 26.
124. Neyrey, *2 Peter, Jude*, 91.

should *keep* their position in God's love.¹²⁵ In verse 24, φυλάσσω ("to keep") is a reference to God's ability to "keep" his readers from stumbling; it is Jude's assurance to his readers that God will protect them from falling into the sinful ways of the false teachers and ensure their final salvation.¹²⁶

Jude's use of this key word has in it the sense of both *to preserve* and *to persevere* in order to reveal his essential meaning. Jude means that God is committed to preserving his people. His people, in turn, have to preserve and to persevere in the apostolic faith handed to them once for all by the apostles. They do so by contending for the faith.

Principles of Biblical Christianity
Implicit Principles of Biblical Christianity

There are three implicit principles of biblical Christianity suggested from a mirror reading of Jude 4–19. Scholars define "mirror reading" as what is written by the biblical author to reflect a problem or situation confronting the church, that is not explicitly spelt out in the text.¹²⁷

From verses 4–19, in contrast to the false teachers' immoral and godless lifestyle that was a dire attack on the moral implications of the gospel, contending for the faith means holding to and defending a theology that reflects both the basic tenets and the moral imperatives of the gospel. This is demonstrated in godly living and praxis. The contrast of the false teachers' theology and praxis in verses 4–19, therefore, yields three implicit principles of biblical Christianity from the text that reflect NT orthodoxy. First, people who identify themselves as being Christians must be truly born again and indwelt by the Holy Spirit (Jude 19; see also Acts 2:38; Rom 8:9b; Eph 1:12–14). Second, since Christians are indwelt by the Spirit of God, they must adhere to basic biblical truths and demonstrate the fruit of the Spirit (Jude 17–23; see also Gal 5:16–25). Third, servant leadership must distinguish the management of the church (Jude 12, 16, 19; see also Matt 20:28).

---

125. Neyrey, 91.
126. Bauckham, *Jude–2 Peter*, 122.
127. Stein, *Basic Guide to Interpreting*, 205–6.

Table 1. Implicit principles of biblical Christianity suggested by the text

Implied Biblical Principle	Location in Text	Opposite of Teaching/ Behaviour of the False Teachers	Description of Character/ Behaviour of the False Teachers
No. 1: New birth in Christ results in indwelling by the Holy Spirit.	Verse 19.	Having the Holy Spirit.	Not having the Spirit of God.
No. 2: Sound biblical doctrine results in godly living.	Verses 4, 8, 10, 16, 17–19.	The fruit of the Holy Spirit.	Denying sound biblical doctrine results in works of the flesh.
No. 3: Selfless servant leadership is essential for the church.	Verses 12–13, 16.	Servant leadership.	Immoral, denying Christ's lordship, self-seeking leadership.

Explicit Principles of Biblical Christianity

There are four explicit principles of biblical Christianity suggested from the core and climax of Jude's appeal to his readers to contend for the faith in verses 19–23. The first of these, explicit in verse 17, is that Jude's readers should remember the teaching of the apostles. This implies a firm commitment to sound doctrine evidenced by a disciplined study of God's Word, both individually and corporately. The second principle, in verse 20, is that the readers are to engage in the habit of Spirit-inspired prayer to build up their faith. The third principle, in verse 21, is that his readers have a duty to actively nurture, in their faith and lifestyles, a positive eschatological expectation of Christ's *parousia*. The fourth principle, in verses 22–23, is that the readers should demonstrate Christian mercy through missions, evangelism, discipleship, and spiritual formation to restore those of their members who may have succumbed to the teaching of the false teachers. Jude was implying that, rather than excluding or excommunicating them, they are to be saved, accepted, and restored.

Table 2. Explicit principles of biblical Christianity suggested by the text

Biblical Principle	Location in Text	Jude's Exhortation
No. 1: Sound biblical doctrine results from disciplined Bible study.	Verse 17.	Remember the apostles' teaching.
No. 2: Engaging in Spirit-inspired prayer is essential for the church.	Verse 20.	Pray in the Holy Spirit.
No. 3: A positive expectation of Christ's *parousia* keeps the church faithful to Christ.	Verse 21.	Waiting for Jesus Christ to bring you to eternal life.
No. 4: Missions, evangelism, and discipleship are essential for the church.	Verse 22–23.	Be merciful.

Summary

Jude's main purpose for writing his epistle, as identified from this chapter's exegesis of the text, was to urge his readers to fight for the preservation of the basic tenets of the Christian gospel. In Jude's understanding, the false teachers' immoral and godless lifestyle was a dire attack on the moral implications of the gospel that call for holy and righteous living. To answer research questions 1, 1A, and 1B, therefore, this chapter concludes that contending for the faith means to uphold, to preserve, and to persevere in the seven principles of biblical Christianity gleaned from the chapter's analysis of Jude's Epistle.

CHAPTER 3

Social Science Literature

Introduction

This chapter addresses research questions 2, 2A, and 2B through a review of the social science literature. This review will first examine what the social science literature reveals about the antecedent religious, socio-economic, and political factors that led to the establishment and growth of the five leading autonomous Ghana Pentecostal-Charismatic Churches (GPCCs) that are highlighted in this study. It will then present and review their current theology and practices. The GPCC, already identified in Chapter 1, are of autonomous Ghanaian origins and are to be distinguished from the larger Pentecostal churches of established denominations like the Assemblies of God, the Church of Pentecost, and the Apostolic Church of Ghana the origins of which are connected to overseas missionary initiatives and involvement.[1]

Most of the more notable social science literature on the GPCC was produced between 1994 and 2004. This was ten to twenty years after their emergence on the Christian scene in Ghana when it became clear to both Bible scholars and social scientists that the GPCC was not a passing phenomenon but one that was going to stay and significantly alter the religious dynamics in the country. On the one hand, the social scientists approached the GPCC with a critical secular perspective while the Bible scholars, on the other hand, took a more sympathetic view. This chapter's review of the social science literature will therefore draw heavily on the work of two research scholars:

---

1. Gifford, "Ghana's Charismatic Churches," 241.

Paul Gifford, who represents the social science perspective of the GPCC,[2] and J. Kwabena Asamoah Gyadu,[3] who represents the more sympathetic theological and pastoral view. Both scholars have undertaken much critical, sustained, and well-received study of the establishment, development, growth, theology, and praxis of the GPCC.

GPCC Development and Growth

Various religious, socio-economic, and political factors account for the establishment, development, and growth of the GPCC. The religious factors include, first, the ways in which Christianity was introduced into the country by European missionaries; second, the emergence of "prophetism" at the turn of the twentieth century; and third, the rise of African Initiated churches in the 1920s. These religious factors, in concert with the socio-economic factors that will be examined below in this chapter, provided the fertile soil in which the seeds of the GPCC would be planted, take root, and grow in Ghana during the 1980s.

Religious Factors

Three main religious factors account for the establishment and growth of the GPCC. The first factor relates to the way in which Christianity was introduced into Ghana. Christianity first arrived in Ghana through the ultimately unsuccessful efforts of Portuguese Roman Catholic missionaries in the fifteenth century.[160] By the mid-1800s, however, through the more successful activities of European Protestant missionaries, mission Christianity had been firmly established in Ghana, then known as the Gold Coast. These Protestant missionaries came from the Basel Mission (1845) and the Bremen Mission (1847)

---

2. Paul Gifford looks critically at the GPCC through the lens of a Western social scientist. He is a senior lecturer in the Department for the Study of Religions at the School of Oriental and African Studies, University of London. Gifford has spent considerable periods in Ghana over the past few years researching the various forms of Christianity in the country today, with special emphasis on the Pentecostal-Charismatic church. In the course of his research he has attended numerous GPCC church functions, spoken to key church leaders and members, and carefully examined the media output of the country's main Pentecostal-Charismatic churches. Gifford's books on the GPCC include *Ghana's New Christianity: Pentecostalism in a Globalizing African Economy*, *African Christianity: Its Public Role*, and *Christianity, Development and Modernity in Africa*.

3. Gifford, 241.

to establish the Presbyterian Church, from the Wesleyan Methodist Mission (1840) to establish the Methodist Church, and from the Church Missionary Society (1870) to establish the Anglican Church.[4]

By the beginning of the twentieth-century, mission Christianity and colonial influences had introduced considerable modernization into the Gold Coast through Western education and medicine, the building of roads, and the beginnings of a rail network, a cash economy, and the establishment of the British colonial civil service. In spite of this, many Africans at that time still viewed the Christian faith with suspicion "as part of the colonist regime" and the establishment of mission Church took place "at the cost of depth," leading to a largely nominal mission church in the country.[5]

Andrew Walls has attributed this nominal Christianity to the fact that the missionaries introduced the faith to the Africans in ways that made them feel out of step with their culture and traditional values.[6] Charles Kraft has explained that, in this period of the missionary era, European and American missionaries held the view that taking the gospel to non-Western peoples involved a basic encounter between the "Christian Euro-America culture" and the "pagan" cultures of the non-Western world.[7] Kraft argues that "the missionaries considered Western institutions such as schools, hospitals and churches as the means to the end of getting non-westerners to think like Euro-Americans and, in the process, to become truly Christian."[8] The missionaries also assumed that producing Christianity in non-Western cultures was their sole responsibility "with little or no participation by the receiving peoples in the process."[9] J. Annorbah-Sarpei holds that this alienation of the Africans from their culture by the missionaries meant that many Africans

---

4. Debrunner, *History of Christianity in Ghana*, 13–102.

5. Debrunner, 317.

6. Walls, "Evangelical Revival: The Missionary Movement in Africa," in *Evangelicalism*, 100.

7. Kraft, "Development of Contextualization Theory in Euro-American Missiology," in *Appropriate Christianity*, 15.

8. Kraft, 16.

9. Kraft, 16.

"became Christians only in the mind but not in their heart."[10] The Ghanaian scholars Abraham Akrong[11] and D. E. K. Amenumey[12] both share this view.

This disenchantment with mission Christianity among the Africans gave rise to the second factor that has been instrumental in the development and growth of the GPCC. This was the inevitable emergence of "African prophets" who were "able to mediate just sufficient Christian wisdom to be understood" and accepted by the African masses.[13] This phenomenon has come to be referred to as "prophetism."[14] These prophets and the movements they engendered, Hastings notes, were "almost always . . . an attempt to reproduce missionary Christianity rather than to reject it. The prophet was essentially taking on the missionary's task . . . basing it on the missionary's book, the Bible."[15] In Ghana, the three prophets who were at the forefront of prophetism were the Prophets William Wade Harris, John Swatson, and Sampson Oppong.

William Wade Harris came from the Kru clan of the Grebo tribe in Liberia. He received his early education in a school of the American Episcopal Church and later became a catechist in that church. Harris's opposition to the rule of the Afro-Americans in Liberia led to his eventual arrest and imprisonment.[16] After his release from prison, Harris became an itinerant preacher, claiming that in prison he had a vision in which a divine voice charged him to preach God's word. In 1914, he left Liberia and traveled widely in neighboring Ivory Coast, then a French colony, and in the eastern parts of British colonial Gold Coast, now Ghana.[17] Everywhere he went Harris preached that "people should abandon fetishism, believe in God and the Cross, be baptized, organize Christian congregations under Church elders called apostles, keep Sunday holy, respect the Bible and wait for missionaries."[18] His ministry spanned the years 1913 to 1915. It involved many miracles of healing,

---

10. Annorbah-Sarpei, "Rise of Prophetism: A Socio-Political Explanation," in *Rise of Independent Churches*, 23–27.

11. Akrong, "'Born Again' Concept," 32.

12. Amenumey, *Ghana: A Concise History*, 178.

13. Hastings, *History of African Christianity*, 531.

14. Quayesi-Amakye, *Prophetism in Ghana Today*, 12.

15. Adrian Hastings, *Church in Africa*, 531.

16. Debrunner, *History of Christianity in Ghana*, 270–271.

17. Debrunner, 271.

18. Debrunner, 271.

deliverance from demons and witchcraft, and the eventual conversion and baptism of as many as 120,000 people in both the Ivory Coast and the Gold Coast. Debrunner observes that "Harris wore a white gown and a turban, and carried a bamboo cross, a Bible and a calabash for baptism"[19] and that as a result of his prophetic and charismatic ministry, "whole villages and tribes did away with all signs of the old pagan religion by burning all the objects connected with it"[20] and enrolling *en masse* in the Methodist church. Harris did not insist on monogamy and traveled everywhere accompanied by two wives.[21]

John Swatson was a native of the eastern Gold Coast area of Nzima who, although originally a member of the Methodist Church, had become a follower of Harris. In 1915, Swatson resigned from the Methodist Church and became an itinerant preacher like his mentor, Prophet Harris, "dressed in a flowing gown and carrying a cross, a Bible and a bowl of baptismal water."[22] Swatson traveled across large areas of the western part of Ghana preaching and converting pagans to Christianity.[23] In 1920, another Prophet named Samson Oppong, described by Hastings as "less instructed," also began an itinerant evangelistic ministry in the forested hinterlands of Ashanti and Brong-Ahafo in the Gold Coast.[24] Amanor notes of Oppong that, "as was characteristic of prophets of his day, he moved about in a white flowing gown with a wooden cross and preached to turn people from idolatry to serve the only true God."[25] Hastings notes that Oppong's "converts were even more numerous, his anti-fetish fervor even more unbounded."[26] Although at this time there was a general distrust of Christianity in this part of the country, Oppong's ministry is thought to have converted as many as ten thousand people to Christ in a period of two years.[27] Oppong's ministry was affirmed

---

19. Debrunner, 271.
20. Debrunner, 271.
21. Debrunner, 272.
22. Jones Darkwa Amanor, "Pentecostalism in Ghana: An African Reformation," 8–9, www.pctii.org/cyberj/cyberj13/amanor.html.
23. Debrunner, *History of Christianity in Ghana*, 276–77.
24. Hastings, *Church in Africa*, 447.
25. Amanor, "Pentecostalism in Ghana," 10.
26. Hastings, *Church in Africa*, 447.
27. Foli, *Christianity in Ghana*, 50–51.

by the Methodist Church, which thus reaped from his evangelistic ministry a dramatic increase in their membership in this part of the Gold Coast.[28]

In their wake, these African prophets and their ministries spawned a wide array of African Initiated Churches that account for the third religious factor in the eventual emergence and growth of the GPCC. The African Initiated Churches are also known as African Independent Churches, African Indigenous Churches, and African Instituted Churches. All of these names have the same acronym, AIC. These churches, which came to be known as the "spiritual churches"[29] or the *sunsum sore* (*spiritual churches*, in Akan, the predominant Ghanaian language)[30] had already began to emerge in the late nineteenth century when African Christians began to separate themselves from the historic mission churches.[31] Scholars have offered three main explanations for this phenomenon that has been referred to as "independency"[32] in the development of Christianity in Africa.

Hastings has noted that the first of these explanations is "colonialism and racism"[33] within the mission churches themselves. This manifested itself in the form of "able and experienced African ministers" remaining "second-class members of the Church, always inferior to even the most junior missionary recently arrived from Europe."[34] He notes that in matters "of authority exercised, of salary, of details of human behaviour such as the sharing of meals,"[35] this racism rankled the Africans, as it portrayed the hypocrisy and insincerity of the missionaries and a disconnection between the theoretical Christianity the missionaries preached and the real Christianity they practiced.[36]

A second factor is the failure of the mission church to adequately address the strong African belief that witchcraft is a cause of sickness and misfortune. Harold Turner has argued that the African belief in witchcraft is a key

---

28. Debrunner, *History of Christianity in Ghana*, 311.
29. Foli, *Christianity in Ghana*, 90–91.
30. Asamoah-Gyadu, *African Charismatics*, 21.
31. Bevans and Schroeder, *Constants in Context*, 265.
32. Hastings, *History of African Christianity*, 493.
33. Hastings, *Church in Africa*, 528.
34. Hastings, 529.
35. Hastings, 529.
36. Hastings, 529.

feature of the African worldview that gave rise to the AICs.[37] Gerhardus Oosthuizen has asserted that the missionaries ignored the African belief in witchcraft because of their skeptical intellectual Western worldview.[38] The religious anthropologist Birgit Meyer, who has undertaken extensive studies of various religious phenomena in Ghana, maintains that, although the European missionaries correctly interpreted witchcraft as an activity of Satan, they dismissed its negative influence in the lives of the Africans as "outmoded superstition."[39] E. A. Asamoa bemoans the missionaries' denial of witchcraft beliefs as being irrational and backward and holds that no amount of denial on the part of the mission churches could eliminate the belief in supernatural powers from the minds of the newly converted African Christians.[40]

Asamoah-Gyadu has argued that the missionaries' "failure to engage constructively with the phenomenon of witchcraft" led to their inability to effectively address "the anxieties, fears, and insecurities that African converts faced regarding witchcraft."[41] He observes that, although the missionaries successfully translated the Scriptures into the vernacular, "negotiated nearly impassible terrains to preach the gospel," and laudably dealt with "the devastating effects of malaria," they unfortunately "dismissed witchcraft as a psychological delusion and a figment of the unscientific indigenous worldview" and thus failed to adequately bring the gospel to address the Africans' "ardent belief in the power of witchcraft."[42] The result of this, Asamoah-Gyadu further notes, was that the Africans referred minor ailments to the medical facilities established by missionaries, but they took more serious ailments, attributed to supernatural causes, to AIC practitioners who offered treatments "infused with the needed spiritual energy."[43] Both Emmanuel Asante[44] and Cephas Omeyo[45] have argued that Ghanaians almost always link healing with AIC

---

37. Turner, *Religious Innovation in Africa*, 10.
38. Oosthuizen, *Healer-Prophet in Afro-Christian Churches*, 120.
39. Meyer, *Translating the Devil*, 41.
40. Asamoa, "Christian Church and African Heritage," 297.
41. Asamoah-Gyadu, "Witchcraft Accusations and Christianity," 24.
42. Asamoah-Gyadu, 24.
43. Asamoah-Gyadu, 24.
44. Asante, "The Gospel in Context," 358.
45. Omenyo, *Pentecost Outside Pentecostalism*, 296.

spirituality. Hastings confirms that all the AICs "had within them a strong element of miraculous faith-healing."[46]

The third reason scholars put forth as accounting for the establishment of the AICs is what Bevans and Schroeder refer to as the "indigenous appropriations of the Christian faith" that were characterized by giving an important place to the Bible, revelation through prophecy, trances and dreams, and the importance of healing.[47] Lamin Sanneh has described this as the African contextualization of Christianity that involved the use of the vernacular African languages[48] and an attempt to submit biblical material to "the regenerative capacity of African perception."[49] Donald Smeeton has commented that these churches had a special appeal for those Africans who wanted an authentically African faith.[50] Noting that "many of these church groups were charismatic by experience and offered excitement, involvement, and miracles,"[51] he sees these AICs as having developed out of the African "desire for unrestricted religious experiences and freedom from foreign domination" and "spontaneous expressions of faith."[52]

C. G. Baeta, the eminent Ghanaian scholar and theologian, carried out an extensive ground-breaking study of a number of AICs in Ghana that included the Church of the Twelve Apostles, the Musama Disco Christo Church, the Saviour Church, the Apostles Revelation Society, the African Faith Tabernacle Congregation, the Eternal Sacred Order of Cherubim and Seraphim Society, and the St. Michael's Spiritualist Temple of Light.[53] Summarizing the findings of his research, Baeta concluded that, in contrast to the historic mission churches who were "constantly straining to look beyond earthly life," these AICs took a very serious view of the material needs of their people in the here and now.[54] Concurring with Baeta's prognosis, Asamoah-Gyadu takes a generally positive view of the phenomenon of the spiritual churches and

---

46. Hastings, *Church in Africa: 1450–1950*, 531.
47. Bevans and Schroeder, *Constants in Context*, 266.
48. Sanneh, *Translating the Message*, 188–89.
49. Sanneh, *West African Christianity*, 180.
50. Smeeton, *Church: From Pentecost*, 244.
51. Smeeton, 244.
52. Smeeton, 244.
53. Baeta, *Prophetism in Ghana*.
54. Baeta, *Prophetism in Ghana*, 138.

argues that, because they emphasized spiritual gifts, healing, and a focus on offering solutions to the practical existential daily problems of Africans, these churches were "authentic indigenous Pentecostal movements dedicated to the renewal of Ghanaian Christianity."[55] He notes that "their zeal and passion initiated a shift from the formal and staid spirituality and theology that had come to characterize the traditional Western mission churches."[56]

Donald Smeeton has noted that many of these churches "formed around the personality of one strong leader whose influence still dominates the group after his death. Sometimes, such a leader is even considered to be somewhat divine."[57] The AICs, he further observes, also demonstrate "doctrinal confusion" and syncretistic practices, mixing "elements of traditional animism with Christian ideas and terms" and frequently condoning such practices as polygamy.[58] Asamoah-Gyadu notes that, for all the positive AIC contributions to Ghanaian Christianity, "there have been problems with their ministry and theology" that have resulted in their decline and even disappearance from the Ghanaian church scene in recent years.[59] He identifies some of these problems as "the persistent public claims of abuse and accusations of fraud, sexual impropriety, the employment of occult healing practices, the perception of some of the prophets as being fraudulent, or religious impostors who indulge in false prophecy, fortune-telling, lying visions and exploitative divination."[60]

These three foregoing religious factors contributed to the rise, development, and growth of the GPCC in the following ways. First, the imperfect transmission of Christianity by European missionaries led to the eventual widespread "nominalism within the ranks" of the mission churches[61] that led to many young people becoming "skeptical of inherited denominational and ecclesiastical traditions" in the period when the GPCC was taking root in the Ghanaian church landscape. Meyer has argued that the emergence of the GPCC was a new Christian project that broke with the past and sought

---

55. Asamoah-Gyadu, *African Charismatics*, 95.
56. Asamoah-Gyadu, 20.
57. Smeeton, *The Church: From Pentecost*, 244.
58. Smeeton, 244.
59. Asamoah-Gyadu, *African Charismatics*, 94.
60. Asamoah-Gyadu, 94.
61. Asamoah-Gyadu, 116.

to correct past missionary errors.⁶² The Ghanaian Bible scholars Kwabena Amanor⁶³ and Emmanuel Asante⁶⁴ have expressed similar views. Second, prophetism laid the groundwork for accepting charismatic church leaders as specially anointed men and women of God. Third, the perceived failures of the AICs created a spiritual gap that the GPCC sought to fill. Asamoah-Gyadu has noted that this is why the GPCC demonstrate such "significant continuities and discontinuities with the beleaguered *sunsum sore*."⁶⁵

Socio-Economic and Political Factors

With a population of approximately 30 million people from a variety of ethnic and religious groups, Ghana is located along the Gulf of Guinea and the Atlantic Ocean, in the sub-region of West Africa.⁶⁶ In 1957, Ghana became the first sub-Saharan African nation to gain political independence from European colonization.⁶⁷ At its independence in 1957, Ghana was led by a political party known as the Convention People's Party (CPP) whose charismatic leader Kwame Nkrumah had negotiated independence from the British. In the years following the country's independence, Nkrumah's government was bedeviled by corruption, nepotism, economic mismanagement, and political oppression. This led to Nkrumah's overthrow in 1966 in a popular military *coup d'etat*.⁶⁸ Between Nkrumah's removal in 1966 and 1981, a series of ill-fated alternating military and civilian governments resulted in the suspension of the Constitution and the banning of political parties.

This period of political instability resulted in severe economic decline and harsh living conditions for most Ghanaians. In 1981, the military government of the day was eventually forced to negotiate a structural adjustment plan with the International Monetary Fund. This led to the beginnings of a tenuous economic recovery for the country from around 2001.⁶⁹ Like most African countries, however, Ghana's primary commodity-based economy is

---

62. Meyer, "Praise the Lord," 95.
63. Amanor, "Pentecostal and Charismatic Churches," 137.
64. Asante, "The Gospel in Context," 357.
65. Asamoah-Gyadu, *African Charismatics*, 95.
66. "Ghana: A Profile." http://www.ghana.gov.gh/.
67. "Legislation Providing for the Grant," 1.
68. Koduah, *Christianity in Ghana Today*, 70–71.
69. Koduah, 70–71.

still subject to the vagaries of international supply and demand for primary commodities. Ghana thus remains a highly indebted country and over the past two decades its economy has oscillated between growth and stagnation. As a result of this, poverty, unemployment, financial hardship, and frustration still characterize the lives of most Ghanaians today.[70]

Gifford argues that the harsh living conditions experienced by Ghanaians during the country's years of socio-economic and political turmoil and transition during the 1970s and 1980s provided the context and fertile ground within which the GPCC took root and began to grow.[71] He notes that the GPCC were well-adapted to their context, promising the hard-pressed Ghanaian population that "change is possible."[72] This, he holds, was a potent message during those years "when illness, deprivation and poverty became major issues" and "any Christianity that purported to address questions of poverty was sure to flourish."[73]

Asamoah-Gyadu shares this view of the immediate socio-economic and political factors that led to the birth of the GPCC in the mid-1980s.[74] He notes that in that period "living conditions became harsh and the political situation so turbulent that it engendered apocalyptic visions in the minds of Christians." He adds that "the troubles seemed to defy human comprehension."[75] He observes that "years of economic mismanagement threw Ghana into economic, social and moral chaos,"[76] and "the economy was on the brink of collapse, with bribery and corruption having led to widespread moral decay in Ghanaian society."[77] This apocalyptic situation, he adds, "was not helped by severe droughts that resulted in nation-wide bush fires, famine, poverty and squalor."[78] Jim Mason of SIM confirms the dire straits in which the country found itself in those years. He recalls that, "due to the severe food and other shortages in the country at that time, SIM Ghana became involved

---

70. Gifford, *Ghana's New Christianity*, 4–12.
71. Gifford, 19.
72. Gifford, *Ghana's New Christianity*, 61.
73. Gifford, 61.
74. Asamoah-Gyadu, *African Charismatics*, 120.
75. Asamoah-Gyadu, 120.
76. Asamoah-Gyadu, 121.
77. Asamoah-Gyadu, 121.
78. Asamoah-Gyadu, 121.

in providing food and medical supplies to various groups" such as orphanages, ante- and post-natal medical facilities, and prisons around the country.[79]

Asamoah-Gyadu explains that, in the face of the impotence of the successive military and civilian governments of those days, in order to address the worsening problems in the country, Ghanaian Christians began to portray the hardship of the times as God's judgment on the nation in general but particularly on the elite in government and in business who were enriching themselves at the expense of the starving masses. He notes that "many churches across the country resorted to prayer, asking for God's intervention to assuage the ills of Ghana."[80]

At the forefront of these national prayer efforts were many young people who, at that time, belonged to inter-denominational evangelical campus and school Christian organizations such as the Scripture Union and the Christian Union in universities and colleges.[81] Anderson notes that these groups later became "fellowships" from whose ranks several young charismatic leaders emerged with significant followings that soon began to grow into full-blown denominations.[82] One of these fellowships was the Kanda Fellowship, an evangelical Bible study fellowship of mostly secondary school and college students that was located in Kanda Estates, a suburb of Accra, out of which a number of GPCC leaders would eventually emerge.[83] Akrong has argued that the emergence of the GPCC in urban Ghana at this time was a timely "alternative to despair among the youth that could easily have led to violent social revolution."[84]

Around this time, in the mid-1970s, Benson Idahosa began to offer scholarship awards to African students from other African countries, including Ghana, to attend his All Nations Bible Seminary in Benin City, Nigeria. An Assemblies of God church leader in Nigeria had converted Benson Idahosa to Charismatic Christianity in the early 1960s.[85] In 1971, Idahosa was sponsored by the American Pentecostal minister Gordon Lindsay to attend Christ

---

79. Mason, *God's Challenge in Ghana*, 112.
80. Asamoah-Gyadu, *African Charismatics*, 122.
81. Anderson, *To The Ends of the Earth*, 234.
82. Anderson, 234.
83. Larbi, *Pentecostalism*, 340–341.
84. Akrong, "'Born Again' Concept," 34.
85. Anderson, *To The Ends of the Earth*, 235.

for the Nations Bible Institute in Dallas. In 1972, Idahosa left this school before completing his course and returned to Nigeria to found the Church of God Mission International in Benin City. By 1975, Idahosa's church had become "one of the first and most influential new churches" in West Africa.[86] With considerable financial support from American Pentecostal-Charismatic sources, Idahosa established "the most popular and influential Bible school in West Africa at the time," the All Nations for Christ Bible Institute. It was from this school that "hundreds of preachers went out into different parts" of the West Africa region, including some of the key leaders of the GPCC highlighted in this study.[87]

In summary, the socio-economic and political factors noted above directly contributed to the development and growth of the GPCC as Ghanaians sought religious succor from the country's failed economy and political structures. Gifford sees a further confirmation of this in the fact that the years that saw the emergence and growth of the GPCC were the same years of political and economic instability that witnessed a decline in Ghana's GDP per capita.[88]

GPCC Profile

As already noted above, the five GPCCs that are the subject of this study are Action Faith Ministries International, International Central Gospel Church, Lighthouse Chapel International, Perez Chapel International, and Global Revival Ministries. A brief profile of each of these five churches is presented below.

Action Faith Ministries International

Action Faith Ministries International, now renamed Action Chapel International, was founded by Nicholas Duncan Williams in 1979. The son of a politician-diplomat, Williams was brought up by his mother, a nurse who worked in northern Ghana. Williams' parents separated while he was still young.[89] By his own confession, Williams had a wild youth, stowing

---

86. Kalu, *African Pentecostalism*, 91.
87. Anderson, *To The Ends of the Earth*, 236.
88. Gifford, *Ghana's New Christianity*, 156.
89. Gifford, "Ghana's Charismatic Churches," 241.

away twice to Europe as a young man. In 1976, he suffered a nervous breakdown and while in hospital was converted to Christ. After his conversion, Williams joined the Church of Pentecost. In 1976, Williams enrolled in Benson Idahosa's Bible College in Benin City, Nigeria. There he completed a basic Bible course in 1978 and returned to Ghana to establish Action Faith Ministries International the following year.[90]

With its main church building and headquarters now located on Spintex Road in the middle-class airport residential area of Accra, the church currently claims a membership of about eight thousand. The church asserts that it has "a global ministry with more than 100 branches worldwide and several affiliate ministries."[91] In recent years, the church has established both Dominion University and Dominion Television on the grounds of its headquarters in Accra.[92]

Now known as Archbishop Duncan Williams, the church's founder has become "a major figure in Ghanaian Christianity."[93] He has developed a reputation for fraternizing with political leaders both in Ghana and abroad; he was one of the clergymen who prayed in the Prayer Service that took place ahead of the inauguration ceremony for the 45th President of the United States, Donald J. Trump.[94]

International Central Gospel Church

Mensa Anamua Otabil, who originally came from an Anglican Church background, founded International Central Gospel Church (ICGC) in February 1984. In the late 1970s, Otabil joined and eventually led the Kanda fellowship. On February 26, 1984, he started the International Central Gospel Church at the Kanda Cluster of Schools in this suburb.[95] The church's first meeting recorded an initial membership of about twenty people. Within two years, meeting in various rented venues, the church had grown in membership to about 180 members. Between 1986 and 1996, the church's meetings were

---

90. Gifford, 241.
91. "Action Faith Ministries International." http://actionchapel.net/?page_id=3187.
92. "Action Faith Ministries International." http://actionchapel.net/?page_id=3187.
93. Gifford, "Ghana's Charismatic Churches," 241.
94. "Archbishop Nicholas Duncan Williams." http://citifmonline.com/2017/01/20/duncan-williams-leads-prayer-at-church-service-for-trumps-inauguration/.
95. "International Central Gospel Church." http://www.centralgospel.com/?root=about.

held at the Baden Powell Memorial Hall in Accra's central business district.[96] During this period, the church grew in membership to approximately four thousand. The church claims that, during those years, it established forty branch congregations across the Accra-Tema metropolitan area as well as branch churches in almost all the major towns and cities of Ghana, with several others in Europe and the United States.[97]

In 1988, the church established a ministerial training institute that offered a six-month certificate course in Christian ministry. This was later developed into the Central University College that the church describes as "a premier private-owned University."[98] In conjunction with the University, the church has established an educational scholarship scheme known as Central Aid to provide financial assistance to needy students in secondary schools. The church describes this scheme as "the largest non-governmental scholarship program for students in pre-tertiary education in Ghana."[99]

Mensa Otabil serves as General Overseer and Senior Pastor of the church's main congregation in Accra, called Christ Temple. His international radio and television broadcast, called the Living Word, is broadcast across Africa.[100] Like Duncan Williams of Action Faith Ministries, Mensa Otabil is considered a leading figure in Ghanaian Christianity today who is best known for his motivational speaking that addresses the various socio-economic and political problems facing the country.[101] In 1998, he won an award for "Best Motivational Speaker."[102] In recent years, Otabil has become known for advocating black pride and consciousness in his extensive travels throughout Africa.[103]

Lighthouse Chapel International

Dr. Dag Heward-Mills founded Lighthouse Chapel International in 1989 in Accra, Ghana. The son of a Ghanaian father and a Swiss mother, Dag

---

96. Gifford, "Ghana's Charismatic Churches," 244.
97. "International Central Gospel Church." http://www.centralgospel.com/?root=about.
98. "International Central Gospel Church." http://www.centralgospel.com/?root=about.
99. "International Central Gospel Church." http://www.centralgospel.com/?root=about.
100. "International Central Gospel Church." http://www.centralgospel.com/?root=about.
101. Paul Gifford, "View of Ghana's New Christianity," 91–92.
102. Gifford, *Ghana's New Christianity*, 119.
103. Anderson, *To The Ends of the Earth*, 238.

Heward-Mills trained as a medical doctor. The church grew out of his fellowship for medical professionals around Accra's main hospital, Korle Bu Teaching Hospital. The church's flagship, Lighthouse Cathedral, is situated near this hospital. Heward-Mills left medical practice for full-time ministry in January 1991.[104] The church's characteristic yellow signboards advertising its many branches can be seen throughout Ghana. The church claims to have 1600 churches around the world today.[105]

Most Lighthouse Chapel pastors serve on a part-time basis. The church's leadership structure comprises of a Bishop's Council, a General Council, and Regional Councils.[106] The church's various ministries include ministry to prison inmates, hospital patients, the needy, homeless people, and orphans. It also places a great deal of emphasis on its youth ministry. The church has a Bible school in Ghana known as Anagkazo Bible and Ministry Training Center.[107]

Dag Heward Mills has an international ministry that has taken him to over a hundred countries around the world. Although he has received no formal theological training, he is also a prolific author who has written almost two hundred Christian books. The subjects of his books include pastoral ministry, prosperity, and church administration.[108]

Perez Chapel International

Charles Agyin Asare founded Perez Chapel International in March 1987. Agyin Asare professes that he was converted to Christ in the Church of Pentecost in 1980 at the age of 18 from a background of "sin, revelry, alcoholism and drug addiction and women-chasing."[109] He claims that in 1983, at a Morris Cerullo School of Ministry function, he received a divine commission to heal. Soon afterwards, he began to preach in open-air meetings. In 1986, he attended Idahosa's Bible school in Nigeria, returning in March 1987 to found World Miracle Bible Church in Tamale in northern Ghana. By 1994, the church had grown to comprise of sixteen branch churches and an extensive

---

104. Gifford, *Ghana's New Christianity*, 25.
105. Gifford, 238.
106. "Lighthouse Chapel International." www.lighthousechapel.org.
107. Reinhardt, "Christian Plane of Immanence," 416.
108. "Dag Heward Mills." www.daghewardmills.org.
109. "Perez Chapel International." https://www.perezchapel.org/founders/.

ministry in northern Ghana. In that year, ethnic disturbances in that part of the country forced Agyin Asare to relocate his base of operations to Accra.[110]

In 1998, the church acquired a large building in Dzorwulu, a suburb of Accra, which used to house the Ghana Meat Marketing Board, and erected a large sanctuary now named Perez Dome. The church claims that on a recent visit to the Perez Dome the former President of Ghana, John Dramani Mahama, described this place of worship as "one of the Seven Wonders of Ghana."[111] The church also asserts that, "the Perez Dome, which is a 14,000-seater auditorium, welcomes thousands of people weekly and is currently regarded as the largest auditorium in Ghana."[112] The church also claims to have fifty branches in Accra and "hundreds of affiliates worldwide."[113]

The founder, now known as Bishop Agyin Asare, travels a great deal, holding evangelistic meetings around the world and preaching regularly in Pentecostal-Charismatic churches in Ghana, including the churches of both Otabil and Duncan Williams. In recent years, he has developed a high-profile television presence, with his programs often featuring his miracle-focused meetings.[114]

Global Revival Ministries

Robert Ampiah Kwofi founded Global Revival Ministries (GRM) in October 1984. Ampiah Kwofi had been a member of the Kanda Fellowship since its inception in 1976 with some of the fellowship meetings taking place in his family's home in Kanda Estate. Mensa Otabil was then a prominent member of this Fellowship. Ampiah Kwofi remained a member of the Fellowship as he left high school and enrolled first at the Kwame Nkrumah University of Science and Technology in Kumasi and later at the University of Ghana in Legon, Accra. Inspired by Morris Cerullo's evangelistic meetings, Ampiah Kwofi began to attend all-night prayer meetings at Nicholas Duncan Williams' Action Faith ministry, quickly becoming a leader in the church's prayer ministry.[115]

---

110. Gifford, *Ghana's New Christianity*, 25.
111. "Perez Chapel International." https://www.perezchapel.org/founders/.
112. "Perez Chapel International." https://www.perezchapel.org/founders/.
113. "Perez Chapel International." https://www.perezchapel.org/founders/.
114. Gifford, "Ghana's Charismatic Churches," 249.
115. "Global Revival Ministries." http://globalrevivalministries.net/history.

Ampiah Kwofi explains that in 1983, he received his call to preach the gospel of Christ through a vision in which he saw the globe engulfed in flames of revival, hence the name Global Revival Ministries.[116] In that same year he was commissioned as an evangelist by Benson Idahosa in Nigeria and began the initial services of GRM in the premises of the Young Women's Christian Association (YWCA) in Accra on Saturdays between 10 a.m. and 2 p.m. In 1985, the church relocated to the Rex Cinema and began Sunday services. GRM's Tuesday evening services and its Friday all-night prayer sessions were held at Legon Hall on the University of Ghana campus.[117] In 1997, GRM relocated to the Baden Powell Memorial Hall, which had recently been vacated. At the Baden Powell Memorial Hall, GRM grew numerically, regularly attracting large numbers of people from other churches to its well-known Friday all-night prayer meetings.[118]

In 1998, the Ampiah Kwofi World Outreach (AKWO) evangelistic ministry was launched. Since its inception, AKWO has developed a reputation for its many evangelistic outdoor meetings held in all of Ghana and other African countries. In 2016, GRM moved its headquarters to Revival City, a 7000-capacity auditorium in Haatso, a suburb of Accra. GRM claims to have over fifty branch congregations across Ghana and in the neighboring countries of Togo and Cote D'Ivoire.[119]

GPCC Theology and Praxis

With their roots in the urban non-denominational evangelical student fellowships of the 1970s and 1980s, the GPCC began with an affirmation of evangelical NT orthodoxy.[120] GPCC statements of faith were Pentecostal and evangelical in emphasis, stressing salvation and Spirit baptism, evidenced by speaking in tongues, and declaring their primary purpose as providing solid Bible-based instruction to equip their members to preach and teach the gospel. The GPCC empowered untrained but spiritually gifted and effective

---

116. *Global Revival Ministries*, 1.
117. *Global Revival Ministries*, 4–5.
118. *Global Revival Ministries*, 4.
119. *Global Revival Ministries*, 5.
120. Asamoah-Gyadu, *African Charismatics*, 129.

Pentecostal leaders to replace the seemingly less spiritual and nominal leaders of the older mission churches.[121] In their formative years, young GPCC members, on the basis of their spiritual gifts, were encouraged to participate in church activities such as leading worship, personal evangelism, and being involved in healing and deliverance ministries.[122]

Anderson notes that during those early years the GPCC emphasized "a personal conversion experience (being 'born again') . . . they advocated long periods of individual and communal prayer, including fasting and prayer retreats, prayer for healing and for individualized problems like unemployment."[123] Over the past thirty years, however, GPCC theology and practices have metamorphosed and changed in many significant ways. Below is a presentation of current GPCC theology and praxis.

Theology

The current theology of the GPCC rests on three main pillars. The first of these is the prosperity doctrine. The second is deliverance from witchcraft. The third is the special powers and anointing of "the man of God."

The Prosperity Doctrine

The first pillar of GPCC theology, the prosperity doctrine, has been defined by Gordon Fee as the teaching that "God wills the financial prosperity of every one of his children and therefore for a Christian to be in poverty is to be outside God's intended will."[124] Charles Hummel defines the prosperity doctrine as the teaching "that we have been created for an abundant life in Christ that includes physical health and material prosperity based on unwavering faith."[125] Hummel explains that this doctrine is also known as the "the word-of-faith, health-and-wealth, positive confession, name-it-and-claim-it" doctrine.[126]

Scholars have offered several reasons for the conspicuous and predominant role of the prosperity doctrine in the theology of the GPCC. Kingsley Larbi, in his seminal examination of the growth of the GPCC, attributes this

---

121. Asamoah-Gyadu, 126–28.
122. Asamoah-Gyadu, 130–31.
123. Anderson, *To The Ends of the Earth*, 234–35.
124. Fee, *Disease of the Health and Wealth Gospels*, 8.
125. Hummel, *The Prosperity Gospel*, 4.
126. Hummel, 4.

to the fact that "Ghanaian Pentecostalism has found a fertile ground in the all-pervasive primal religious traditions of the people of Ghana, especially in its cosmology and in its concept of salvation," which relates "to the *existential here and now*" that "embodies the enjoyment of long life, health, a life of happiness and felicity; the enjoyment of prosperity; that is, wealth, riches, including children, a life of peace and tranquility."[127] Larbi argues that the continuity between the traditional Ghanaian concept of salvation and the Pentecostal understanding of salvation lies in the fact that Pentecostals view salvation "as the key to abundant life" and "the enjoyment of prosperity, which includes wealth, health and fertility."[128]

Anderson argues that the prosperity doctrine has become a central plank of GPCC theology because, as the GPCC expanded, they began to develop concepts of material success and prosperity based on the American Word of Faith doctrine that addressed the felt needs of Ghanaians in the "impoverished cities" of the country.[129] Joel Robbins explains that the prosperity doctrine was attractive to the many struggling young urban Ghanaians because, considering themselves to be missing out on the promises of modern urban Ghanaian affluence, the doctrine "offers ecstatic escape, hope for millennial redress, and an egalitarian environment in which everyone is eligible for the highest religious rewards."[130]

Ogbu Kalu explains that the GPCC leaders were originally exposed to the prosperity doctrine in Benson Idahosa's school in Nigeria in the mid-1980s that had become "a breeding camp for adherents of the prosperity gospel" that Idahosa's "flamboyant career had made visibly fashionable."[131] Asamoah-Gyadu concurs with this view by noting that the GPCC generally share the underlying principles of the prosperity doctrine because in the formative years of the GPCC Ghanaian students returning from Idahosa's Bible school became symbolic embodiments of Idahosa's theology that was based on the teaching of the apostles of the prosperity doctrine in North America.[132] Gifford equally attributes the health and wealth emphasis in the GPCC to the

---

127. Larbi, *Pentecostalism*, 424.
128. Larbi, 424–25.
129. Anderson, *To The Ends of the Earth*, 234.
130. Robbins, "Globalization of Pentecostal and Charismatic Christianity," 120.
131. Kalu, *African Pentecostalism*, 257.
132. Asamoah-Gyadu, *African Charismatics*, 204–5.

influence of the teachings of leaders of the American faith movement such as Kenneth Hagin and Kenneth Copeland.[133]

Gifford explains that the GPCC theology of material prosperity is saturated with the words "inheritance, breakthrough, destiny, season, manifestation, claim, victory, power, abundance, and increase."[134] Asamoah-Gyadu observes that the GPCC prosperity theology "preaches material abundance as a sign of right standing with God."[135] He defines the strong American prosperity doctrine influence on GPCC theology as the "internationalism" of the GPCC that is an "inevitable consequence of religious globalization."[136]

The declarations, sermons, assertions, and writings of GPCC leaders confirm the cardinal place of the prosperity doctrine in their theology. Gifford has noted that in the book entitled *You Are Destined to Succeed* Duncan Williams quotes from Genesis 1:29–30 to make the claim that "God never planned for (us) or any of mankind to have sickness, fear, inferiority, defeat or failure."[137] Again from this book, Duncan Williams, quoting from the American "high priests of the prosperity movement" asserts that "the Word of God is a tree of life that will produce riches, honour, promotion and joy."[138] Gifford quotes Mensa Otabil as declaring in a sermon, "God blesses us according to our deposits. If you haven't deposited anything, you have no right to ask for anything" and then goes on to declare that people should give to the church "so the God of Abraham, Isaac, and Jacob will meet all your needs."[139]

In a sermon preached by Agyin Asare on "the anointing," Gifford observes that Agyin Asare claimed that the requirement for having one's needs met was to sow financially into anointed ministries like his.[140] In a four-day conference hosted by Robert Ampiah-Kwofi of Global Revival Ministries in April 2001, Gifford notes that he urged those attending "to sell cars, houses and

---

133. Gifford, *Ghana's New Christianity*, 115.
134. Gifford, *Christianity, Politics and Public Life*, 113.
135. Asamoah-Gyadu, *African Charismatics*, 99.
136. Asamoah-Gyadu, 99.
137. Gifford, "Ghana's Charismatic Churches," 243.
138. Gifford, 243.
139. Gifford, 244.
140. Gifford, *Ghana's New Christianity*, 62.

property and close bank accounts, before the fundraising on Sunday, and give to the church."[141]

In his book entitled *Unbeatable Prosperity*, Gifford observes that Heward-Mills argues that prosperity is provided by divine provision and asserts confidently that "any time you minister personally to a man of God you invoke the laws of divine provision."[142] Gifford further notes that in Heward-Mills' book entitled *Name It! Claim It! Take It!* he declares that "the master key to your blessing is to name it, claim it, take it."[143]

Deliverance from Witchcraft

A second pillar of GPCC theology today is deliverance from witchcraft. Opoku Onyinah has observed that "the main agenda of . . . Ghanaian Pentecostals is deliverance, which is based on the fear of spirit forces, especially witchcraft."[144] Hans Debrunner, the Basel Mission church historian, has defined witchcraft as "the idea of some supernatural power of which [human beings] become possessed, and which is used exclusively for evil and antisocial purposes."[145] Jon P. Kirby, a Catholic missionary and anthropologist who worked in Ghana for thirty-six years, explains that in Ghana today, as in the past, "witchcraft beliefs seem to be the filter through which modern social institutions, including Christianity, are colored, interpreted, given new meanings, and dealt with."[146] Gifford has referred to this Ghanaian obsession with witchcraft as the result of a persistent "enchanted religious imagination."[147] He explains that the GPCC emphasis on deliverance from witchcraft is due to the fact that "the ills that beset Ghanaians are often explained in terms of spiritual forces, and many of these religious leaders claim the powers to control these forces."[148] Meyer concurs with this view by noting that the GPCC have constructed narratives

---

141. Gifford, 63.
142. Gifford, 152.
143. Gifford, 165.
144. Onyinah, "Deliverance as a Way." http://www.pctii.org/cyberj/cyberj10/onyinah.html.
145. Debrunner, *Witchcraft in Ghana*, 1.
146. Kirby, "Toward a Christian Response," 19.
147. Gifford, *Christianity, Development and Modernity*, 14.
148. Gifford, *Ghana's New Christianity*, 196.

of evil powers that enables them to present themselves as "the purveyors of true knowledge" and deliverance.[149]

Commenting on the GPCC preoccupation with witchcraft, Asamoah-Gyadu explains that "for the churches in Africa, evil preeminently includes witchcraft" and "successful Christian ministry . . . is impossible unless one takes into account the supernatural evil implied by the word 'witchcraft.'"[150] He argues that GPCC leaders have been further encouraged to see traditional African ideas of witchcraft causality as resonating with biblical teaching by the recent interest in spiritual warfare by various American Charismatic church leaders.[151] He notes that this "warfare language fits well with the African understanding of witchcraft."[152] Recent advertisements for Archbishop Nicholas Duncan-Williams show him wielding a sword, "suggesting his power over negative spiritual forces."[153]

The Man of God

The third pillar of GPCC theology is what Ogbu Kalu has called the syndrome of "the big man of the big God."[154] Gifford notes that this syndrome, promoted by both the GPCC prosperity doctrine and its emphasis on witchcraft, relies on the GPCC idea that there are demonic forces everywhere blocking the personal success of African Christians and their members can only appropriate the health and wealth being preached by faithfully and regularly giving their tithes and offerings to their church leaders. This, he argues, places "the person of the Man of God" at the center of church life and activities.

The special "man of God" is understood to have the "anointing" to conquer these forces and to "reverse the curse" that is holding back the success of African Christians. Gifford describes this as an "aggressive, theologically driven quest for funds"[155] and "a religious entrepreneur phenomenon" at the heart of which is "the seed" theology,[156] and he quotes a concerned observer

---

149. Meyer, "Delivered from the Powers of Darkness," 244.
150. Asamoah-Gyadu, "Witchcraft Accusations and Christianity in Africa," 26.
151. Asamoah-Gyadu, 26.
152. Asamoah-Gyadu, 26.
153. Asamoah-Gyadu, 26.
154. Kalu, *African Pentecostalism*, 105.
155. Gifford, *Ghana's New Christianity*, 70.
156. Gifford, 70.

who laments that the prosperity being preached by the GPCC enriches only the pastors and the new bishops.[157]

Praxis

The current profile of GPCC praxis is largely defined by their ecclesiology, their missiology, and their leadership styles. GPCC ecclesiology was originally shaped by the ethos of the student evangelical fellowships from which their leaders emerged, such as the Kanda Fellowship whose activities comprised mainly of corporate prayer, small group Bible study, and inviting guest speakers to teach on various biblical topics.[158] As the GPCC has grown and expanded over the last thirty years its ecclesiology has significantly evolved beyond that early simplicity.

GPCC Ecclesiology

The Sunday Worship Service

In most GPCC congregations today, there is usually one main service on Sunday morning that lasts four to five hours. These GPCC Sunday services, delivered primarily in English, with occasional translations into the vernacular, are made up of three parts: praise and worship, offerings, and the sermon.[159] The praise and worship sessions, usually very participatory, last for about an hour and are led by groups of several musicians who play mostly Western instruments. The songs, often simple and repetitive, are predominantly in the English language with frequent variations in the vernacular Ghanaian languages.[160] Gifford describes the GPCC praise and worship sessions as being "a significant element in the whole experience," that frequently brings "considerable numbers dancing down to the front."[161] Asamoah-Gyadu adds that most GPCC congregations are "youthful and worship is very exuberant, high in musical content and participatory."[162] Anderson notes that GPCC services "are usually emotional and enthusiastic, featuring electronic

---

157. Gifford, 70.
158. Larbi, *Pentecostalism*, 340–41.
159. Gifford, *Ghana's New Christianity*, 26–28.
160. Gifford, 26–28.
161. Gifford, 27.
162. Asamoah-Gyadu, *African Charismatics*, 119.

musical instruments."¹⁶³ The exuberance of GPCC worship sessions reflects what Debrunner has described as the "boisterous and lively" character of Ghanaians in general and their "immense zest for life."¹⁶⁴ Carolyn Worthge sees the festive atmosphere in GPCC services as being redolent of the music, drumming, and rhythmic dancing that in earlier times characterized religious ceremonies in traditional Ghanaian religion.¹⁶⁵

GPCC sermons, usually the principal focus of most GPCC services, typically last for at least an hour. Gifford notes that the preaching of GPCC leaders is neither expository nor doctrinal, with their sermons drawn predominantly from Old Testament narratives. He adds that, although the name of Jesus is often invoked in these sermons, little sustained use is made of Christ's teaching or his life.¹⁶⁶ The taking of offerings, usually after the sermon, is a prominent part of GPCC ecclesiology. The choirs, often consisting of young women, go into action and people dance exuberantly to the front to put their offerings in the offering boxes placed in the front area of the church. This can happen several times during the service and take up to half an hour.¹⁶⁷

GPCC Extracurricular Activities

GPCC ecclesiology involves more than the attendance of Sunday services. Church members are expected to attend several mid-week functions that include Bible teaching sessions and meetings of various church ministries and departments.¹⁶⁸ Gifford notes that these include "the welfare, children, prayer, outreach to prison or hospital, counseling, music, professionals' and women's fellowships and departments."¹⁶⁹ He adds that "almost every evening there are meetings: zonal, departmental or sectional meetings, or prayer meetings for specific groups."¹⁷⁰ During GPCC prayer meetings and vigils, Asamoah-

---

163. Anderson, *To The Ends of the Earth*, 234.
164. Debrunner, *History of Christianity in Ghana*, 1.
165. Worthge, "Praying for Prosperity," 9.
166. Gifford, *Ghana's New Christianity*, 28.
167. Gifford, "View of Ghana's New Christianity," 86–87.
168. Gifford, "Ghana's Charismatic Churches," 242.
169. Gifford, 242.
170. Gifford, 242.

Gyadu notes that "witches are resisted in prayer as demons who afflict God's people and fire is invoked from heaven to burn them."[171]

GPCC Conventions and Conferences

Another noticeable characteristic of GPCC ecclesiology is the importance placed on church conventions and conferences. GPCC leaders frequently travel abroad to attend conventions held by other Pentecostal-Charismatic churches and they also welcome leaders from other Pentecostal-Charismatic churches from around the world to attend their church conventions and conferences. Anderson describes this as the GPCC link to the "wider international networks of independent Charismatic preachers."[172] Rijk Van Dijk sees the adding of the words "international," "global," and "world," to GPCC names as reflecting their growing sense of being connected to this global movement.[173]

The GPCC church conventions and conferences often offer variations on the prosperity doctrine and are given themes such as "Winning Ways."[174] In recent years, some of the well-known Charismatic speakers who have featured in these functions include Mike Murdock, the late Myles Munroe, Creflo Dollar, and Matthew Ashimolowo.[175] These thematic conventions and conferences are frequently advertised on huge and costly signboards that have become ubiquitous landmarks in Ghana's main cities. These larger-than-life posters and signboards invariably display smiling GPCC leaders and their guest speakers in expensive-looking attire.

GPCC Use of Modern Media

Another significant aspect of GPCC ecclesiology is its widespread use of modern media technologies.[176] Meyer explains that the opportunity for the GPCC to use the media as widely as they do today arose from the liberalization of the Ghanaian media in the 1992 Constitution as the country moved

---

171. Asamoah-Gyadu, "Witchcraft Accusations and Christianity," 26.
172. Anderson, *To The Ends of the Earth*, 234.
173. Van Dijk, "Time and Transcultural Technologies," 221.
174. Gifford, *Ghana's New Christianity*, 53.
175. Gifford, 53.
176. Hackett, "Charismatic/Pentecostal Appropriation," 1.

towards a semblance of democracy.[177] Anderson notes that the GPCC have "a prominent media focus" that includes the publishing of their own literature, glossy booklets, and broadcast radio and television programs.[178] Marlene De Witte has argued that the GPCC spend the considerable funds they do to get themselves on TV because, in the TV culture, dramatic and visual effect create strong impressions on the public mind.[179] Gifford observes of GPCC leaders that, "whatever else they are," they are also entertainers who "have to compete in a crowded field. The repeated screening of their programs has made them media personalities and stars."[180] De Witte explains that the GPCC's use of media technology includes the appropriation of radio programs, audio and videocassette tapes containing GPCC sermons, and church magazines and newsletters.[181] Gifford observes that the widespread GPCC use of the media includes the publishing of books by GPCC leaders that are often ghostwritten.[182]

Profile of GPCC Congregations

GPCC ecclesiology and theology, in contrast to that of the traditional mission churches, has drawn into its ranks "the new urbanized generation of Africans," who are "younger, more educated, and consequently more Westernized professionals and middle-class urbanites."[183] Gifford notes that these aspiring middle class Ghanaians are noticeable by their expensive cars, "the hairstyles and hair-coverings of the women, the number of men in formal traditional clothes, the use of English, and the obtrusiveness of mobile phones."[184]

Asamoah-Gyadu explains that the GPCC dress code is modern and fashion-conscious because being "well dressed is considered an affirmation of God's blessing and prosperity and to some extent a measure of right standing with God."[185] Gifford argues that many aspiring Ghanaian middle-class

---

177. Meyer, "Praise the Lord," 92.
178. Anderson, *To The Ends of the Earth*, 234.
179. De Witte, "Spectacular and the Spirits," 314.
180. Gifford, *Ghana's New Christianity*, 32–33.
181. De Witte, "Spirit Media," 57.
182. Gifford, *Ghana's New Christianity*, 37.
183. Anderson, "Pentecostal Hermeneutics: Part 1," 234.
184. Gifford, "A View of Ghana's New Christianity," 84.
185. Asamoah-Gyadu, *African Charismatics*, 119.

professionals find the GPCC attractive for two reasons. First, because of the GPCC's theology of "ambition, achievement and opportunity, directly geared to the upwardly mobile," and second, because the GPCC leaders offer themselves as role model "entrepreneurs who have developed" successful religious enterprises.[186]

Asante has argued that, in a culture that is already very communal in its ethos and worldview, a key feature of GPCC ecclesiology is the social networking and the sense of community it engenders in the urban Ghanaian context.[187] D. J. Antwi equates this sense of communality in the GPCC with NT *koinonia*.[188] Kobena Hanson takes a more pragmatic view by noting that relationships established in the GPCC church context can be crucial for gaining business and employment opportunities in an economy in which most employment is found within the private informal sector.[189] Worthge argues that, for many young urban Ghanaians, GPCC social networking provides "contacts, friends, and potential spouses."[190] She adds that GPCC communality is particularly important for "women who are generally confined to the home doing housework each day since the church offers an escape from the mundane, and a place where they can take on a role other than housewife."[191]

GPCC Missiology

Concerning its missiology, scholars have commented that the GPCC began with an emphasis on missions and evangelism. In its formative years, for example, Gifford notes that Mensa Otabil's IGCC was "distinguished for its evangelism," and explains that those attending the church's early Sunday service would conduct a coordinated evangelism program beforehand and those attending the latter services would then conduct a similar exercise afterwards. In recent years, however, Gifford argues that its emphasis has shifted to an inordinate interest in "this world."[192] The GPCC now appear to display a noticeable lack of interest in "the end times" with "very little focus

---

186. Gifford, *African Christianity*, 91.
187. Asante, "The Gospel in Context.," 362–65.
188. Antwi, "A Sense of Community," 68.
189. Hanson, "Landscapes of Survival and Escape," 1305.
190. Worthge, "Praying for Prosperity," 24.
191. Worthge, 24.
192. Gifford, "Ghana's Charismatic Churches," 244.

on heaven or hell."[193] He notes that ,for this reason, the GPCC "have grown not by converting non-Christians but by attracting members" of the mainline churches and the moribund AIC's.[194]

This GPCC failure to emphasize missions but instead to grow by poaching members from the traditional mission churches has also been commented on by Asamoah-Gyadu. He notes that, in a recent poll of four hundred members of four GPCCs, more than 90 percent of them conceded that they came from Anglican, Methodist, Presbyterian, or Roman Catholic backgrounds.[195] He attributes the GPCC's success in drawing away members from the mission churches into their own ranks, instead of engaging in missions, to two reasons. He explains that first, in the period when the GPCCs were taking root in the Ghana church landscape, the GPCC appealed to many young people "to leave their 'dead' and 'irrenewable' churches" because mission churches held "negligible emphasis on salvation as a conscious personal experience," and their "virtual silence on the Holy Spirit."[196] Secondly, he notes that, ignoring the "abiding contribution [of] both to the spread of Christianity and to the socio-economic and political development" of the mission churches in Ghana, the GPCC mounted "attacks on the traditional mission churches that were derisive, unsympathetically sharp and scathing."[197]

By doing this, Asamoah-Gyadu argues, the GPCC's "created a gulf between themselves and the mission churches that did not help Christian witness in Ghana."[198] The GPCC, he adds, overlooked the fact that they had been able to establish themselves and grow in the country "only in areas where traditional mission churches already exist as testimony to the important foundations that these older churches have laid for the gospel in Ghana."[199]

GPCC Leadership

With reference to GPCC leadership, Asamoah-Gyadu has noted that in its early days the general GPCC understanding was that the leaders were

---

193. Gifford, *Ghana's New Christianity*, 81.
194. Gifford, 38.
195. Asamoah-Gyadu, *African Charismatics*, 117.
196. Asamoah-Gyadu, 116.
197. Asamoah-Gyadu, 124.
198. Asamoah-Gyadu, 125.
199. Asamoah-Gyadu, 125.

expected to lead the body of Christ "by virtue of their special calling, but most importantly they are only expected to inspire others in the employment of their gifts."[200] Anderson observes that, although they had begun as non-denominational evangelical groups, with their growth and expansion, the GPCCs developed "denominational structures" and "episcopized" their leaders who then began to assign to themselves ecclesiological titles such as archbishops, bishops, and prophets.[201] The GPCC leaders, Gifford maintains, "have thus become increasingly important figures" in Ghana with "their otherness trumpeted quite unashamedly."[202] Gifford adds that, to "entrench their personal control," several GPCC leaders "have brought their wives into leadership positions."[203]

Gifford cites the case of Otabil's IGCC where many of his pastors maintain that Otabil "used his increasing stature to make himself totally unaccountable."[204] Dag Heward-Mills has written several books about loyalty and makes his teaching about loyalty a key feature of his ministry. As a result, Heward-Mills rails against any contrary opinion expressed by his subordinates, and calls them "traitors, villains, anarchists, mutineers, rebels, betrayers."[205] Of this evident lack of servant leadership, Gifford notes that "many of these new churches have absolutely nothing except the pastor's vision."[206]

Summary

This chapter has addressed research questions 2, 2A, and 2B through a review of the social science literature. This review has examined what the social science literature reveals about the antecedent religious, socio-economic, and political factors that led to the establishment and growth of the five leading autonomous Ghana Pentecostal-Charismatic Churches (GPCCs) that are highlighted in this study. This chapter has also presented and reviewed what the social science literature reveals about the current theology and practices of the GPCC.

---

200. Asamoah-Gyadu, 129.
201. Anderson, *To The Ends of the Earth*, 234.
202. Gifford, *Ghana's New Christianity*, 186.
203. Gifford, 187.
204. Gifford, 187.
205. Gifford, 188.
206. Gifford, 188.

CHAPTER 4

Methodology

Introduction

This chapter provides a description of the duly triangulated methodological framework for this study. It explains the procedures and instruments that have been involved in obtaining and analyzing the data for addressing the study's research questions.

Overview of Exegetical Study

In his brief epistle, Jude describes biblical Christianity as "the faith that was once for all delivered to the saints" (Jude 3 ESV). The proposed research problem in this study is as follows: From an evangelical and Pentecostal understanding of Jude's Epistle, how should Ghanaian Pentecostal-Charismatic Christians, in their theology and praxis, "contend for the faith that was once for all delivered to the saints" (Jude 3 ESV) in demonstration of biblical Christianity? The purpose of this study is to identify principles of NT Christianity from Jude's Epistle that can be used to advocate for a more contextualized biblical Christianity in the Ghana Pentecostal-Charismatic church. The goal is to ensure that sound biblical doctrine (as revealed in the NT) is better understood, more widely accepted, and authentically lived out by Ghanaian Pentecostal-Charismatic Christians who desire to do so.

The Nature of this Study

This research study used an interdisciplinary qualitative research methodology. This methodology is particularly appropriate for this study because its examination of the theology and practices of the GPCC involved efforts to obtain information on the perceptions of the churches from within the churches themselves "through a process of deep attentiveness, of empathetic understanding."[1] This methodology has conformed to John Swinton and Harriet Mowat's definition of qualitative research as the study of things in their natural settings, attempting to make sense of, or interpret, phenomena in terms of meanings people bring to them.[2] This has also corresponded to Keith Punch's understanding that, in qualitative research, the researcher's role is to gain "a 'holistic' overview of the context under study."[3] This is especially applicable to this study because it proposes to be primarily exegetical in nature, supplemented by the social science literature and field research of the views and teaching of GPCC leaders.

The interdisciplinary nature of this study has been reflected in its use of exegetical/hermeneutical and empirical social science research methodologies. This use of exegetical/hermeneutical and empirical social science research methodologies, Marvin Gilbert observed, has ensured that "the Truth of the Word rightly divided and the truth of empirical research credibly executed can be effectively integrated to challenge, empower, and guide the Church in the pursuit of God's mission."[4] The advantages of such interdisciplinary research include the commitment to discipline-specific, best-practice methods; the generation of conclusions that are fact-driven and not preconceived ideas; and the elimination of guesswork and existing prejudicial beliefs.[5]

---

1. Punch, *Introduction to Research Methods*, 117.
2. Swinton and Mowat, *Practical Theology and Qualitative Research*, 29.
3. Punch, *Introduction to Research Methods*, 117.
4. Gilbert and Johnson, "Interdisciplinary Research," 1.
5. Gilbert and Johnson, 2.

Research Questions 1, 1A, and 1B

Research question 1 (RQ1) asked: What principles of biblical Christianity emerge from an exegetical study of the Greek text of the epistle of Jude? RQ1A asked: What is Jude's meaning of the phrase "contending for the faith once for all delivered to the saints" in relation to the teaching and behaviour of the false teachers? RQ1B asked: What accepted evangelical interpretations have arisen from various scholars' exegesis of the text?

Exegetical Study

The research methodology that has addressed research questions 1, 1A, and 1B was an exegetical analysis of the Greek text of Jude's epistle. This methodology is cardinal to this study because of its primary focus to identify principles of biblical Christianity from Jude's epistle that can be offered as recommendations for promoting contextualized biblical Christianity in the GPCC.

In seeking to ascertain the meaning of Jude, both for its original readers or hearers and for the GPCC today, this study's exegetical analysis was based on the primary assumption of the authority and unity of scripture.[6] Establishing Jude's meaning has been carried out with the aid of the appropriate commentaries, grammars, and the other theological tools listed in Chapter 2. This has involved establishing the historical, cultural, socio-economic, political, and geographic context of Jude.[7] It has also entailed a discovery of the original theological meaning of the text because this was critical to determining what Jude's text meant to those to whom his epistle was originally addressed. After ascertaining what the text meant to the original audience, this meaning has since been applied to today's GPCC.[8]

An important place has been given to the review of applicable scholarly commentaries on Jude and the wider theological literature, with a view to discovering how other Bible scholars have interpreted and understood the meaning of Jude's text to its original recipients. This has enabled the study to corroborate its understanding of the text with the conclusions of the wider

---

6. Vyhmeister, *Quality Research Papers for Students,* 141–50.
7. Vyhmeister, 147.
8. Vyhmeister, 148.

theological community.⁹ This has been particularly important in this research study since its intention was to identify principles of biblical Christianity from Jude's Epistle in its review of how the church has interpreted Jude historically and as it has examined what accepted evangelical views have arisen from the exegesis of recognized scholars.

Research Questions 2, 2A, and 2B

Research question 2 (RQ2) asked: What does the social science literature reveal about the theology and practices of the five leading autonomous Pentecostal-Charismatic churches in Ghana? RQ2A asked: What does the social science literature reveal about the antecedent religious, socio-economic, and political factors that led to the establishment and growth of the GPCC? RQ2B asked: What does the social science literature reveal about the theology and practices of the GPCC?

Integrative Critical Analysis

These research questions have been addressed through a review of the social science literature informed by integrative critical analysis (ICA). Marvin Gilbert has defined ICA as a research method useful for producing a well-crafted, credible, and comprehensive review of precedent literature.[10] He has argued that the primary strength of ICA is that "it allows the integration of the findings reported in *multiple* bodies of knowledge."[11] Gilbert explains that ICA can be applied to both the relevant biblical-theological and the social science literature without the researcher "being easily convinced by one theological or empirical position or another."[12] In this study, the use of ICA has involved the application of critical thinking skills while interacting with both the theological and social science literature.

Gilbert notes that the first goal of ICA is the creation of a big-picture overview of the literature that empowers the reader to grasp the complexity of the

---

9. Vyhmeister, 148.
10. Gilbert, "Integrative Critical Analysis," 1.
11. Gilbert, 2.
12. Gilbert, 3.

interdisciplinary literature. The second goal, he notes, is strategic sequencing in the literature review that builds a "case" based on published findings and theories. These two goals of ICA have enabled this research to "empower the reader to reach evidence-based conclusions that build convincingly throughout the review."[13] The third goal of ICA, Gilbert explains, "is the identification of what *does not* appear in the literature."[14] This has also enabled this study to build a credible case for its research by distinguishing between what the academy knows and what it does not yet know.[15]

Research Questions 3, 3A, and 3B

Research question 3 (RQ3) asked: What does GPCC leaders' own output reveal about their theology? RQ3A asks: What does the content of GPCC leaders' teachings and writings reveal about their theology? RQ3B asked: What do GPCC leaders' own points of view reveal about their theology? RQ3 was a collective question that has been answered by the integration and analysis of the results from RQ3A and RQ3B. RQ3A has been answered by the content analysis of the teachings and writings of GPCC leaders and RQ3B has been answered by Q Methodology. Below is a brief overview of Q Methodology and an explanation of how the study used this methodology to answer RQ3B.

Q Methodology

Steven R. Brown has described Q Methodology as a methodology "that provides perhaps the most thoroughly elaborated basis for the systematic examination of human subjectivity."[16] This means that this study's use of Q Methodology has enabled the subjective understanding of GPCC leaders about their theology to be observed, understood, and described, as part of the process of answering RQ3B. This use of Q Methodology has also enabled the study to separate its own subjectivity from the subjectivity of GPCC

---

13. Gilbert, 4.
14. Gilbert, 5.
15. Gilbert, 4.
16. Brown, "Q Methodology," 699.

leaders. Braswell has observed that this is one of the great advantages of Q Methodology.[17]

The first of the five steps involved in this study's Q Methodology analysis was the identification of a "concourse."[18] Brown defines a concourse as "the volume of common communicability with regard to any topic"[19] that can be gathered from "the media, interviews, and the internet."[20] In this study, the concourse has comprised of the published sermons, teachings, and writings of GPCC leaders.

The second of the five Q Methodology steps in this study involved a sampling of the entire concourse through generating thirty-five statements from the teachings and writings of GPCC leaders that has been used to assess their points of view.[21] Braswell explains that this structured sampling is known as "the "Q-set" and is administered as a "Q-sort" by constructing "a target grid in the shape of a flattened normal curve."[22] In this study, the instructions that have guided the sorting of the statements were divided into several columns from "Most Like My View" on the far right to "Most Unlike My View" on the far left, with the column in the middle saved for statements that are neutral.[23]

The third step involved collecting the Q-Sort data. In this study, the persons, normally referred to as the "P-set," who undertook the sorting were selected because of their leadership roles and positions in the GPCC. These comprised of four senior officials from each of the five churches in this study. Each participant was personally offered an explanation of the sorting assignment. Built into the administration of the Q-Sort was a certain degree of "follow-up interviewing to validate the Q-set and to better understand what participants were thinking during the sort."[24]

The fourth step involved the statistical analysis of the collected Q-Sort data through the use of an online software program called PQMethod. This enabled comparison and identification of sorting patterns commonly known

---

17. Gilbert et al., *Research Methods and Proposal Development*, 97.
18. Braswell, "Q Methodology," 107.
19. Brown, "Q Methodology," 699.
20. Brown, "Q Methodology," 699.
21. Brown, 700.
22. Braswell, "Q Methodology," 108.
23. Brown, "Q Methodology," 566.
24. Braswell, "Q Methodology," 109.

as "factors."[25] The software calculated the "averaged" sort for each factor that identified "what the pattern-defining sorts had in common,"[26] and additionally indicated "what statements were most influential for each factor, including which statements were treated in significantly different ways by different factors."[27]

The fifth and final step involved the objective interpretation of the factors that emerged from the statistical analysis of the collected Q-Sort data. The factors represented a point of view shared by the sorts. These points of view were then interpreted in the given context to emphasize the statements that were important in explaining and defining the factor.[28] This use of Q Methodology to understand GPCC leaders' subjective understanding of their theology has enabled this study to compare and analyse the Q Methodology outputs with what has been identified above as Jude's principles in Chapter 2 and thereby fully address RQ3B.

Validity and Reliability

The qualitative research methods used in this study were an exegetical study of the epistle of Jude, the use of integrative critical analysis to review the social science literature, and the use of Q Methodology. This research has ensured that both its design and the way it has been applied meet accepted validity and reliability criteria. Edgar Elliston notes that validity may relate to both the design of the research as well as to the way it is applied.[29] He further explains that reliability is a "subset" of validity that establishes the consistency and accuracy of a research instrument or method.[30]

The threat to the validity and reliability of the exegetical study of the epistle of Jude would have been the inadequate exegesis and hermeneutical analysis of the text, and an eisegetic analysis, interpretation, and application of the text. To address this, the research drew primarily from highly recognized and credible commentaries and scholars on the epistle. The study also adhered

---

25. "FlashQ." http://www.hackert.biz/flashq/demo/.
26. Braswell, "Q Methodology," 109.
27. Braswell, 109.
28. Brown, "Q Methodology," 700.
29. Elliston, *Introduction to Missiological Research Design*, 56.
30. Elliston, 62.

to Gordon Fee's recommendation that biblical exegetical studies should be defined by a historical investigation into the meaning of the biblical text with the aim of applying one's exegetical understanding of the text to the contemporary church and world.[31]

The threat to the validity and reliability of the use of integrative critical analysis to review the social science literature in this study could have come from an absence of high quality selected social science literature and an inadequate integration of biblical theological analysis with social science/literature review conclusions. To counter this, careful thought went into both the selection of appropriate social science literature and the adequate integration of theological analysis with the conclusions drawn from the review of social literature.

The threat to the validity and reliability of the Q Methodology would have come from inadequate care being taken in the statistical analysis of the Q-Sorts. This could have resulted in less-than-accurate factor interpretation. This threat has been addressed by ensuring that the Q-Sort allowed the participants to make their subjective judgments observable enough.[32] This has enabled the research "to comprehend the patterns among sorts using statistical tools."[33] The end result has been sufficient validity and reliability that has ensured that this research method has yielded "a structured, relatively objective path to deeper understanding of the views"[34] of the GPCC with reference to their theology and praxis.

Research Ethics and Informed Consent Protocol

This research was committed to principles of best practice ethical research with human subjects. Towards this end, the research ensured that its overall conduct and, more specifically, its data collection have been carried out, in the words of Denscombe, "in a way that protects the interests of the participants; ensures that their participation is voluntary and based on informed consent; avoids deception and operates with scientific integrity; and complies with the

---

31. Fee, *New Testament Exegesis*, 1–2.
32. Braswell, "Q Methodology," 109.
33. Braswell, "Q Methodology," 109.
34. Braswell, 109.

laws of the land."[35] Adequate information about the research was provided to participants, specifying to them what kind of commitment was being required of them.[36] A draft copy of the consent for participation in the Q Methodology research outlined above is attached as appendix A.

Summary

The methodological framework described above clarifies this research's choice of an interdisciplinary qualitative research approach to address its research questions.

---

35. Denscombe, *Good Research Guide*, 331.
36. Denscombe, 333.

CHAPTER 5

Results and Analysis

Introduction

This chapter analyses the results and findings obtained from the research data. First to be submitted will be the findings from the exegetical study of the Greek text of Jude's epistle aimed at answering RQ1 and its sub-questions. Next to be offered will be the findings from the study's review of the relevant social science literature to address RQ2 and its sub-questions. Third, the results obtained from a Q-Sort analysis will be analysed to identify and understand the shared perceptions of GPCC leaders, in answer to RQ3B.

The analysis of the study's research results that will be undertaken in this chapter, and the subsequent conclusions and recommendations for praxis change that will also be offered in the next chapter, will cite from a narrow range of secondary scholarship that has not been situated in the context of the larger discussions of which they are a part. This is for three reasons. First, doing so is outside the scope of this study. Second, these sources have been chosen because they offer evangelical theological perspectives that effectively counter various aspects of the GPCC theology and praxis presented and discussed in the foregoing chapters. Third, the views of these scholars have, in recent years, had a significant impact on the evangelical understanding of the issues addressed herein.

Findings

Research Questions 1, 1A, and 1B

Research questions 1, 1A, and 1B sought to discover what principles of biblical Christianity would emerge from an exegetical study of the Greek text of the epistle of Jude; what Jude's meaning of the phrase "contending for the faith once for all delivered to the saints" was in relation to false teachers; and what accepted evangelical interpretations have arisen from various scholars' exegesis of Jude. An exegetical analysis of the Greek text of Jude's epistle was undertaken in Chapter 2 to address this first set of research questions. This involved establishing the historical, cultural, socio-economic, political, and geographic context of Jude, and discovering what Jude's text meant to those to whom his epistle was originally addressed. The study's exegetical analysis yielded the following understanding of the text.

In verses 1–2, Jude opens his epistle with a salutation. Following this salutation, in verses 3–5, Jude explains that he wrote to urge his readers to fight for the preservation of the basic tenets of the Christian gospel in opposition to the errant teaching and the ungodly influence of false teachers who had infiltrated the congregation with heretical teaching. In Jude's understanding, these false teachers' immoral and godless lifestyle was a direct attack on the moral implications of the gospel that call for holy and righteous living. From verses 5–7, he reminds his readers of God's judgments in the past against such godlessness. In verses 8–19, Jude describes the godless character of the false teachers and God's forthcoming judgment of them. Between verses 19 and 23, Jude presents a number of ways in which his readers should "build up their most holy faith" and contend for it. He concludes the epistle with an inspiring doxology of praise to God in verses 24–25. In the process of ascertaining Jude's meaning and what the text meant to the original audience, seven principles of biblical Christianity were identified in the epistle and extensively discussed above in Chapter 2.

RQ2, RQ2A, and RQ2B

Research questions 2, 2A, and 2B set out to identify what the social science literature reveals about the origins, the theology, and the practices of the five leading autonomous Pentecostal-Charismatic churches in Ghana, what the literature reveals about the antecedent religious, socio-economic, and political factors that led to the establishment and growth of these churches, and what the literature discloses about their current beliefs and practices.

That review concluded that the creation of the GPCC was an attempt, during a period of much socio-political turbulence in Ghana, to address the felt religious needs of Ghanaians that older mission churches and AICs had not met. As Ghana's socio-economic and political situation stabilized, to remain relevant to the interests of the Ghanaian middle class of professionals, the theology and praxis of the GPCC changed from its initial evangelical and Pentecostal fervor to a more accommodative theology that emphasized material affluence and upward mobility.[1]

With growing congregations and the establishment of institutional church structures came the need for the GPCC to secure and reinforce sources of predictable income. Gifford confirms this by noting that the GPCC's "buildings, pastors, programs, vehicles, instruments and sound systems have had to be paid for."[2] Arguably, this sense of financial pressure could very well be one of the reasons that led to the current GPCC emphasis on the prosperity doctrine. These emphases, soon to be discussed, inspired giving in the GPCC. Concomitant with the institutionalization of the GPCC was the establishment of leadership structures that mirror the dictatorial characteristics of most African political leadership. Table 3 below diagrams the similarities and differences between GPCC theology and praxis and Jude's principles of biblical Christianity.

---

1. Asamoah-Gyadu, *African Charismatics*, 1.
2. Gifford, *Ghana's New Christianity*, 80.

Table 3. Similarities and differences between GPCC theology and praxis and Jude's principles of biblical Christianity

Jude's Biblical Principles	Similar to or Different from	Explaining GPCC Similarity/Difference
No. 1: New birth in Christ results in the indwelling by the Holy Spirit.	Similar	GPCC statements of faith affirm the acceptance of new birth in Christ resulting in indwelling by the Holy Spirit. e.g.: IGCC.[3]
No. 2: Sound biblical doctrine results in godly living.	Different	The GPCC focuses primarily on the prosperity doctrine.
No. 3: Selfless servant leadership is essential for the church.	Different	The GPCC lacks expressions of NT servant leadership.
No. 4: Sound biblical doctrine results from disciplined Bible study.	Different	GPCC theology is characterized by the prosperity doctrine.
No. 5: Spirit-inspired prayer is essential for building up the church.	Different	GPCC praying focuses on material prosperity and deliverance from witchcraft.
No. 6: A positive expectation of the *parousia* keeps the church faithful to Christ.	Different	This is noticeably lacking in current GPCC theology that emphasizes a lifestyle of material affluence in the here and now.
No. 7: Missions, evangelism, and discipleship are essential for the church. Jude's concern was to bring back into the church Christians who have compromised their faith.	Different	The GPCC lacks focused evangelism directed at non-Christians and effective discipleship to bring backsliding members back into the church.

---

3. "International Central Gospel Church." http://www.centralgospel.com/?root=about.

RQ3, RQ3A, and RQ3B

Research questions 3, 3A, and 3B sought to identify what GPCC leaders' own output (their teachings, points of view, sermons, and writings) reveals about their theology. RQ3 and RQ3A have already been addressed in Chapter 3 in the review of the social science literature. The review presented the teachings and writings of GPCC leaders. Presented below to address RQ3B are the results obtained from a Q-Sort analysis aimed at identifying and understanding the shared perceptions of GPCC leaders.

Q-Sort Data for Addressing Research Question 3B

Research Question 3B asks: What do GPCC leaders' own points of view reveal about their theology? This research question is addressed by Q Methodology as previously explained in Chapter 4. Below are, first, a presentation of the process that has been involved; second, the research data that has been produced; and third, the analysis and interpretation of the data obtained from using Q Methodology to address this research question.

PQMethod, the statistical software program specifically designed for Q Methodology studies, was used in this exercise. Originally developed by John Atkinson under the guidance of the Q Methodology expert Steven R. Brown, PQMethod has been adapted and maintained by Peter Schmolck as a free download from the Internet.[4] Watts and Stenner observe that the PQMethod "facilitates data input, generates the initial by-person correlation matrix, and make processes of factor extraction, rotation and estimation very straightforward."[5]

The Process

Brown explains that the process involved in using PQMethod to analyse and interpret Q-Sort data is as follows: "each Q sort produces a set of scores (typically ranging from +4 to −4) representing the degrees of preference for all statements."[6] This allows each person's individual subjective response to be "statistically correlated with every other"[7] with "the magnitude of the

---

4. Schmolck, "PQMethod." http://schmolck.userweb.mwn.de/qmethod/pqmanual.html.
5. Watts and Stenner, "Doing Q Methodology," 80.
6. Brown, "Q Methodology," 701.
7. Brown, 701.

correlation coefficients indicating the degree of similarity among the various perspectives."[8] Brown further explains that "the factor analysis of the correlations reveals the number of qualitatively different ways in which the various Q sorts have been organized, that is, the number of different viewpoints (or attitudes, identities, narratives, schemata, etc.) inherent in the population."[9]

As already explained in Chapter 4, twenty GPCC leaders were given thirty-five cards with a statement typed on each card. The thirty-five statements were formulated from two sources. The first source was the seven principles of biblical Christianity obtained from this study's exegetical-hermeneutical analysis of Jude. The second source was the writings, sermons, and teachings of GPCC leaders as well as generally-held GPCC theological perspectives as indicated in the social science literature. The GPCC leaders were asked to sort the cards according to how much the statements on the cards represented their own views of their respective church's theological beliefs.

There were several steps involved in using PQMethod to produce an analysis of this study's Q-Sort data. First, PQMethod enabled the editing of a file into which was entered the text of the Q-Sort statements. Second, PQMethod enabled a routine called QENTER that allowed the direct entry of data from the Q-Sorts. Third, PQMethod created a correlation matrix from the raw Q-Sort data. PQMethod next provided a choice between two methods of factor analysis: QCENT for a Centroid factor analysis, or QPCA for Principal Component analysis. Watts and Stenner note that, although "there often seems little reason for preferring one system over another," most researchers use QPCA because it's a "more recently developed" analytic technique.[10] Braswell explains that "a reason for preferring PCA is that it extracts a factor with the largest possible variance first, then extracts the next largest uncorrelated factor, and so on, so that unrotated PCA is the best solution when all sorts load on a single factor."[11]

Fourth, after running the PCA analysis, the option for judgmental rotation was opened. Only two rotating factors were chosen. This was chosen as a new rotation, not a continuation of any previous rotation. The rotation

---

8. Brown, 701.
9. Brown, 700.
10. Watts and Stenner, "Doing Q-Methodology," 80.
11. Braswell, "GPCC Q-Sorts Analysis," 31st January 31st, 2018, 1. Personal E-Mail to Researcher.

screen was then entered to obtain a screen capture of the scatterplot. This was done to assist with the interpretation of the factors. Finally, QAnalyze was run to get an output file (LIS) based on the above choices. Schmolck notes that "this differentiates the factors based on the original Q-sort statements."[12]

The Data Generated

PQMethod yielded a number of files and tables from the Q-Sort data. It provided a table that illustrated the loadings of the participant Q-Sorts on all the extracted and rotated factors. The significant loadings were marked with an asterisk (*). The eigenvalues[13] and the percentage of the study variance explained by each factor were provided. A table entitled "Factor Correlations" indicated the inter-correlations of the various factor arrays that arose, which were the most important files gathered. This table gives the basic indication of the relationships between the factors. These were provided as tables entitled "Factor Scores." All the data tables produced are presented in Appendix B.

The Q-Sort data indicated that most of the GPCC participants sorted the thirty-five statements in a highly correlated manner. Brown notes that this is an indication of a commonly held outlook and that this explains why the correlations yielded are as highly positive as they are, clearly pointing to the fact that only one main factor is in evidence in this study.[14] A factor is a composite sort, created by the software that is based on the agreements among the (flagged) sorts that load on it. Watts and Stenner explain that in Q Methodology a conventional practice is "to select only those factors with an eigenvalue in excess of 1.00."[15] This, they argue, "is a generally accepted means of safeguarding factor reliabilities, and factors which go below this minimum will ultimately serve no data-reductive purpose as they explain less of the overall study variance than would any single Q sort."[16]

The much larger eigenvalue of Factor 1, in contrast to the eigenvalues for Factors 2 and 3, indicates that Factors 2 and 3, obtained from the initial

---

12. Schmolck, "PQMethod." http://schmolck.userweb.mwn.de/qmethod/pqmanual.html.
13. An eigenvalue is the sum of the squared loadings of the sorts.
14. Brown, "Q Methodology," 702.
15. Watts and Stenner, "Doing Q Methodology," 81.
16. Watts and Stenner, 84.

extraction, may not be meaningful factors. Their small eigenvalues and strong correlation with Factor 1 confirm this.

The scatterplot below, with its one main cluster of points, demonstrates visually that the sorting data represents one main single factor. A scatterplot shows the relationship between two variables on a horizontal and a vertical axis. The relationship between the two variables on the scatterplot shows the correlation between the two variables. The overall agreement on Factor 1 is represented on the scatterplot as the single cloud of points all in the vertical direction from the horizontal axis. The disagreements within the agreement are represented by the left end and right end of the cloud of points at some horizontal distance from each other on the scatterplot. The cluster is spread out so that the respondent with the largest positive loading on Factor 2 is all the way at the right while the other respondents loading negatively on Factor 2 are all the way at the left. The position of an asterisk on the scatterplot indicates that more than one sort shares that position on the scatterplot.

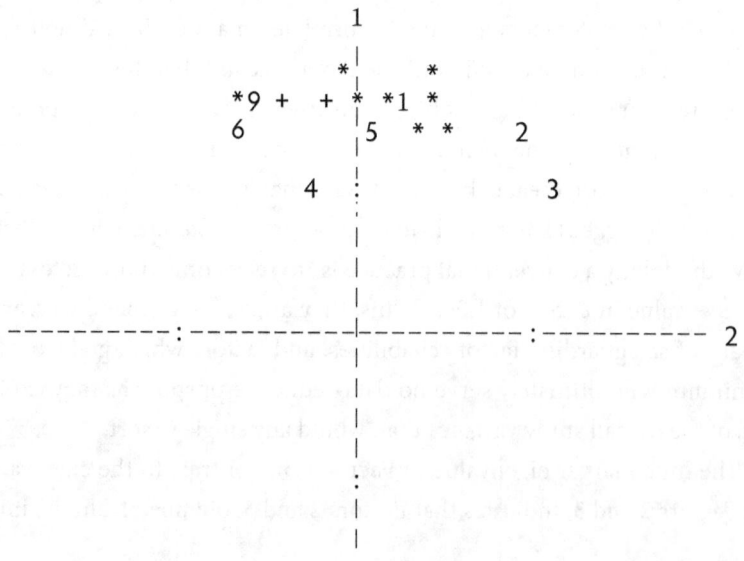

Figure 1. The scatterplot

To understand the range of views within F1, a second LIS file was produced by flagging the two rightmost sorts of the scatterplot in what is listed above in Table 1 as Factor 2, to represent sub-factor A. A mirror image copy of this factor was made. It was rotated by 180 degrees so that the two sides of the scatterplot were flipped to enable subfactor B to be understood in its natural direction rather than as negative loadings on subfactor A. Two representative sorts were flagged to represent subfactor B. These two subfactors, representing the right and left ends of the scatterplot loadings, were thus generated to help in understanding the nature of the disagreements within the overall agreement of Factor 1.

Interpreting the Data

In interpreting Q-Sort data, Brown notes that "the meaning and significance of each statement is entirely in the hands of participants."[17] He adds that, in the interpretive process, "[first], the investigator is constrained by the factor scores – that is, the scores (typically from +4 to −4) registering the degree of agreement or disagreement with the statements within each of the factors."[18] He then adds that the interpretive process must reflect "the entire pattern of scores"[19] because the pattern of all statements affects the meaning of particular statements.

Brown explains that this is what makes it possible for what began as an undifferentiated concourse to end with a pattern of meaning "that explains why the volume of subjective communicability displays this particular form and content."[20] Watts and Stenner explain that "the interpretative task in Q-Methodology involves the production of a series of summarizing accounts, each of which explicates the viewpoint being expressed by a particular factor"[21] with "reference to the positioning and overall configuration of the items in the relevant 'best-estimate' factor arrays."[22] Figure 2 presents the grid showing the composite GPCC sort and Table 2 that follows presents the 35 statements. On the basis of this composite GPCC sort Factor 1 and the two sub-factors are analysed, interpreted, characterized, and named below.

---

17. Brown, "Q Methodology," 701.
18. Brown, 702.
19. Brown, 702.
20. Brown, 701.
21. Watts and Stenner, "Doing Q Methodology," 82.
22. Watts and Stenner, 82.

-4 Most Unlike My View	-3 Very Strongly Unlike My View	-2 Strongly Unlike My View	-1 Unlike My View	0 Neutral	1 Like My View	2 Strongly Like My View	3 Very Strongly Like My View	4 Most Like My View
8	11	1	12	4	16	2	14	17
9	13	6	22	5	20	3	15	24
	30	10	23	7	25	19	28	
		18	27	21	26	35		
			31	92	33			
				32				
				34				

Figure 2. Grid showing the composite GPCC sort

Table 4. The thirty-five statements sorted by the GPCC leaders

Statement	No.
The gospel is that Christ died to deliver us from poverty and disease.	1
I am a true Christian because I am indwelt by the Holy Spirit.	2
Christ calls all Christians to engage in evangelism and discipleship.	3
Not paying my tithes and offerings is robbing God.	4
Pentecostal-Charismatic sermons accurately interpret the Bible.	5
Praying aloud in tongues is Spirit-inspired prayer.	6
Healing the sick is evidence of an anointed man of God.	7
The gospel is that Christ died to make us rich and successful.	8
I am a Christian because I speak in tongues.	9
My active participation in church proves I am a serious Christian.	10
I must pay my tithes to properly prepare for Christ's second coming.	11
Paying my tithes and offerings affirms my Christian faith.	12
As a Christian suffering should not be my portion in life.	13
My faith in Christ's death and resurrection makes me a Christian.	14
The fruit of the Holy Spirit demonstrates my Christian maturity.	15
Church leaders must demonstrate humility and self-sacrifice.	16
The Holy Spirit guides us to pray according to God's will.	17
A mega church is evidence of the anointing of the man of God.	18
Discipleship is teaching Christians to faithfully follow Jesus.	19
Sound biblical doctrine results from disciplined Bible study.	20
A Bible text's meaning intended by the original author applies to me.	21
Pentecostal-Charismatic pastors must exemplify personal success.	22
Praying in tongues is more effective than praying silently.	23
The church's mandate is to make disciples of all nations.	24
Pentecostal-Charismatic pastors must practice servant leadership.	25
Looking forward to Christ's second coming keeps Christians faithful.	26
As a Christian, I can, by faith, name and claim prosperity.	27
The gospel is that Christ died and rose again for our salvation.	28
Spiritual transformation prepares me for Christ's second coming.	29
The mission of the church is to end poverty in the lives of Christians.	30
Discipleship is teaching Christians to be loyal church members.	31
Not paying my tithes and offerings is forfeiting my blessings.	32
The second coming of Christ is the church's blessed hope.	33
Evangelism and discipleship demonstrate Christian mercy.	34
Christians must eagerly anticipate Christ's second coming.	35

Factor 1: Assent to NT Orthodoxy

As already noted above, the Q-Sort data generated in this study reveals that most of the GPCC participants sorted the thirty-five statements in a highly correlated manner. This indicates a high level of agreement in their sorts. Watts and Stenner note that an important part of the interpretive process in Q Methodology is a careful review of the sorts at the two "poles" of a factor because this is where one finds the items that the participants who loaded on the factor feel particularly strongly about.[23] The statements that characterize the two ends of Factor 1 (+4 and -4), presented below in Table 3, lead us to characterize and name Factor 1 as "Assent to NT Orthodoxy."

Table 5. The two ends of Factor 1: Assent to Jude's principles and NT orthodoxy

No.	Statement	Ranking	Z-Score
24	The church's mandate is to make disciples of all nations.	+4	1.559
17	The Holy Spirit guides us to pray according to God's will.	+4	1.387
8	The gospel is that Christ died to make us rich and successful.	-4	-1.400
9	I am a Christian because I speak in tongues.	-4	-1.584

These four statements at the two ends of Factor 1 lead us to characterize and name Factor 1 as "Assent to NT Orthodoxy" because they reflect the counsel of the NT as a whole. The first of the two statements on the far right that the GPCC leaders most agreed with, Statement 24 ("The church's mandate is to make disciples of all nations"), ranked as +4 (Most like my view), corresponds to Jude's seventh principle of biblical Christianity (Missions, Evangelism and Discipleship are essential for the church). This statement corresponds to the words of Jesus Christ in Matthew 28:18–20[24] that call on his disciples to go and make disciples of all nations. This command by Christ has come to be known as the Great Commission. The sorting of the GPCC

---

23. Watts and Stenner, "Doing Q Methodology," 82.

24. Although this study is focused principally on Jude, as already noted in chapter 2, the study takes the view that "the faith once and for all delivered to the saints" reflect apostolic witness and principles of biblical Christianity found throughout the NT corpus.

leaders, therefore, indicates their commitment to the Great Commission. The second of the two statements on the far right that the GPCC leaders most agreed with, Statement 17 ("The Holy Spirit guides us to pray according to God's will"), also ranked as +4 (Most like my view), corresponds to Jude's fifth principle of biblical Christianity (Engaging in Spirit-inspired prayer is essential for the church). This statement reflects NT orthodoxy by corresponding to Paul's thought in Romans 8:26–27 that the Holy Spirit enables Christians to pray according to the will of God.

The two statements at the far left of the grid equally demonstrate the GPCC leaders' assent to NT orthodoxy. The first of the two statements on the far left of the grid that the GPCC leaders most disagreed with is Statement 8 ("The gospel is that Christ died to make us rich and successful"), ranked as -4 (Most unlike my view). This unbiblical statement, frequently condemned by scholars, reflects a foundational idea of the prosperity doctrine.[25] The second of the two statements on the far left of the grid that the GPCC leaders most disagreed with was Statement 9 ("I am a Christian because I speak in tongues"), which they also ranked as -4 (Most unlike my view). Their disagreement reflects NT orthodoxy because Paul's definition of a Christian is a person who has "the Spirit of Christ" (Rom 8:9), not necessarily one who speaks in tongues. This definition of a Christian as a person who has the Spirit of Christ was the first principle of biblical Christianity identified by this study as being suggested by Jude 19. This first principle states that people who identify themselves as being Christians must be truly born again and indwelt by the Holy Spirit. To declare that one is a Christian because they speak in tongues demonstrates ignorance of this fundamental NT doctrine.

In keeping with Watts and Stenner's explanation that the two ends of a factor reveal what the participants who loaded on the factor feel particularly strongly about, a review was carried out of the statements that the GPCC leaders' sorted as very strongly like their view (+3) and very strongly unlike their view (-3) to ascertain how these line up with this study's characterization and interpretation of the two ends of Factor 1 as reflecting, on the whole, the GPCC leaders' assent with NT orthodoxy. The six statements that were ranked as +3 and -3 are presented below.

---

25. Fee, *Disease of the Health and Wealth Gospels*, 7.

Table 6. Further demonstration of assent to Jude's principles and NT orthodoxy

No.	Statement	Ranking	Z-Score
28	The gospel is that Christ died and rose again for our salvation.	+3	1.361
15	The fruit of the Holy Spirit demonstrates my Christian maturity.	+3	1.311
14	My faith in Christ's death and resurrection makes me a Christian.	+3	1.257
11	I must pay my tithes to properly prepare for Christ's second coming.	-3	-1.390
13	As a Christian suffering should not be my portion in life.	-3	-1.388
30	The mission of the church is to end poverty in the lives of Christians.	-3	-1.253

The three statements above that the GPCC leaders sorted as very strongly like their view (Statements 28, 15, and 14) all equally demonstrate the leaders' assent to NT orthodoxy because they reflect an understanding of the NT's teaching about salvation and the marks of Christian maturity. The three statements above that the leaders sorted as very strongly unlike their view (Statements 11, 13, and 30) all repudiate principles that underlie the prosperity doctrine and, in equal measure, contradict NT orthodoxy.

Competing Views

On the scatterplot, sorts 2 and 3, at the far-right end of the scatterplot, represent subfactor A. Sorts 6 and 14, at the far-left end of the scatterplot, represent subfactor B. These two groups represent two competing views within the overall agreement on F1. These competing views within the overall agreement on F1 show how, in their views, the pastors who loaded on these subfactors differ in emphasis from one another, and from the main agreement in Factor 1.

Tables 7 and 8 below present the two ends of both subfactor A and subfactor B to show what these pastors feel strongly about. The similarities of views between the two groups are evident. Following the tables below is a brief analysis and interpretation of their differences and how they can thus be characterized and named.

Table 7. Subfactor A

No.	Statement	Value	Z-Score
17	The Holy Spirit guides us to pray according to God's will.	+4	1.647
15	The fruit of the Holy Spirit demonstrates my Christian maturity.	+4	1.530
24	The church's mandate is to make disciples of all nations.	+3	1.320
21	A Bible text's meaning intended by the original author applies to me.	+3	1.308
4	Not paying my tithes and offerings is robbing God.	+3	1.215
27	As a Christian, I can, by faith, name and claim prosperity.	+3	-1.203
18	A mega church is evidence of the anointing of the man of God.	-3	-1.320
12	Paying my tithes and offerings affirms my Christian faith.	-3	-1.308
9	I am a Christian because I speak in tongues.	-4	-1.530
30	The mission of the church is to end poverty in the lives of Christians.	-4	-1.869

Table 8. Subfactor B

No.	Statement	Ranking	Z-Score
14	My faith in Christ's death and resurrection makes me a Christian.	+4	1.809
24	The church's mandate is to make disciples of all nations.	+4	1.524
28	The gospel is that Christ died and rose again for our salvation.	+3	1.314
17	The Holy Spirit guides us to pray according to God's will.	+3	1.295
32	Not paying my tithes is forfeiting God's blessing.	+3	1.276
30	The mission of the church is to end poverty in the lives of Christians.	-3	-1.029
23	Praying in tongues is more effective than praying silently.	-3	-1.029
22	Pentecostal-Charismatic pastors must exemplify personal success.	-3	-1.276
9	I am a Christian because I speak in tongues.	-3	-1.314
13	As a Christian suffering should not be my portion in life.	-4	-1.563
11	I must pay my tithes to properly prepare for Christ's second coming.	-4	-1.791

Disagreements Within the Overall Agreement

As already noted above, on the whole, the Q-Sort data indicates that most of the GPCC participants sorted the thirty-five statements in a highly correlated manner. Overall, the two ends of Factor 1 lead to the conclusion that this factor can summarized, characterized, and interpreted as generally reflecting the GPCC leaders' assent with NT orthodoxy. As shown in Tables 5 and 6, the same can be said of subfactors A and B, although their positions on the far-left and the far-right ends of the scatterplot gives an indication of emphasis on differing aspects of the theology and praxis of the GPCC. Some of these differences in emphasis are reviewed below to explain how the study has therefore characterized and named these two subfactors.

Characterizing and Naming the Subfactors

As noted above, the positions of subfactors A and B on the far-right and the far-left ends of the scatterplot gives an indication of their emphasis on differing aspects of the theology and praxis of the GPCC. These differences are very clearly displayed in the values the two subfactors assigned to statements 14 and 27.

To statement 14 ("My faith in Christ's death and resurrection makes me a Christian"), subfactor A assigned a value of -2 (Strongly unlike my view). Subfactor B, on the other hand, assigned a value of +4 (Most like my view) to this statement. Factor 1 equally assigned to this statement a high value of +3 (Strongly like my view). This statement, as Paul confirms in Romans 10:9–10, is a fundamental tenet of NT orthodoxy. The value assigned by Factor 1 to this statement further affirms this study's earlier characterization and interpretation of the two ends of Factor 1 as reflecting, on the whole, the GPCC leaders' assent with NT orthodoxy. Subfactor B, by assigning +4 (Most like my view) to this statement, also reflects NT orthodoxy. The pastors who loaded on subfactor A, on the other hand, by sorting this statement as being strongly unlike their view (-2), demonstrate a sharp variance from NT orthodoxy and a fundamental misunderstanding of some of the basic tenets of the gospel.

The same observation can be made about statement 27 ("As a Christian, I can, by faith, name and claim prosperity"). To this statement, subfactor A assigned a value of +3 (Very strongly like my view). Subfactor B assigned to it a value of -2 (Strongly unlike my view), and Factor 1 assigned to it a value of -1 (Unlike my view). Once again, while both Factor 1 and sub-factor B demonstrate NT orthodoxy in their sorting of this statement, subfactor A takes a variant view that strongly affirms the prosperity doctrine.

Highlighting above the stark differences in the way subfactors A and B ranked statements 14 and 27 demonstrates that the two groups do indeed represent two competing views within the overall agreement on F1 as shown on the scatterplot, and generally in the Q-Sort data. Subfactor B evidently shares the general NT orthodoxy of Factor 1 and can thus appropriately be characterized and named in this study as "Conventional Pentecostal Charismatic Views."

The pastors who loaded on subfactor A, on the other hand, in the words of Gordon Fee, seem to have "misunderstood the basic nature of the gospel."[26] Fee, in his exegesis of 1 Corinthians 1:18–3:4, uses this phrase to describe the Corinthian Christians who seemed to have forgotten that "the gospel has a crucified Messiah, risen from the dead, at its very heart"[27] and were therefore placing a greater emphasis, in their theology and praxis, on material human values and human wisdom. Fee concludes that as a result of their misunderstanding of the gospel the Corinthian Christians had also misunderstood "what it means to be a person of the Spirit" and had therefore adopted "a triumphalist view of life."[28]

The triumphalist misunderstanding of the gospel evinced by the Corinthian Christians and the subfactor A pastors explains why these GPCC pastors would give a low value of -2 (Strongly unlike my view) to statement 14 ("My faith in Christ's death and resurrection makes me a Christian") but give to statement 27 ("As a Christian, I can, by faith, name and claim prosperity") a high value of +3 (Very strongly like my view). For this reason, subfactor A is hereby characterized and named in this study as "Triumphalist Pentecostal Charismatic Views."

This process of interpreting the differences between the main factor and the two subfactors was followed with all the statements listed in the tables of distinguishing statements for the factors. In doing so, the same pattern of sometimes nuanced differences as well as strong differences were continually observed.

The Jude Sort

To enable the objective comparison of the GPCC sorts with Jude's principles of biblical Christianity obtained from the exegetical-hermeneutical analysis of Jude in Chapter 2, a sorting of the thirty-five statements that explicitly accords with Jude's principles of biblical Christianity were undertaken by this researcher. The same procedure outlined above for entering the GPCC sorting data in PQMethod was used for the Jude sort. The data tables are presented in Appendix C. The Jude sort did not change the overall data analysis that was previously yielded without the Jude sort. The similarities between the

---

26. Fee and Stuart, *Bible For All Its Worth*, 64.
27. Fee and Stuart, *Bible Book by Book*, 326.
28. Fee and Stuart, 326.

information in Table 1 (above) and Table 9 (below) demonstrate this. The average reliability coefficient of Factor 1 in the data without the Jude sort is .80 and the composite reliability is .98.[29] These exact same figures applied to the data with the Jude sort, confirming that the Jude sort did not change the overall data analysis.

Table 9. Eigenvalues and percentage of variation with the Jude sort added

Factor	Eigenvalues	% Expl. Var.
1	12.3897	59
2	1.3171	6
3	0.9815	5

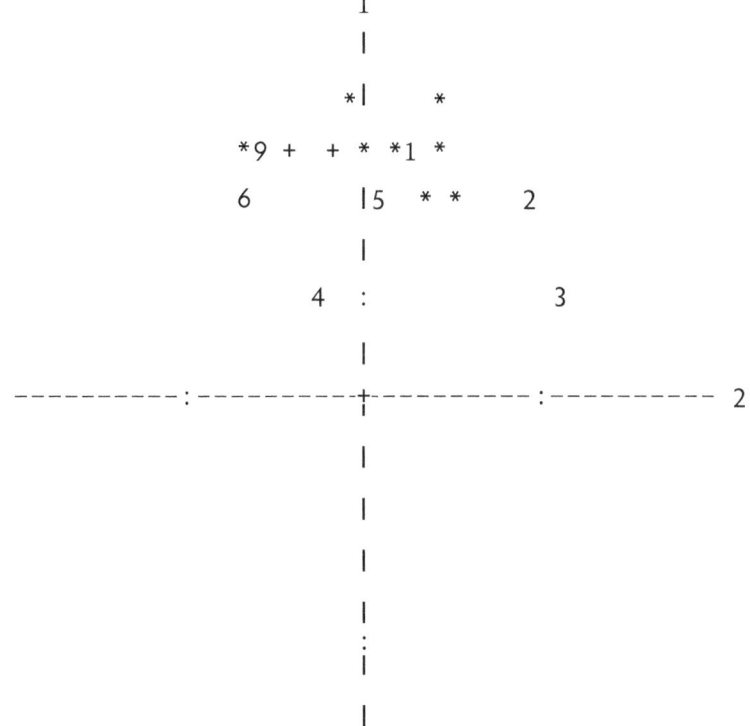

Figure 3. The scatterplot without the Jude sort

---

29. Braswell confirms the reliability of these statistics in this Q Methodology study that yielded similar results: Braswell, "Passing Down Pentecost," 13.

-4 Most Unlike My View	-3 Very Strongly Unlike My View	-2 Strongly Unlike My View	-1 Unlike My View	0 Neutral	1 Like My View	2 Strongly Like My View	3 Very Strongly Like My View	4 Most Like My View
8	30	5	32	20	33	17	24	28
1	13	10	18	26	2	16	29	19
	27	22	7	15	21	25	14	
		31	4	6	3	35		
			11	9	34			
				12				
				23				

Figure 4. Grid showing the Jude sort

The list of statements numbered in the grid has already been presented above on page 96. Drawn from the grid above, Table 10 below presents the two ends of the Jude sort.

Table 10. The two ends of the Jude sort

No.	Statement	Ranking
28	The gospel is that Christ died and rose again for our salvation.	+4
19	Discipleship is teaching Christians to faithfully follow Jesus.	+4
8	The gospel is that Christ died to make us rich and successful.	-4
1	The gospel is that Christ died to deliver us from poverty and disease.	-4

Statements 28 ("The gospel is that Christ died and rose again for our salvation") and 19 ("Discipleship is teaching Christians to faithfully follow Jesus") were assigned a Q-Sort value of +4 (Most like my view) because they are both fundamental NT tenets of the gospel that Jude wrote to urge his readers to contend for. These two statements therefore affirm, respectively, Jude's first and seventh principles of biblical Christianity. Statements 8 ("The gospel is that Christ died to make us rich and successful") and 1 ("The gospel is that Christ died to deliver us from poverty and disease") were equally assigned a Q-Sort value of -4 (Very strongly like my view), because they contradict both NT orthodoxy and instead affirm the theological leaning of the false teachers in Jude's Epistle that he wrote to warn his readers against.

Differences Between the Jude and GPCC Sorts

The differences between the two ends of the Jude sort and the GPCC sorts are presented below in Table 11 and discussed below.

Table 11. The different ranking of statements by the GPCC and Jude sorts

No.	Statement	Factor 1 Value	Subfactor A Value	Subfactor B Value	Jude Sort Value
28	The gospel is that Christ died and rose again for our salvation.	+4	+1	+3	+4
19	Discipleship is teaching Christians to faithfully follow Jesus.	+2	+2	+2	+4
8	The gospel is that Christ died to make us rich and successful.	-4	-3	0	-4
1	The gospel is that Christ died to deliver us from poverty and disease.	-2	-2	0	-4

On the far-right end of the grid, to statement 28 ("The gospel is that Christ died and rose again for our salvation"), the Jude sort assigned a Q-Sort value of +4 (Most like my view) but subfactor A assigned a value of +1 (Like my view) to this statement. This indicates a lower emphasis on this fundamental tenet of NT theology by the GPCC pastors who loaded on this factor than the Jude sort. Both Factor 1 and subfactor B assigned respectively to this statement the values of +4 (Most like my view) and +3 (very strongly like my view), indicating that they share with the Jude sort a similarly positive view about this important NT belief. To statement 19 ("Discipleship is teaching Christians to faithfully follow Jesus"), the Jude sort once again assigned a Q-Sort value of +4 (Most like my view) but all the GPCC pastors, loading on the other three factors, assigned a value of +2 (Like my view) to this statement. This shows a weaker emphasis on this view by the GPCC pastors than the Jude sort. The Jude sort prioritized this statement, because in Luke 9:23, Jesus Christ stated that being his disciple means denying oneself, taking up one's cross daily, and following him. Jude's seventh principle of biblical Christianity equally affirms discipleship as being essential for the church.

On the far-left end of the grid, to statement 8 ("The gospel is that Christ died to make us rich and successful"), the Jude sort assigned a strong Q-Sort value of -4 (Most unlike my view), as did Factor 1, to show a strong disagreement with this view that contradicts NT orthodoxy. To statement 1 ("The gospel is that Christ died to deliver us from poverty"), the Jude sort assigned a strong Q-Sort value of -4 (Most unlike my view). Both Factor 1 and subfactor A assigned a weaker value of -2 (Strongly unlike my view) to the statement.

The differences between the Jude sort and the GPCC sorts are equally evident in the statements that the GPCC leaders sorted as very strongly like their view (+3) and very strongly unlike their view (-3). The six statements in these two categories are presented and briefly reviewed below.

The six statements in the two ranking categories presented above further reveal the differences in theological emphasis between the GPCC sorts and the Jude sort. Once again, as already noted above, statement 14 ("My faith in Christ's death and resurrection makes me a Christian") and statement 27 ("As a Christian, I can, by faith, name and claim prosperity"), in particular, highlight these differences. To statement 14, the Jude sort assigned a value of +3 (Very strongly like my view) but sub-factor A assigned a value of -2 (Strongly unlike my view) to it. To statement 27, the Jude sort assigned a value of -3 (Very strongly unlike my view) but subfactor A assigned a value of +3 (Very strongly like my view) to it. While the Jude sort repudiated this statement, the pastors who loaded on subfactor A evidently affirm this quintessential prosperity doctrine view in no small measure. This further confirms the characterization and naming assigned to this subfactor in this study. These differences are statistically significant because they demonstrate a difference of at least three categories in the Q-Sort values assigned to them by the two groups being compared.[30]

Table 12. Further evidence of differences between the GPCC and Jude sorts

No.	Statement	Factor 1 Value	Subfactor A Value	Subfactor B Value	Jude Sort Value
24	The church's mandate is to make disciples of all nations.	+4	+3	+4	+3
29	Spiritual transformation prepares me for Christ's second coming.	0	+1	0	+3
14	My faith in Christ's death and resurrection makes me a Christian.	+3	-2	+4	+3
30	The mission of the church is to end poverty in the lives of Christians.	-3	-4	-3	-3
13	As a Christian suffering should not be my portion in life.	-3	-1	-4	-3
27	As a Christian, I can, by faith, name and claim prosperity.	-1	+3	-2	-3

Addressing RQ3B

Q Methodology was used in this study to address research question 3B that asks what GPCC leaders' own points of view reveal about their theology.

---

30. Watts and Stenner, "Doing Q Methodology," 88.

The comparison between the GPCC and the Jude Q-Sorts indicates that, although there are similarities between the two, there are also significant differences of emphasis between them. The conclusion this study draws from this data analysis, therefore, is that although the GPCC sorts demonstrate a general intellectual assent to NT orthodoxy and Jude's principles of biblical Christianity, the theological differences between them are significant enough to warrant a more careful examination of the underlying reasons that explain what the GPCC leaders' own points of view, as revealed by their sorts, reveal about their theology.

Analysis: GPCC Theology and Praxis

The findings from research questions 1, 1A, and 1B yielded the understanding that Jude wrote his epistle to urge his readers to fight, in their doctrinal confession and lifestyles, for the preservation of the basic tenets of the Christian gospel in opposition to the errant teaching and influence of false teachers who had infiltrated the congregation with heretical teaching. The findings from research questions 2, 2A, 2B, 3, and 3A showed the similarities with and the differences between GPCC theology and praxis and Jude's principles of biblical Christianity. The findings from research question 3B obtained from the Q-Sort analysis of the shared perceptions of GPCC leaders indicated the lack of a coherent and consistently orthodox theology in the GPCC. Some of the beliefs revealed from the sorting ostensibly align with Jude's principles, while others reflect the GPCC's current theological emphasis on the prosperity doctrine, deliverance from witchcraft, and the special powers and anointing of "the man of God."

Jude wrote to warn his readers of false teachers who had "crept in stealthily" (Jude 4) into the ranks of his readers. In the case of the GPCC, it appears that it is false teaching that has been allowed to "creep in stealthily" into these churches in the form of theological points of view and doctrinal influences that differ from Jude's principles of biblical Christianity. This is evident from the lack of a coherent and consistently orthodox theological belief system in the GPCC that emerged from their sorts. The underlying reason for this inconsistency appears to be the GPCC's continuing emphasis on the three main pillars of their theology already noted above. Presented below, therefore, is an examination of the different ways in which these pillars of GPCC theology and praxis are at odds with Jude's principles of biblical Christianity.

The Prosperity Doctrine

In the GPCC Q-Sorts, five statements were directly related to the prosperity doctrine. These were statement number 1 ("The gospel is that Christ died to deliver us from poverty and disease"), statement number 8 ("The gospel is that Christ died to make us rich and successful"), statement number 13 ("As a Christian suffering should not be my portion in life"), statement number 22 ("Pentecostal-Charismatic Pastors must exemplify personal success"), and statement number 27 ("As a Christian, I can, by faith, name and claim prosperity"). The Q-Sort values that the GPCC leaders respectively assigned to these statements in the main factor, Factor 1, are -2, -4, -3, -1, and -1. Although the GPCC leaders' ranking of these statements indicates that these statements are not like their views, Asamoah-Gyadu confirms in a recent overview of the GPCC's current theology that the GPCC still strongly advocate and promote the prosperity doctrine.[31]

The prosperity doctrine, which has already been defined in Chapter 3, is at odds with Jude's principles of biblical Christianity in a number of significant ways. First, the prosperity doctrine supports its theology on the foundation of a consistent misinterpretation of Scripture.[32] Kenneth Mbugua confirms this by noting that "the falsehood of the prosperity gospel is rooted in the misinterpretation of the Bible."[33] This contradicts Jude's fourth principle of biblical Christianity, gleaned from verse 17 of his epistle, that a commitment to disciplined Bible study, both individually and corporately, results in sound biblical doctrine.

The sound interpretation of Scripture calls for the discovery of the original meaning of a biblical text as it was intended by the original author and understood by his original readers. This is done through a careful study of the text's historical, cultural, and literary contexts. The interpreter then identifies timeless implications and principles based on the author's original intention that can be applied in the historical, social, and spiritual context of contemporary

---

31. Asamoah-Gyadu, *Sighs and Signs*, 163–76.
32. Fee, *Disease of the Health and Wealth Gospels*, 9.
33. Mbugua et al., *Prosperity?*, 16.

Christians.³⁴ Prosperity doctrine preachers generally ignore these principles of biblical interpretation by reading their own intended meaning into the biblical text to support their teaching.³⁵ Asamoah-Gyadu refers to this as the practice of "selective hermeneutics"³⁶ in the GPCC that relies on proof texts to interpret the Scriptures "without due attention to context."³⁷

Second, the prosperity doctrine contradicts Jude's seventh principle of biblical Christianity obtained from verses 22–23 of his epistle. This principle is that the church must demonstrate Christian mercy through missions, evangelism, discipleship, and spiritual formation. One prominent African prosperity preacher, David Oyedepo of Winners Chapel, represented the general GPCC prosperity doctrine ethos when he claimed that God has specifically instructed him that God's mission today is to "make my people rich."³⁸ Femi Adeleye has criticized this as a distortion of the mission of Jesus Christ that was primarily to save lost humanity from sin.³⁹ Bible scholars have warned that a serious danger of this troubling distortion of the mission of God is that the current numerical growth of the African church may in the end sadly "be relegated to the status of a footnote of church history."⁴⁰ This distortion of the mission of God has diverted GPCC members from an active participation in the true mission of God. Asamoah-Gyadu notes that this distortion of God's mission has prevented the GPCC from seeking to plant churches in the rural parts of the country where the difficult economic conditions of most rural Ghanaian hinder the kind of giving that feeds the prosperity doctrine in urban areas.⁴¹

More seriously, perhaps, the prosperity doctrine has created many GPCC churchgoers who mistakenly believe that they are genuine Christians when they are not (Matt 7:21–23).⁴² Individuals, having been told that Jesus could give them the relief they seek from poverty, sickness, and despair if they

---

34. Klein, Blomberg, and Hubbard, *Introduction to Biblical Interpretation*, 8–13.
35. Fee, *Disease of the Health and Wealth Gospels*, 8.
36. Asamoah-Gyadu, *Sighs and Signs*, 168.
37. Asamoah-Gyadu, 174.
38. Adeleye, *Preachers of a Different Gospel*, 91.
39. Adeleye, 161.
40. York and Block, *MIS 9253: Leadership and Training*, 8.
41. Asamoah-Gyadu, *Sighs and Signs*, 166–67.
42. Musyimi, *Counterfeit Gospel*, 143.

repeat a certain prayer, have done so without a genuine sense of conviction (Acts 2:38) and without a pure desire to follow Jesus (Luke 9:23–26).[43] The preponderance of non-Christians within the GPCC violate Jude's first principle of biblical Christianity, obtained from verse 19 of his epistle, that people who identify themselves as being Christians must be truly born again and indwelt by the Holy Spirit.

Third, the prosperity doctrine contradicts Jude's sixth principle of biblical Christianity suggested by verse 21 of his epistle. This principle asserts that Christians must actively nurture faith into their lifestyles, a positive eschatological expectation of Christ's *parousia*. Through the work of Christ on the cross to break the power of sin and Satan, the kingdom of God is now a spiritual reality in human history in the lives of men and women who, by faith, have submitted their lives to Christ. This kingdom of God will be fully manifested in power and glory with the return of Christ to restore God's original kingdom purposes for His creation. Now, however, Christians live prayerfully in the tension of the already and not yet (Col 3:4; 1 John 3:2) as they eagerly look forward to Christ's second coming to consummate the kingdom of God in which God will once again dwell with His people in His kingdom here on earth (Rev 11:15; 21:1–4).[44] This will then become a world without pain, suffering, sorrow, or death. The prosperity doctrine taught in the GPCC is that as "the King's kids"[45] in the kingdom of God, Christians are now entitled to perfect lives of material prosperity and perfect health in this fallen world.

Alfred Koduah has described the prosperity doctrine as the GPCC's "new gospel" that preaches a "problem-free and a suffering-free" Christianity.[46] This "new gospel" preached in the GPCC displays serious ignorance about the already/not yet reality of the Christian life that scholars have labeled as "over-realized eschatology."[47] Mark Vander Pol defines over-realized eschatology as expecting the eternal blessings of the "not-yet" eschatological period in the "already" of today.[48] Vander Pol argues that "over-realized eschatology takes

---

43. Platt, *Follow Me*, 3–24.
44. Fee, *Disease of the Health and Wealth Gospels*, 42–43.
45. Fee, 9.
46. Koduah, *Christianity in Ghana Today*, 132.
47. Vander Pol, "An Over-Realized What?," 1.
48. Vander Pol, 1.

a Christian's eyes off of the cross of Christ and looks to one's own situation as the measure of what God has done and is doing for us."[49]

Gordon Fee sees an over-realized eschatology as being the root problem behind the non-Christian behaviour of the Corinthian church that contradicted the moral imperatives of the gospel.[50] Fee observes that "they were arguing that they should be living out their new eschatological existence."[51] He notes that this "Corinthian false theology"[52] can be attributed to their "over-realized eschatology informed by an improper understanding of spiritual enthusiasm."[53] A. C. Thiselton concurs with this view by noting that "the Corinthians were behaving as if the age to come were already consummated . . . For them there is no 'not yet' to qualify the 'already' of realized eschatology."[54] Matthew R. Malcolm adds that "the Corinthians were behaving as though they could lay claim to eschatological arrival."[55] Malcolm labels this Corinthian behaviour as "premature triumphalism."[56]

In the above analysis of the Q-Sort data, the GPCC pastors who loaded on subfactor A have already been characterized as demonstrating pronounced triumphalist Pentecostal Charismatic views similar to the over-realized eschatology views of the Corinthian Christians. This over-realized eschatology in the GPCC has resulted in what Asamoah-Gyadu describes as an "emphasis on health, wealth, promotion, advance, privilege, and power in the gospel of prosperity that necessarily implies that those who preach it have a weak theology of pain and suffering."[57] Their over-realized eschatology has also hindered the GPCC from actively nurturing the kind of positive eschatological expectation of Christ's *parousia* that Jude urges upon his readers.

Fourth, Asamoah-Gyadu notes that GPCC leaders preach the prosperity doctrine "in support of their extravagant and materialistic lifestyles."[58] He

---

49. Vander Pol, 2.
50. Fee, "1 Corinthians 7:1 in the NIV," 313.
51. Fee, 313.
52. Fee, 313.
53. Fee, 313.
54. Thiselton, "Realized Eschatology at Corinth," 525.
55. Malcolm, "Premature Triumphalism in Corinth," 115.
56. Malcolm, 115.
57. Asamoah-Gyadu, "Witchcraft Accusations and Christianity," 25.
58. Asamoah-Gyadu, *Sighs and Signs*, 164.

observes that recently one GPCC leader "opened his house and wardrobe to a local TV station to film his luxurious estate and expensive cars."[59] This theology and praxis of covetousness calls to mind Jude's denunciations of the sybaritic and godless antinomianism of the false teachers (Jude 4, 16) because it "distorts the person of Christ by portraying Jesus as one who was materially rich."[60] It may very well have been a similar distortion of the person of Christ that provoked Jude's sharp denunciation of the false teachers for perverting the grace of God into sensuality and denying the truth about "our only Master and Lord, Jesus Christ" (Jude 4).

Deliverance from Witchcraft

The GPCC teaching and understanding of deliverance from witchcraft was reviewed in Chapter 3. Yusuf Turaki attributes the ubiquitous focus on witchcraft in the African church to the continuing influence of ATR in the worldview of African Christians.[61] Wilbur O'Donovan notes that even today, witchcraft is a source of great fear in the lives of many church-going Africans.[62] Keith Ferdinando has noted that, because African Christians confront their problems through the prism of such ATR thinking, they still seek the services of a specialist, a diviner, "who is supposed to be able to penetrate the unseen world of spirits and occult power to discern what is taking place there."[63] Reference has already been made in Chapter 3 to Birgit Meyer's observation that in the GPCC the church founders offer themselves as modern day diviners with special powers to deliver church members from witchcraft by constructing narratives of evil powers that enable them to present themselves as "the purveyors of true knowledge."[64] This bears an uncanny resemblance to the false teachers in Jude's epistle, whom he condemned for offering up their dreams as visions to justify their godless teaching and behaviour (Jude 8).[65] Ferdinando also observes that, because witchcraft is perceived in the African worldview as explaining suffering and misfortune, in recent years

---

59. Asamoah-Gyadu, 167.
60. Asamoah-Gyadu, 175.
61. Turaki, *Foundations of African Traditional Religion*, 117–18.
62. O'Donovan, *Biblical Christianity in Modern Africa*, 330.
63. Ferdinando, *Battle Is God's*, 13.
64. Meyer, "Delivered from the Powers of Darkness," 244.
65. Kelly, *Commentary on the Epistles of Peter*, 260–61.

African churches such as the GPCC have demonstrated a vested interest in maintaining witchcraft fears because it helps them to attract members.[66]

Ferdinando has noted a number of ways in which this "unwholesome preoccupation with the powers of evil . . . rather than with God himself" harms the church. He notes that, first, it denies the NT understanding that "the Christian is a person who has been redeemed, forgiven, born again, and delivered from Satan's power by the work that God has accomplished through Christ"[67] as Jude affirms in the very first verse of his epistle. Second, Ferdinando notes that the inordinate obsession with witchcraft overlooks the fact that Christians have the assurance of God's "constant presence and of the indwelling power of the Holy Spirit in their lives to guide and sustain them" because their "struggle with the world, the flesh and the devil takes place because they have *already* been saved through the death and resurrection of Jesus Christ."[68]

Ferdinando asserts that, thirdly, the GPCC's focus on witchcraft harms the church by sustaining "misguided cultural and theological preconceptions,"[69] a false theology of fatalism and passivity, encouraging church members to "evade personal responsibility for failure,"[70] attribute all their sinful habits, trials, and difficulties to witchcraft, stir division, hostility, fear, and hatred in the church community when individuals are wrongly accused of using witchcraft to harm others.[71] Jude denounces such division within the church community in verse 19 of his epistle. These various ways in which the GPCC obsession with witchcraft harms the church also negate Jude's conviction that the Lord is able to protect his people and to present them blameless before "the presence of his glory with great joy, through Jesus Christ" (Jude 24–25).

The Man of God

In the GPCC Q-Sorts, five statements were directly related to the GPCC "man of God" syndrome. These were statement number 7 ("Healing the sick is evidence of an anointed man of God"), statement number 16 ("Church

---

66. Ferdinando, *Battle Is God's*, 22.
67. Ferdinando, 82.
68. Ferdinando, 83.
69. Ferdinando, 92.
70. Ferdinando, 22.
71. Ferdinando, 102.

leaders must demonstrate humility and self-sacrifice"), statement number 18 ("A mega church is evidence of the anointing of the man of God"), statement number 22 ("Pentecostal-Charismatic pastors must exemplify personal success"), and statement number 25 ("Pentecostal-Charismatic pastors must practice servant leadership"). The Q-Sort values that the GPCC leaders respectively assigned to these statements in the one main factor (Factor 1) are 0, 1, -2, -1, and 1. The GPCC leaders' low ranking of these statements is revealing.

The GPCC emphasis on their church leaders being special men of God has already been reviewed in Chapter 3. That review noted that scholars have described this phenomenon as the syndrome of "the big man of the big God"[72] that places "the person of the Man of God" at the center of church life and activities.[73] Gottfried Osei-Mensah notes that "such leaders have no real conception of serving others; they promote themselves and have no thought of being examples of godliness. Instead they lord it over those in their trust."[74]

The scholars Hiebert, Shaw, and Tienou have called attention to the tendency in young churches and church movements such as the GPCC to develop personality cults around charismatic and frequently authoritarian church leaders.[75] They note that this creates church members who are merely followers with "an uncritical trust in their leaders" and who attribute healings, prophecies, and miracles to these leaders who are then easily tempted "to take credit for the work, encourage the adoration of their followers, and not be accountable to others."[76] The profile of GPCC leadership that emerges from the social science literature fits this description.

This evident lack of servant leadership in the GPCC is a clear contradiction of Jude's third principle of biblical Christianity, derived from verses 12, 16, and 19 of his epistle, which affirms that selfless servant leadership must distinguish the management of the church. In these verses of his epistle, Jude strongly castigates the grasping for power by the false teachers within the faith community to serve their own selfish ends.

---

72. Kalu, *African Pentecostalism*, 105.
73. Gifford, *Ghana's New Christianity*, 70.
74. Osei-Mensah, *Wanted: Servant-leaders*, 25.
75. Hiebert, Shaw, and Tienou, "Responding to Split-Level Christianity," 9.
76. Hiebert, Shaw, and Tienou, 9.

Summary

This chapter has submitted the results obtained from the research data. First, it has presented the findings from the exegetical-hermeneutical study of the Greek text of Jude's Epistle aimed at answering RQ1 and its sub-questions. Next, it has presented the findings from the study's review of the relevant social science literature that addressed RQ2 and its sub-questions. Third, the results obtained from a Q-Sort analysis to identify and understand the shared perceptions of GPCC leaders about their theology and praxis to address RQ3B have been described and analysed through the prism of Jude's principles of biblical Christianity.

CHAPTER 6

Conclusions and Recommendations

Introduction

This chapter submits the study's conclusions and recommendations for praxis change and additional research. First, a summary of the results obtained to address the study's three research questions will be presented. Second, implications will be drawn from these research results. Third, recommendations will be offered for implementing changes in GPCC theology and praxis to align these more fully with Jude's principles of biblical Christianity. Fourth, recommendations will be offered for further study on the problem highlighted in this study.

Addressing the Research Questions
Research Questions 1, 1A, and 1B

Research questions 1, 1A, and 1B were addressed in Chapter 2 by the exegetical review of Jude's message. Jude's letter, sent with prophetic love and concern to his first-century readers, warns them of the danger of false teachers and their false teachings. It exhorts his readers to let correct doctrine guide their holy living and spiritual growth.

This study's analysis of Jude has concluded that the epistle's defining statement in verse 3, "to contend for the faith," means to uphold, to preserve, and to persevere in the seven principles of biblical Christianity that have been identified from the epistle, supported by the counsel of the NT corpus, and analysed in the preceding chapters.

Research Questions 2, 2A, and 2B

Research questions 2, 2A, and 2B were addressed in Chapter 3 by a review of what the social science literature discloses about the theology and praxis of the GPCC. That review concluded that numerical growth and the establishment of institutional church structures in the GPCC brought with them the need for these churches to secure and reinforce sources of predictable income by emphasizing the prosperity doctrine, deliverance from witchcraft, and the special powers and anointing of "the man of God." These three pillars of the GPCC, it was noted in Chapter 5, differ in significant ways from Jude's principles of biblical Christianity.

Research Questions 3, 3A, and 3B

Research questions 3 and 3A were addressed in Chapter 3 through a presentation of the content of GPCC leaders' teachings and writings. Research question 3B was addressed by the results obtained from a Q-Sort analysis to identify and understand the shared perceptions of GPCC leaders. That analysis concluded that the GPCC leaders' shared perceptions of their theology revealed a troubling triumphalist and over-realized eschatology belief system in their churches that demonstrates divergence from Jude's principles. A confirmation of this was the fact that, as already pointed out in Chapter 5, the GPCC sorts in several cases, as with the prosperity doctrine, glaringly contradict the current prevailing theology and praxis of these churches. In a recent article, Asamoah-Gyadu has described the GPCC's current theology and praxis as having resulted in a lack of "transformational discipleship" in these churches that "needs to be dealt with for the optimization of Christian impact in Africa."[1]

Answering the Problem Statement

The problem statement of this study, identified in Chapter 1, is: From an evangelical and Pentecostal understanding of Jude's epistle, how should Ghanaian Pentecostal Charismatic Christians "contend for the faith that was once for all delivered to the saints" demonstrating authentic biblical Christianity in their

---

1. Asamoah-Gyadu, "'Go Near and Join Thyself,'" 355.

theology and praxis? The study's data obtained from its theological, social science, and field research has generated the answer to the problem statement.

In order for Ghanaian Pentecostal-Charismatic Christians to "contend for the faith that was once for all delivered to the saints," first, they must put into practice the seven principles of biblical Christianity which were determined exegetically from this study of Jude's Epistle. The seven principles embody the "faith" Jude references in verse 3. Second, the focus of GPCC praxis must be discipleship and spiritual formation that redirect the worldview, faith, and godly living of their members to reflect the biblical orthodoxy for which Jude strongly advocates throughout his epistle. This conclusion gives rise to the implications that follow. It informs the recommendations for praxis change, and it leads to the recommendations for additional research that follow thereafter.

Implications: GPCC Theology and Praxis

The triumphalist and over-realized eschatology belief system in the GPCC that has emerged from the research data implies the existence of two disturbing realities at work in the theology and praxis of these churches. A review of these two theological realities is offered below with a view to using this understanding to guide the recommendations for implementing changes in GPCC theology and praxis that will follow.

GPCC Syncretism

In the GPCC, the prevalence of the prosperity doctrine, the focus on deliverance from witchcraft, and the insistence on the special powers and anointing of the "man of God" reflect the mixing of Christian assumptions with ATR worldview assumptions that are incompatible with biblical Christianity. Scholars refer to this theological reality as syncretism.[2] Syncretism manifests itself in the GPCC in two primary ways. First, syncretism is seen in the GPCC's reinterpretation of the gospel in terms of current African urban aspirations of material affluence.[3] This has promoted in the GPCC a syn-

---

2. Kraft, "Culture, Worldview and Contextualization," 405.
3. Meyer, "Pentecostalism and Neo-Liberal Capitalism," 13.

drome of "andro-centrism"[4] in which church members "see themselves as the center of the world, and everything revolves around them and their lives."[5] This syndrome fosters the understanding in these churches that Christianity provides ways for church members "to get what they desire by bribing or begging God"[6] through their tithing and offerings. In their narrow focus on themselves, the pursuit of personal health and wealth are seen as ultimate ends in themselves. This is a departure from biblical Christianity in which disciples of Jesus Christ are called away "from feeling they need to be in control of their lives to entrusting themselves completely to God's mercy and totally submitting their lives to his will."[7] This syndrome of andro-centrism often leads to various forms of "authoritarian leadership, competition, divisions and spiritual pride"[8] that are sadly all too common in the GPCC.

Second, syncretism is displayed in the GPCC by the ATR-influenced focus on experience-based theology and praxis in which "the sign of spiritual life and vital worship *is* feelings of excitement, health, and prosperity" instead of basing their experiences on Scripture itself.[9]

GPCC Christo-Paganism

Scholars refer to the second disturbing theological reality at work in the theology of the GPCC as "Christo-paganism" and "split-level Christianity."[10] A corollary of syncretism, Christo-paganism is characterized by church members assigning to ostensibly Christian rituals and terminology meanings influenced by non-Christian beliefs.[11] Christo-paganism is seen in the GPCC in two ways. First, Christo-paganism is displayed in the magical mentality, in contradistinction from biblical faith, which is very prominent in the GPCC. Gifford has referred to this as the GPCC's "enchanted religious imagination."[12] Hiebert, Shaw, and Tienou note that this magical mentality is a throwback

---

4. Hiebert, Shaw, and Tienou, "Responding to Split-Level Christianity," 8.
5. Hiebert, Shaw, and Tienou, 8.
6. Hiebert, Shaw, and Tienou, 8.
7. Hiebert, Shaw, and Tienou, 8.
8. Hiebert, Shaw, and Tienou, 8.
9. Hiebert, Shaw, and Tienou, 8.
10. Hiebert, Shaw, and Tienou, 7.
11. Kraft, "Culture, Worldview and Contextualization," 405.
12. Gifford, *Christianity, Development and Modernity in Africa*, 14.

to the ATR's need to gain "control over nature, supernatural powers, and even God, through the practice of proper rites."[13] They observe that this ATR inclination betrays the tendency of fallen human beings to want to be in control of their destiny whereas in "Christianity they are called to submit unconditionally to God and his will."[14]

In the GPCC, the magical mentality is evident in the unashamed selling of "anointed olive oil and water" and the practice of church members carrying their Bibles in their pockets or placing them under their pillows like amulets in the belief that these will protect them from harm.[15] Femi Adeleye has explained that the GPCC magical mentality can be blamed partly on the prosperity doctrine's emphasis on people having "faith in their faith"[16] as the means of obtaining what they desire from God. Adeleye points out that, in contrast to this, faith in God as taught in the Bible is a continuing personal attitude of trust and confidence in God. This is expressed in the life of a Christian through obedience to God and submission to his sovereign will at all times and in all circumstances.[17]

Second, Christo-paganism is manifest in the GPCC in its practice of public prayer. This involves a contrived, guttural, abrasive, and throaty chanting of words that are repeatedly and loudly blasted out of loudspeakers. This is more reminiscent of ATR chanting than the Spirit-anointed prayer the GPCC mistakenly take it for.[18] Hiebert, Shaw, and Tienou argue that when Christians resort to coercive methods in prayer that include saying "the right things in the right tone of voice accompanied by certain right words and actions to be assured of the right results," as happens in the GPCC, they are demonstrating Christo-paganism and split-level Christianity.[19] In the GPCC, the inability of most church members to attain the material affluence promised by their church leaders results in the leaders calling for prayer meetings at which the members' shortfalls of prosperity are supposed to be addressed through prayer characterized by "imprecations upon family members, witches and

---

13. Hiebert, Shaw, and Tienou, "Responding to Split-Level Christianity," 7.
14. Hiebert, Shaw, and Tienou, 7.
15. Asamoah-Gyadu, *Contemporary Pentecostal Christianity*, 167–77.
16. Adeleye, *Preachers of a Different Gospel*, 73.
17. Adeleye, 73.
18. Asamoah-Gyadu, *Contemporary Pentecostal Christianity*, 35–57.
19. Hiebert, Shaw, and Tienou, "Responding to Split-Level Christianity," 7.

demons that are supposed to be hindering the breakthroughs being sought by the church members."[20]

In contrast to this misguided understanding of prayer, Packer argues that if Christians want to see God at work answering their prayers, their "task is not to screw themselves up to self-induced certainty that what we ask for is going to happen, just because we have assured ourselves that it will."[21] He argues that "our task is, rather to . . . allow him to show us . . . how we should pray 'thy will be done' following Jesus' path of prayer in Gethsemane."[22] Such was the story of George Müller, the nineteenth-century Christian leader who, through faith in God and prayer to God alone, housed and fed thousands of orphans in England.[23]

Implications of GPCC Syncretism and Christo-Paganism

As already noted in the first chapter of this study, Birgit Meyer has argued that the influence of the GPCC in Ghana is now a "central factor in the country's public culture."[24] Both Paul Gifford[25] and Asamoah-Gyadu[26] have equally argued that the theology and practices of the GPCC have had far-ranging effects on Christianity as a whole in Ghana. These scholars' observations imply that the two theological realities of syncretism and Christo-paganism at work in the theology and praxis of the GPCC carry religious, socio-economic, and political implications for Ghana as a whole. Some of these religious, socio-economic and political implications are examined below.

Religious Implications

As already noted in Chapter 5, the three pillars of GPCC theology and praxis are spawning large numbers of nominal Christians in the country because they are creating Ghanaian churchgoers who mistakenly believe that they are genuine Christians when they are not (Matt 7:21–23).[27] These church mem-

---

20. Asamoah-Gyadu, *Sighs and Signs*, 168.
21. Packer, *Passion For Holiness*, 232.
22. Packer, 232.
23. Steer, *George Müller*, 98–100.
24. Meyer, "Pentecostalism and Neo-Liberal Capitalism," 13.
25. Gifford, *African Christianity*, 77.
26. Asamoah-Gyadu, *African Charismatics*, 60–63.
27. Musyimi, *Counterfeit Gospel*, 143.

bers are in the GPCC because they have been told that Jesus will give them relief from poverty, sickness, and despair if they come forward and repeat a certain prayer. They have done this without genuine biblical repentance (Acts 2:38), and without a real understanding of what it means to follow Jesus (Luke 9:23–26). This spread of nominal Christianity ironically belies the GPCC leaders' decrying, in the formative years of their churches, the nominal Christianity they saw as prevailing in the country's mainline churches. The leaders' strident calls at that time for young people to abandon what the leaders saw as the mainline churches' moribund and nominal Christianity was in fact one of the factors that gave impetus to the GPCC's rise and establishment.[28] The Ghanaian scholar Jones Amanor reports that a recent survey conducted by Operation World shows that 64 percent of Ghanaians were Christians.[29] Amanor notes, though, that "the extent to which the population was truly Christianized has, however, come under some scrutiny since the discovery, by the Ghana Evangelism Committee, that nominalism is the greatest problem of Christianity in Ghana today."[30]

Christian witness in Ghana is increasingly at stake as a result of this lack of spiritual transformation and genuine discipleship in the GPCC. In both the print media and, more recently, in the social media, the widespread criticism of the GPCC's image as being nothing other than a commercial enterprise aimed at enriching its founders has further eroded Christian witness in Ghana and turned many non-Christians away from the church.[31] In 2016, the Kenyan government introduced "a raft of tough new measures"[32] to change the way religious institutions such as churches are run in the country. This was the government's response to "widespread public outrage"[33] over reports of fake miracles and promises made by Kenyan Pentecostal-Charismatic church leaders to defraud the public.

The GPCC would do well to try to avoid a similar response from the Ghanaian government, as the Ghanaian public grows increasingly disillusioned with the churches' commercial image. The unchecked continuation

---

28. Asamoah-Gyadu, *African Charismatics*, 116.
29. Amanor, "Pentecostalism in Ghana," 2. www.pctii.org/cyberj/cyberj13/amanor.html.
30. Amanor, 5.
31. Gifford, *Ghana's New Christianity*, 40–41.
32. Githae, "Tough Laws to Now Tame," 1.
33. Githae, 4.

of this decline in biblical Christianity in Ghana could also very well lead to a duplication of the fate of Christianity in western Europe where the result of widespread nominalism, in the words of the social scientist Philip Jenkins, is that "the era of Western Christianity has passed within our lifetimes."[34]

Socio-Economic Implications

In his landmark study of the socio-economic and political impact of the introduction of missionary Christianity on developing countries in Asia and Africa, Robert Woodberry has demonstrated historically and statistically that the biblical Christianity promoted by evangelical conversionary Protestant missionaries significantly influenced the rise and spread of stable democracies in these countries. "The development and spread of religious liberty, mass education, mass printing, newspapers, voluntary organizations, and colonial reforms" created the conditions that led to modernization, socio-economic development and growth.[35] In one notable example provided by Woodberry, he narrated his startling discovery of the contrast in educational development between Ghana and Togo, because in Ghana "British missionaries had established a whole system of schools and printing presses. But France, the colonial power in Togo, severely restricted missionaries."[36] The result of this was that "more than 100 years later, education was still limited in Togo. In Ghana, it was flourishing."[37] Arguably, if the introduction of biblical Christianity in African countries contributed to the establishment of education, a notable feature of socio-economic development, the GPCC's growing shift away from biblical Christianity bodes ill for Ghana's socio-economic future.

Political Implications

On the political front, Gifford has argued that the glaring lack of servant leadership in the GPCC works against socio-political reform in Ghana. Gifford's reason for this observation reason is that the GPCC leaders "operate on neo-patrimonial or patronage rather than accountable bureaucratic lines,

---

34. Jenkins, *The Next Christendom*, 3.
35. Woodberry, "Missionary Roots of Liberal Democracy," 244.
36. Dilley, "Surprising Discovery about Those Colonialist," 2.
37. Dilley, 2.

encouraging the emergence of the 'Big Man.'"[38] This is the same philosophy of leadership that prevails in the secular polity of the country.

This trend, Gifford further argues, impedes the realization of Ghana's aspiration to "join the modern world economy"[39] because the eventual fulfillment of this national aspiration requires the development of "transparent and accountable structures, systems, procedures and institutions to regulate all aspects of society."[40] Gifford, no doubt, rightly bases his assessment of these requirements for successful economic development on the models of governance that prevail in the more economically affluent countries of Europe and North America.

This inability to provide a godly example in the political affairs of Ghana also means that the GPCC fails to demonstrate that it is an "outpost of God's reign on earth and should manifest the social order of the kingdom of God, which is based on love, reconciliation, servant-hood and submission to Christ."[41] This failure should be of concern to the GPCC.

Recommendations for Change: Applying Jude's Principles of Biblical Christianity

The recommendations for implementing changes in GPCC theology and praxis that follow will be guided by the seven principles of biblical Christianity suggested by Jude's Epistle that have been identified and discussed in the preceding chapters of this study.

Principle No. 1

The first principle of biblical Christianity identified by this study as suggested by Jude's Epistle was verse 19 of the epistle. This first principle states that people who identify themselves as being Christians are born again and are sealed by the Holy Spirit (Eph 1:13–14). In this part of his epistle, Jude concluded that the false teachers' ungodly lifestyles betrayed them as not possessing the Spirit of God (πνεῦμα μὴ ἔχοντες). Because ἔχοντες is a present

---

38. Gifford, *Ghana's New Christianity*, 197.
39. Gifford, 197.
40. Gifford, 197.
41. Hiebert, Shaw, and Tienou, "Responding to Split-Level Christianity," 12.

participle, it implies that this was the current condition of the false teachers, indicating that they lived purely on the level of carnal, unredeemed life (ἐπιθυμίας, "carnal desires"). Jude was evidently implying that the attitudes and actions of the false teachers, ruled as these were by their ungodly lusts, and their worldly-mindedness, showed them to be without the Spirit of God, and far from salvation.

The GPCC will need to recapture this foundational NT truth about who a Christian really is which formed an integral part of its theology in its formative years.[42] To do this, the GPCC will need to intentionally move away from preaching that "tithing works whether the person is a believer or not, because it is God's formula for success,"[43] because this preaching, as observed in Chapter 5, violates Jude's first principle, suggesting that many GPCC churchgoers mistakenly believe that they are genuine Christians when in reality they are not (Matt 7:21–23).[44]

Principle No. 2

The second principle of biblical Christianity identified by this study as being suggested by Jude's epistle was in verses 17–23. This principle, in agreement with the overall counsel of the NT, notes that, indwelt by the Spirit of God, Christians are to adhere to basic biblical truths and demonstrate the fruit of the Spirit (Gal 5:16–23). In these verses, Jude exhorts his readers to hold firmly to the gospel truths, τῇ ἁγιωτάτῃ ὑμῶν πίστει, originally handed down to them once for all (Jude 3) by the apostles. Packer affirms this principle by noting that, "when God through the Holy Spirit calls sinners to faith in Christ, their hearts are changed. Henceforth the heart-changing Spirit *indwells* them"[45] to sustain in their hearts and lives "a constant energizing, empowering, Christ-imparting relationship to them at the core of their being."[46] Packer further observes that this is because "holy living is only ever achieved by divine grace, power, and help, through the Holy Spirit."[47]

---

42. Anderson, *To The Ends of the Earth*, 235.
43. Asamoah-Gyadu, *Sighs and Signs*, 176.
44. Musyimi, *Counterfeit Gospel*, 143.
45. Packer, *Passion For Holiness*, 103.
46. Packer, 103.
47. Packer, 109.

This reality of the Holy Spirit motivating and empowering Christians in the core of their beings to desire to adhere to basic biblical truths and to demonstrate the fruit of the Spirit has been a cardinal result of genuine spiritual revival throughout church history. Colin Whittaker defines revival as "those times of divine visitation when God the Holy Spirit quickens and stirs" his slumbering church so that "believers are set ablaze for Christ and unbelievers are convicted by the Holy Spirit, leading them to turn, in repentance, to faith in Christ."[48] Selwyn Hughes adds that revival "is the Christian church going back again to the God-given norm."[49]

Throughout the Christian centuries, God has sent revivals to spiritually revitalize his church whenever it has been threatened by nominalism.[50] The most notable revival in Africa is what has come to be known as the East Africa Revival (EAR). That revival began in the 1920s and spread across East Africa, dramatically impacting and transforming the church and indigenous communities across the region. The EAR began with the focused, determined prayer of the missionary Dr. Joe Church and his African co-workers of the Ruanda Mission, an arm of the British Church Missionary Society. Burdened by growing nominalism and syncretism in the Anglican mission church, they unceasingly asked God for a visitation of the Holy Spirit.[51] The results of the revival, when it finally came in 1927, were countless healings, miracles, and deliverances from witchcraft.[52] Revived Christians throughout East Africa professed their experience of conversion and stressed the importance of the lordship of Christ over all areas of their lives.[53] Prayer and church unity became a hallmark of the East Africa church and the spiritual life of entire congregations of Presbyterians, Anglicans, and Methodists in East Africa were revitalized and transformed for fifty years.[54] Three compelling reasons lead this study to conclude that if the GPCC is to live up to the spirit of Jude's second principle of biblical Christianity, what is required is a reviving visitation of God such as characterized the EAR.

---

48. Whittaker, *Great Revivals*, 21–22.
49. Hughes, *Revival: Times of Refreshing*, 14.
50. Whittaker, *Great Revivals*, 25–125.
51. Church, *Quest for the Highest*, 130–37.
52. Shaw, *Global Awakening*, 93–111.
53. Ward and Wild-Wood, *East African Revival*, 3–7.
54. Reed, *Walking in the Light*, 10.

First, Colin Reed, whose analysis offers a fairly reliable consensus view among scholars of the EAR, notes that the revival "was a powerful work of God" and "a spontaneous response to God the Spirit" and an "activity of God, unplanned by humans, renewing the church, extending the faith to outsiders and reforming communities, as lives are changed by the Gospel."[55] This is what the GPCC requires, in contrast to its many contrived programs that yield contrived responses from its members.

Second, Colin Reed notes that "the conviction of sin was another crucial component" of the EAR, "which almost always drove people to their knees in prayer and repentance. Repentance and regular public confession of sin were a key component to the East African Revival."[56] This is critical for the GPCC because in its overriding focus on the prosperity doctrine, the concept of sin is almost completely ignored.

Third, Reed notes that in the EAR it was easy to see "the power of God at work in the lives of those who were being touched by the Holy Spirit" because the center of the revival "was Jesus Christ and its message above all, that of his great saving work on the cross for people's salvation."[57] The GPCC seems to have lost focus of this central tenet of NT theology.

The result of this, Reed adds, was that there was an "overwhelming response that was a deep sense of repentance, as the conviction of sin became almost intolerable, accompanied by open confession of sins, often with tears."[58] Every saved Christian was then "expected to have a living testimony, a story of how Jesus had saved them, and from what."[59] This is, at present, markedly absent in the GPCC.

A revival in the GPCC would enable it to fulfill its potential that inspired scholars, in the GPCC's formative years, to refer to it as "a renewal movement."[60] It could then become a group of Pentecostal churches that can affirm the Pentecostal imperative to "unashamedly proclaim a non-pluralistic message: there is salvation in no other name, but the name of Jesus Christ."[61]

---

55. Reed, 10.
56. Reed, 12.
57. Reed, 12.
58. Reed, 12.
59. Reed, 12.
60. Asamoah-Gyadu, *African Charismatics*, 1–3.
61. Lowenberg, *Reading the Bible with Help*, 4.

The GPCC could then acknowledge that, "preparation for one's eternal destiny is significantly more important than one's temporal health [and] prosperity . . . and the imminent return of Jesus calls for an urgent missional response to reach the unengaged peoples of our world."[62] A revival would make the GPCC a company of Ghanaian Christians who "are secure in their identity as Pentecostals, pursuing a Spirit-filled life marked by supernatural giftings and miracles."[63]

Principle No. 3

The third principle of biblical Christianity identified by this study as being suggested by Jude's Epistle comes from verses 12, 16, and 19 of the epistle. Although Jude does not specifically mention servant leadership in the text, in agreement with the counsel of the NT as a whole, servant leadership was selected as being perhaps the most effective way of addressing the self-focused and disruptive attitudes of the false teachers mentioned in Jude's letter. This third suggested principle insists that selfless servant leadership must distinguish the management of the church. In these verses, Jude implies that the false teachers are like the shepherds of Ezekiel 34, who looked only after their own interests, not caring for the sheep entrusted to their care – who, in short, lacked a spirit of servant leadership. In contrast to this, Richard Gehman asserts that "a Christian leader who is a servant leader serves God preeminently and others – not himself."[64]

As already noted in Chapters 3 and 5, servant leadership is conspicuously absent in the GPCC. GPCC leaders must begin to develop servant leadership guided by the following three biblical recommendations. First, Osei-Mensah advocates that African church leaders must allow the Bible to judge their African culture so that they can jettison ungodly African models of leadership that are incompatible with biblical principles of servant-leadership.[65] This is critical because, as George Janvier notes, there are many aspects of African leadership that contradict biblical servant leadership.[66]

---

62. Lowenberg, 4.
63. Lowenberg, 4.
64. Gehman, *Learning to Lead*, 204.
65. Osei-Mensah, *Wanted: Servant-leaders*, 55.
66. Janvier, *Understanding Leadership*, 61.

Second, because the GPCC leaders confess to having had genuine conversion experiences, they must allow the new nature that Christ gives to his disciples by his Holy Spirit when they are born again, to make them willing to humble themselves to serve the congregation of God's people as they learn to cultivate the mind of Christ and develop a spiritual dimension that transforms both their worldview and their behaviour.[67]

Third, GPCC leaders need to cultivate a lifestyle of obedience to God. Such obedience, Edgar Elliston observes, will be displayed by their faithfulness to God's word and their submission to God's clear guidance.[68] Such obedience will show that GPCC leaders are persons of integrity, that they are trustworthy, and that they are accountable stewards of God's flock (1 Cor 4:1–2; 1 Pet 5:1–4). Their trust in and obedience to Christ will enable the GPCC leaders to "mature internally in spiritual formation and externally in ministering."[69] Osei-Mensah notes that, when African Christian leaders develop "a lifestyle of exemplary obedience" to Christ, "the people [they] are called to lead are more likely to cooperate and submit if they know it is to the Lord they are submitting, and if they see [them] showing the way by bowing [their] knee to king Jesus."[70]

Principle No. 4

The fourth principle of biblical Christianity identified as being suggested by Jude's epistle comes from verse 17 of the epistle. This principle is that a commitment to disciplined Bible study, both individually and corporately, results in sound biblical doctrine. In verse 17, Jude's use of the plural, ὑμῶν, implies this communal, corporate, and committed study of the Word of God. In most African churches today, the kind of communal, corporate, and committed study of the Word of God that Jude is calling for takes place in church cell groups.[71]

In the GPCC's church model (the prevalent church model), church cell groups are not prioritized. Daniel Sinclair has defined the prevalent church

---

67. Osei-Mensah, *Wanted: Servant Leaders*, 26.
68. Elliston, *Home Grown Leaders*, 162.
69. Elliston, 162.
70. Osei-Mensah, *Wanted: Servant Leaders*, 33.
71. Holtum and Holtum, *Cell Church Experience*, v.

model as being characterized by a group of Christians who meet on Sundays in a building dedicated for that purpose, who engage in other activities during the week, and are led by professional, paid clergy.[72] In this church model, Sinclair notes that the church building serves as the center of activity for the believer, with virtually all activities related to the church happening there.[73] In this model, also, Alan Johnson observes that trained professionals carry out the ministry of the church, with the members of the congregation seeing themselves primarily as "consumers" of this ministry.[74] This, he believes, has resulted in a largely passive laity who "can sing, listen, and give, but other than that, they do not participate."[75] This is very descriptive of the GPCC. If the GPCC is to make Jude's fourth principle a reality of their ecclesiology, there is a need for their leaders to consider how elements of the cell church model can be incorporated into their current prevalent church model. In the cell church model, an important element of their ministry to one another is a commitment to the kind of disciplined Bible study that Jude calls his readers to engage in.[76]

In the GPCC, the sound biblical doctrine that will result from such an individual and corporate commitment to disciplined Bible study is likely to lead to a departure from the GPCC's current emphasis on the prosperity doctrine which, as explained in Chapter 5, is based on eisegetic interpretations of the Bible.[77] A possible salutary benefit of this could very well be a change in the current preaching style of GPCC leaders from their current unstructured, non-contextual preaching to the preaching of expository sermons, in which "each sermon is the explanation, interpretation or application of a single dominant idea from one passage or several passages of Scripture."[78] As Douglas Lowenberg notes, "The meaning of the text has boundaries and cannot mean all things to all people."[79] GPCC leaders are evidently unaware of this.

---

72. Sinclair, *Vision of the Possible*, 212.
73. Johnson, *Strategies for Reaching Unreached*, 65.
74. Johnson, 65–66.
75. Johnson, 65–66.
76. Sinclair, *Vision of the Possible*, 213.
77. Fee, *Disease of the Health and Wealth Gospels*, 8.
78. Robinson, *Biblical Preaching*, 35.
79. Lowenberg, *Reading the Bible with Help*, 30.

Principle No. 5

The fifth principle of biblical Christianity identified as being suggested by Jude's Epistle comes from verse 20 of the epistle. This principle is that engaging in Spirit-inspired prayer is essential for the church. In Jude's three-part exhortation to his readers in verses 20–21, he urges them to continue to pray in the Holy Spirit as an important means of building themselves up in their faith. Arguably, by Spirit-inspired prayer, Jude may very well be echoing Paul's thought in 1 Corinthians 14:4 that this involves Christians praying in tongues as a way of edifying themselves. As already noted above, in the GPCC, the practice of public prayer involves a contrived, guttural, abrasive, and throaty chanting of monosyllabic words that is more reminiscent of ATR chanting than the Spirit-anointed prayer the GPCC mistakenly take it for.[80] This chanting, as already noted, betrays the GPCC's Christo-pagan tendency "to manipulate God into doing our will when our will is not his."[81]

Two recommendations can be offered to address this evident misunderstanding of prayer in the GPCC. First, the GPCC needs to align its understanding of prayer with the traditional Pentecostal understanding that praying in tongues is a God-given capacity that is valuable because, in the place of prayer, it heightens a Christian's mood of praise, penitence, and petition.[82]

Second, GPCC leaders need to understand and to teach their members that prayer is not an effort to change God's mind or twist his arm, but instead, that Christian prayer "generated and sustained as it is by God himself, becomes the means by which His people enter into God's mind"[83] because Christians end up "asking God to do what he had planned all along to do."[84] Heeding this wise biblical counsel will doubtlessly bring the GPCC more into alignment with Jude's fifth principle of biblical Christianity.

Principle No. 6

The sixth principle of biblical Christianity identified as being suggested by Jude's Epistle is to be found in verse 21 of the epistle. This principle notes

---

80. Asamoah-Gyadu, *Contemporary Pentecostal Christianity*, 35–57.
81. Packer, *Passion For Holiness*, 231.
82. Packer, *Keep in Step with the Spirit*, 144.
83. Packer, 144.
84. Packer, 144.

that Christians must actively nurture, in their faith and lifestyles, a positive eschatological expectation of Christ's *parousia*. In this verse, Jude counsels his readers that contending for the faith in the ways in which he has explained in the preceding verses will demonstrate on their part a positive eschatological expectation of Christ's merciful salvation at the *parousia*, in contrast to the false teachers whose disobedience would only merit the Lord's severe judgment upon his second coming.[85]

One of the defining characteristics of the EAR was its emphasis on the imminent return of Christ. This focus on the *parousia* "created a sense of urgency to live in right relationship with the Lord daily and to proclaim the gospel to those who had not yet come to Christ."[86] This is the shift that is needed in the GPCC to move it away from the prosperity doctrine that advocates a perfect life of health and wealth in the here-and-now in this fallen world, and diverts attention from the *parousia*.

Packer notes that this diversion of focus from the *parousia* has created a church that has a "shockingly little sense of the reality, pervasiveness, shame, and guilt of sin"[87] and instead cherishes "shockingly strong illusions about having a right to expect from God health, wealth, ease, excitement, and sexual gratification."[88] In a church movement like the GPCC which is clearly guilty of Packer's charge, adhering to Jude's sixth principle of biblical Christianity will focus the hearts and minds of church members on the *parousia* of Christ when they are made to understand that "ease is for heaven, not earth" because "life on earth is fundamentally out of shape and out of order by reason of sin."[89]

Principle No. 7

The seventh and final principle of biblical Christianity identified from this study as suggested by Jude's Epistle is found in verse 22–23 of the epistle. This last principle states that the church must demonstrate Christian mercy through missions, evangelism, discipleship, and spiritual formation. In these verses, Jude urges the members of the community to faithfully disciple those

---

85. Kelly, *Commentary on the Epistles of Peter*, 287.
86. Reed, *Walking in the Light*, iii.
87. Packer, *Passion For Holiness*, 250.
88. Packer, 250.
89. Packer, 254.

in their midst who may have been swayed by the false teachings. Such discipleship would involve seeking to ground the errant members once again in "the faith that was once for all delivered to the saints" (Jude 3 ESV) by reminding them of basic Christian doctrines and disciplines such as the assurance of salvation, prayer, Bible study, and the Spirit-filled life. Mel Lawrenz refers to such grounding as "spiritual formation" that involves "the progressive patterning of a person's inner and outer life according to the image of Christ through intentional means of spiritual growth."[90]

This is noticeably absent in the GPCC today, where what prevails instead is "mindless prayers, mechanical Bible studies and impressive edifices that kill real spiritual life."[91] The GPCC will need to change this moribund approach to discipleship by seeking to make disciples of Christ "who are continually being reshaped in thought, word, and deed"[92] as they daily take up their cross and follow Jesus (Luke 9:23)[93] on the life-long Christian journey of being conformed to the image of Christ (Rom 8:29).[94]

The discipleship that Jude calls for as a demonstration of Christian mercy also implies the demonstration of godly mercy through the church's active involvement in missions, evangelism, and social action. John Stott defines Christian mission as "the loving service that God sends his people into the world to render."[95] Stott adds that "of primary importance within this mission of sacrificial service is 'evangelism', the sharing with others of God's good news about Jesus."[96] Christopher Wright affirms this primacy of evangelism in the church by noting, "It is not so much the case that God has a mission for his church in the world but that God has a church for his mission in the world."[97]

Mention has already been made above of the GPCC's troubling misunderstanding of the mission of God. The GPCC will need to reorient its understanding of the mission of God to reflect the missional views of Stott and Wright presented above. It will need to turn away from its current emphasis

---

90. Lawrenz, *Dynamics of Spiritual Formation*, 15.
91. Lawrenz, 16.
92. Lawrenz, 16.
93. Boa, *Conformed to His Image*, 117.
94. Boa, 281.
95. Stott, *Christian Mission in the Modern World*, 109.
96. Stott, 82.
97. Wright, *Mission of God*, 62.

on the prosperity doctrine and motivational teachings that "offer practical information for personal development,"[98] and return to the fervent preaching of the gospel of its formative years because, as Stott notes, "men without Christ are perishing."[99]

The GPCC will also need to repent of its current lack of social action that is reflected in its indifference to the needs of the poor and struggling members in their congregations.[100] Stott argues that social action demonstrates Christian mercy as "a partner of evangelism" because "the two belong to each other and yet are independent of each other" as expressions of God's unfeigned love.[101] Stott notes that "there will be times when a person's material need is so pressing that he would not be able to hear the gospel if we shared it with him."[102] A concerted effort to thus demonstrate Christian mercy through missions, evangelism, discipleship, spiritual formation, and social action is how the GPCC could show conformity to Jude's seventh principle of biblical Christianity.

Recommendations for Further Study

The recommendations for further study that follow are informed by both the implications presented above from the study's research findings, and the recommendations offered above for implementing changes in GPCC theology and praxis to align these more fully with Jude's principles of biblical Christianity. Three areas will be highlighted below as particularly requiring further study on the problem identified in this study. The first is how to restore the biblical and Pentecostal imperatives that characterized the early days of the GPCC. The second is how to effectively address, through contextualization, the syncretism and Christo-Paganism that have become troubling hallmarks of the GPCC. The third is how to establish contextual biblical training for GPCC leaders that will enable them to align their theology and praxis with Jude's principles of biblical Christianity.

---

98. Asamoah-Gyadu, *Sighs and Signs*, 17.
99. Stott, *Christian Mission in the Modern World*, 28.
100. Asamoah-Gyadu, *African Charismatics*, 227.
101. Stott, *Christian Mission in the Modern World*, 27.
102. Stott, 28.

Restoring Pentecostal Imperatives in the GPCC

The first area requiring further study is how to restore the Pentecostal imperatives that characterized the early days of the GPCC when its young leaders exhibited the strong evangelical, Pentecostal, and missional influences of para-church organizations such as the Scripture Union[103] and SIM (Sudan Interior Mission)[104] from which they emerged. This background explains the GPCC leaders' continuing assent to NT orthodoxy displayed in their Q-Sorts. Asamoah-Gyadu sees the appearance of the GPCC on the Ghanaian religious scene at that time as offering the possibility of being used by the Spirit of God to engender a renewal of Christianity in Ghana at a time when the faith was waning under the weight of nominalism and growing secularism. This renewal, he argues, "Did not occur through human planning and strategizing" but rather "through yielding to the Spirit of God."[105] He adds that God chose the GPCC "to renew the flagging spirit of his church."[106]

In contrast to this great and laudable potential to become a movement that would engender the renewal of Christianity in Ghana, the GPCC has today become a largely nominal religious institution in which its leaders clamour for social recognition through the self-conferring of high-sounding ecclesiastical titles; hobnobbing with politicians; erecting large, architecturally impressive church buildings; furnishing plush suites of offices; wearing clerical robes and collars; and seeking honorary academic degrees.[107] In its formative years, GPCC leaders had condemned all these as being "un-scriptural and un-spiritual."[108]

By allowing doctrines and practices to insidiously "creep in" (Jude 4) that deviate from biblical Christianity, the GPCC now demonstrates what Packer has described as:

> A feeble grasp of the moral realities of redemption, of the significance for our discipleship of self-denial, accepted weakness and apparent failure, and of the spiritual values that belong to

---

103. Barker and Boadi-Siaw, *Changed by the Word*, 28.
104. Mason, *God's Challenge in Ghana*, 5.
105. Asamoah-Gyadu, *African Charismatics*, 248.
106. Asamoah-Gyadu, 246.
107. Asamoah-Gyadu, 230.
108. Asamoah-Gyadu, 230.

hard thought, frustrated endeavor, pain accepted, loss adjusted to, and steady faithfulness in life's more humdrum routines.[109]

Further study is therefore urgently required into how GPCC leaders can be convinced to take practical steps that will see that their movement becomes one in which emphasis is placed on true spiritual renewal characterized by biblical faith in a living God, a focus on clear and Spirit-empowered preaching of the true gospel of redemption through faith in Christ, biblical discipleship through "learning of God from God through Scripture, openness to the indwelling Spirit, close fellowship in prayer and praise" and "expecting God actively to answer prayer and change things for the better."[110]

Addressing Syncretism and Christo-Paganism in the GPCC

The second area requiring further study is how to effectively address the evidence of syncretism and Christo-paganism in the GPCC through effective forms of contextualization. A generation ago, Byang Kato sounded an early warning about the serious dangers that syncretism and Christo-paganism posed to biblical Christianity in Africa.[111] Kato was an African evangelical leader who, in his brief thirty-nine years, strongly opposed all the various forms of syncretism and Christo-paganism that he saw as a threat to the African church in his day. His concern then was what he saw as the rush by African scholars to justify and defend ATR ideas and practices that were definitely incompatible with biblical teaching.[112] Kato's bold and forceful efforts to insist on upholding biblical Christianity in the African church earned him many enemies but it also earned him the sobriquet, "the Founding Father of African Evangelical Theology."[113]

Kato saw the effective contextualization of the gospel as one of the solutions to syncretism and Christo-paganism in the African church. He defined contextualization as making "the Gospel relevant in every situation everywhere without compromising it"[114] and "employing compatible modes of

---

109. Packer, *Keep in Step with the Spirit*, 186.
110. Packer, 183.
111. Kato, *Biblical Christianity in Africa*, 11.
112. Kato, 42.
113. Shaw, *Kingdom of God in Africa*, 330.
114. Kato, *Biblical Christianity in Africa*, 24.

expression"[115] to advance the gospel. Effective contextualization, Kato believed, would "make Christianity culturally relevant while holding fast to its ever-abiding message" in Africa.[116] Such effective contextualization, Kato argued, will succeed in finding Christianity a home in Africa through the adopting of "local hymnology, and using native language, idioms and concepts to express the unchanging truths" of Christianity.[117] Douglas Lowenberg concurs with this view and adds that, in the African context, effective contextualization should relate to the content and the methods of biblical teaching, preaching, singing, church architecture, and other aspects of Christian life in Africa.[118]

The church in Ghana already has a rich history of this kind of contextualization. Casely Essamuah has noted that Ghanaians first received the gospel with "great ingenuity" by appropriating it as their own through the singing of traditional mission church hymns translated into the local languages.[119] He observes that in the Methodist Church of Ghana this became the church's "most definite characteristic as a popular movement."[120] The translation into local Ghanaian languages of the historic hymns of the mainline mission churches helped to create in the early Ghanaian Christians a sense of the historic continuity of the Christian faith because these historic hymns are characterized by "theologically and poetically accomplished words"[121] that contain and teach the foundational truths of the Bible.

Syncretism and Christo-paganism in the African church, as already noted above, have as their foundation the continuing influence of an ATR worldview in African Christians. To wean new believers off their old, non-Christian beliefs and practices, such as is seen in the GPCC, Hiebert, Shaw, and Tienou advocate a form of contextualization they refer to as "critical contextualization" that calls for an examination of church members' traditional beliefs and practices that will enable church leaders to address "both the issues that emerge out of the study of Scripture and those that emerge in the daily lives

---

115. Kato, 29.
116. Kato, 31.
117. Kato, 38.
118. Lowenberg, *Current Issues in New Testament Interpretation*, 88.
119. Essamuah, *Genuinely Ghanaian*, 133.
120. Essamuah, 133.
121. Packer, *Keep in Step with the Spirit*, 146.

of the people."¹²² Such critical contextualization, Hiebert, Shaw, and Tienou argue, can ensure that there is an appropriate evaluation of old beliefs and practices in the light of biblical truth.

These scholars note that the aim of critical contextualization is not just the replacement of the old, non-Christian beliefs with formal Christianity, but instead to develop a vibrant Christianity that is rooted in the gospel.¹²³ They argue that, applied effectively, this form of critical contextualization will result in the establishment of ministries that transform individuals and churches, moving them from where they are to where God wants them to be.¹²⁴ They assert that it will also enable the Christian faith, for new believers, to go beyond the mere knowledge of biblical truths to its practical application in their lives.¹²⁵ Further study that offers effective means and methods of using such forms of contextualization to address syncretism and Christo-paganism in the GPCC will result in the realization of Kato's dream that, "It is God's will that Africans, on accepting Christ as their Savior, become Christian Africans."¹²⁶

Establishing Contextual Biblical Training for GPCC Leaders

The third area requiring further study is how to establish contextual biblical training for GPCC leaders that will enable them to align their theology and praxis with Jude's principles of biblical Christianity. The phenomenal numerical growth of the African church has created a crisis of rising demand for leadership training on the continent. This need to train pastors for the burgeoning African church presents a real challenge because at the present time there is a dearth of balanced, contextual, evangelical, and Pentecostal training programs and resources dedicated to this task. John Elliott has called attention to the fact that this current lack of adequately trained leaders and training programs is resulting in both stunted church growth and the rise of new cults, "as untrained pastors syncretize Christian beliefs with beliefs common to the local culture."¹²⁷ Richard Gehman has equally argued that syncretism

---

122. Hiebert, Shaw, and Tienou, "Responding to Split-Level Christianity," 178.
123. Hiebert, Shaw, and Tienou, "Responding to Split-Level Christianity," 178.
124. Hiebert, Shaw, and Tienou, 179.
125. Hiebert, Shaw, and Tienou, 180.
126. Kato, *Biblical Christianity in Africa*, 42.
127. Elliott, "Leadership Development in the Early Church," 1.

and Christo-paganism are on the rise in the African church today because of the "inadequate biblical teaching" of African church leaders which is leading to the spread of "a deficient gospel" and "unconverted second-generation Christians."[128] This appears to be the troubling situation in the GPCC today.

A number of GPCC churches, as already noted in Chapter 3, have established Bible schools to train their pastors. This implies that GPCC church leaders see a need for their pastors to receive some measure of theological training, although, as already noted in Chapter 3, the GPCC church founders themselves have had little or no formal theological training. A review of the curricula of courses offered in the GPCC Bible schools reveals the standard staple of courses offered in most Pentecostal Bible schools in Africa today.

Writing about one of the cardinal challenges facing theological training in Ghana today, Victor Atta-Baffoe, the former Dean of St. Nicholas Seminary, a leading Anglican training institution in Ghana, notes that there is a marked inconsistency between theological education and parish life among the trained clergy.[129] He sees this as being a sign of the breakdown of "the theological paradigm for doing and communicating theology in Africa today."[130] He notes that, although the staff at the seminary is indigenous, the training programs offered by the school are Western and imported. The result of this, he laments, "is that ministerial formation has failed to meet the needs of the people of Ghana."[131] If this is true of the Bible school of a mainline church in the country, it seems fair to conjecture that it must be all the more true of the GPCC-sponsored Bible schools.

Further study is required to discover how to convince the GPCC of the need to turn these Bible schools into institutions that provide effective and relevant theological training for their pastors. This would be training that is contextual, biblical, Pentecostal, and missional in its focus, its methods, and its purpose. This is what would make what Lowenberg refers to as "a hermeneutic that is thoroughly Pentecostal, biblically based, and culturally relevant"[132] a reality in their ministries.

---

128. Gehman, *African Traditional Religion*, 280–82.
129. Atta-Baffoe, "Ministerial Formation and Theological Education," 41.
130. Atta-Baffoe, 42.
131. Atta-Baffoe, 44.
132. Lowenberg, *Reading the Bible with Help*, 5.

In keeping with Michael Anthony's view that "a truly Christian education should help us to understand and appreciate the authority of God's Word,"[133] the training advocated here would also help GPCC leaders to preach and teach the Bible more accurately in its original context.[134] A review of their sermons, available on the internet,[135] confirms their dire need of this.

The missionaries who first brought the Christian faith to Ghana accomplished the goal of getting the early Ghanaian Christians to understand and appreciate the authority of God's word through the widespread use, in their mission churches and schools, of contextualized traditional church liturgies and catechisms[136] such as the Westminster Shorter Catechism (Presbyterian), the Thirty-Nine Articles (Anglican), and the Christian creeds.[137] These, together with the Bible itself, had been translated into the local Ghanaian languages.[138]

These contextualized traditional liturgical and catechetical tools and methods provided the early Ghanaian Christians with biblical and theological moorings that are missing today in the GPCC. Further study, therefore, is needed into how these tried and tested methods can be adapted today to establish contextual biblical training for both GPCC leaders and laity that will give to them the kind of biblical and theological foundations that will help them to distinguish between sound doctrine and spurious and heretical teaching.

---

133. Anthony, *Introducing Christian Education*, 33.

134. Keener, *Biblical Interpretation*, 7.

135. ICGC sermons: *https://www.youtube.com/watch?v=zqB7Sj51pqY*. GRM sermons: *www.preachub.com/visionpurpose-rev-dr-robert-ampiah-kwofi_190a11cbc.html*. Perez Chapel sermons: *https://www.youtube.com/watch?v=JlrpA1wipzc*. Action Chapel sermons: *www.godsword4us.com/speaker/8-archbishop-nicholas-duncan-williams.html*. Lighthouse Chapel sermons: *www.godsword4us.com/speaker/20-bishop-dag-heward-mills.html*.

136. A catechism is a summary of basic Christian doctrines used from New Testament times to the present. Catechisms are often in the form of questions followed by answers to be memorized by new Christians to provide to them a systematic and organized introduction to the basics of the Christian faith.

137. The Christian creeds are confessions and statements of faith such as the Nicene Creed and the Apostles Creed, developed throughout church history to remind the church of the basic tenets of the faith.

138. Ekem, "Wesleyan Methodism and Bible Translation," 81–91.

Summary

This chapter has submitted the study's conclusions and recommendations for praxis change and additional research. First, a summary of the results obtained to address the study's three research questions has been presented. Second, implications have been drawn from these research results. Third, recommendations have been offered for implementing changes in GPCC theology and praxis to align these more fully with Jude's principles of biblical Christianity. Fourth, three recommendations have been offered for further study on the problem highlighted in this study.

Adeyemo has urged the church in Africa today, in the face of the "growing Christo-paganism and widespread syncretism"[139] in its ranks, to heed Jude's "intense, sustained, and powerful call to contend for the faith"[140] on the continent today. This study is offered with a similar hope because it is the heeding of Adeyemo's call that will enable Jude's principles of biblical Christianity to become a transformative reality in the GPCC that turns its members into true Christian Africans.

---

139. Adeyemo, "Jude," 1593.
140. Adeyemo, 1593.

APPENDIX A

Q Methodology Data of the GPCC Sorts

Correlation Matrix between Sorts

SORTS	1	2	3	4	5	6	7	8	9	10	11	12	13	14	15	16	17	18	19	20
1 LC 01	100	65	40	42	54	50	54	57	57	73	52	42	56	62	51	69	64	56	56	57
2 LC 02	65	100	39	29	49	29	42	49	35	47	51	51	56	41	54	62	59	35	51	61
3 LC 04	40	39	100	19	31	35	39	44	36	45	42	49	57	18	47	57	47	39	19	32
4 AC 03	42	29	19	100	51	46	32	41	42	48	37	30	54	36	41	39	41	41	51	30
5 AC 02	54	49	31	51	100	44	44	52	46	69	56	61	61	55	41	61	65	66	60	64
6 AC 01	50	29	35	46	44	100	58	62	68	57	63	37	47	61	49	52	65	71	64	49
7 AC 04	54	42	39	32	44	58	100	71	59	66	69	45	69	68	61	74	53	63	68	51
8 PR 01	57	49	44	41	52	62	71	100	68	64	76	61	68	73	54	69	67	69	74	69
9 PR 02	57	35	36	42	46	68	59	68	100	77	62	52	61	73	50	56	54	71	65	64
10 PR 03	73	47	45	48	69	57	66	64	77	100	60	69	69	67	59	70	61	76	66	62
11 GR 01	52	51	42	37	56	63	69	76	62	60	100	51	69	70	55	65	70	70	65	56
12 GR 02	42	51	49	30	61	37	45	61	52	69	51	100	59	56	44	57	47	57	52	64
13 GR 03	56	56	57	54	61	47	69	68	61	69	69	59	100	57	69	77	63	68	62	54
14 GR 04	62	41	18	36	55	61	68	73	73	67	70	56	57	100	38	68	64	71	70	58
15 GR 05	51	54	47	41	41	49	61	54	50	59	55	44	69	38	100	64	63	51	61	47
16 IC 05	69	62	57	39	61	52	74	69	56	70	65	57	77	68	64	100	76	74	71	62
17 IC 04	64	59	47	41	65	65	53	67	54	61	70	47	63	64	63	76	100	65	72	63
18 IC 03	56	35	39	41	66	71	63	69	71	76	70	57	68	71	51	74	65	100	68	64
19 IC 02	56	51	19	51	60	64	68	74	65	66	65	52	62	70	61	71	72	68	100	71
20 IC 01	57	61	32	30	64	49	51	69	64	62	56	64	54	58	47	62	63	64	71	100

Unrotated Factor Matrix

SORTS/Factors	1	2	3	4	5	6	7	8
1 LC 01	0.7568	0.1247	0.1604	0.0847	-0.1850	0.4844	-0.1973	-0.1045
2 LC 02	0.6501	0.4693	0.3180	0.0039	-0.3478	0.0318	-0.0512	0.1038
3 LC 04	0.5340	0.5840	-0.3899	-0.1114	0.3029	0.1722	0.1814	0.0160
4 AC 03	0.5457	-0.1281	0.0620	0.7399	0.1878	-0.0739	-0.0463	0.0435
5 AC 02	0.7384	0.0234	0.4098	0.1537	0.2255	-0.0827	0.1912	-0.2523
6 AC 01	0.7279	-0.3471	-0.2684	0.0981	-0.0115	0.2116	0.2907	0.1687
7 AC 04	0.7827	-0.0879	-0.3090	-0.1157	-0.1654	-0.1709	-0.2816	-0.1374
8 PR 01	0.8481	-0.1026	-0.0840	-0.1722	-0.0535	-0.1579	0.0499	0.0897
9 PR 02	0.7867	-0.2985	-0.0904	-0.0991	0.1643	0.1998	-0.1602	0.2648
10 PR 03	0.8557	-0.0279	0.0709	0.0156	0.2548	0.1873	-0.2506	-0.0033
11 GR 01	0.8158	-0.0883	-0.1626	-0.1105	-0.1163	-0.1493	0.1728	-0.1289
12 GR 02	0.7070	0.1856	0.2388	-0.2607	0.4064	-0.1941	-0.0583	0.1394
13 GR 03	0.8345	0.2159	-0.1597	0.1414	0.1147	-0.2111	-0.1316	-0.1272
14 GR 04	0.7994	-0.3673	0.0777	-0.2051	-0.0777	0.0378	-0.1229	-0.1818
15 GR 05	0.7154	0.2781	-0.2627	0.2221	-0.1740	-0.1315	-0.1058	0.2664
16 IC 05	0.8704	0.1986	-0.0582	-0.0473	-0.1103	-0.0019	-0.0345	-0.2400
17 IC 04	0.8263	0.08 5	0.0193	0.0786	-0.2211	0.0916	0.3687	-0.0640
18 IC 03	0.8421	-0.2211	-0.0604	-0.0777	0.1847	0.0453	0.1099	-0.1431
19 IC 02	0.8361	-0.2335	0.1063	0.0904	-0.2145	-0.1971	0.0073	0.1268
20 IC 01	0.7750	0.0045	0.3640	-0.2156	-0.0360	-0.0386	0.1130	0.2744
Eigenvalues	11.7982	1.2738	0.9737	0.9141	0.8259	0.6255	0.6068	0.5428
% expl.Var.	59	6	5	5	4	3	3	3

Cumulative Communalities Matrix

SORTS/Factors	1	2	3	4	5	6	7	8
1 LC 01	0.5728	0.5883	0.6141	0.6212	0.6555	0.8901	0.9290	0.9399
2 LC 02	0.4226	0.6428	0.7439	0.7439	0.8649	0.8659	0.8685	0.8793
3 LC 04	0.2852	0.6263	0.7783	0.7907	0.8824	0.9121	0.9450	0.9452
4 AC 03	0.2978	0.3142	0.3181	0.8656	0.9009	0.9063	0.9085	0.9104
5 AC 02	0.5452	0.5458	0.7137	0.7374	0.7882	0.7950	0.8316	0.8952
6 AC 01	0.5298	0.6503	0.7223	0.7319	0.7321	0.7768	0.8613	0.8898
7 AC 04	0.6127	0.6204	0.7159	0.7293	0.7566	0.7858	0.8651	0.8840
8 PR 01	0.7193	0.7298	0.7369	0.7665	0.7694	0.7943	0.7968	0.8048
9 PR 02	0.6188	0.7079	0.7161	0.7259	0.7529	0.7928	0.8185	0.8886
10 PR 03	0.7322	0.7329	0.7380	0.7382	0.8031	0.8382	0.9010	0.9010
11 GR 01	0.6655	0.6733	0.6997	0.7119	0.7254	0.7477	0.7776	0.7942
12 GR 02	0.4998	0.5346	0.5916	0.6596	0.8248	0.8625	0.8659	0.8853
13 GR 03	0.6964	0.7434	0.7690	0.7889	0.8021	0.8466	0.8640	0.8801
14 GR 04	0.6391	0.7740	0.7801	0.8221	0.8282	0.8296	0.8447	0.8778
15 GR 05	0.5118	0.5892	0.6582	0.7075	0.7378	0.7551	0.7663	0.8372
16 IC 05	0.7576	0.7970	0.8004	0.8027	0.8148	0.8148	0.8160	0.8736
17 IC 04	0.6827	0.6893	0.6897	0.6959	0.7448	0.7532	0.8891	0.8932
18 IC 03	0.7092	0.7581	0.7617	0.7678	0.8019	0.8039	0.8160	0.8365
19 IC 02	0.6991	0.7536	0.7649	0.7731	0.8191	0.8579	0.8580	0.8741
20 IC 01	0.6006	0.6006	0.7331	0.7796	0.7809	0.7824	0.7952	0.8705
cum% expl.Var.	59	65	70	75	79	82	85	88

Factor Matrix with an X Indicating a Defining Sort

QSORT/Loadings	1	2	3
1 LC 01	0.7568X	0.1247	-0.1247
2 LC 02	0.6501X	0.4693X	-0.4693
3 LC 04	0.5340X	0.5840X	-0.5840
4 AC 03	0.5457X	-0.1281	0.1281
5 AC 02	0.7384X	0.0234	-0.0234
6 AC 01	0.7279X	-0.3471	0.3471X
7 AC 04	0.7827X	-0.0879	0.0879
8 PR 01	0.8481X	-0.1026	0.1026
9 PR 02	0.7867X	-0.2985	0.2985
10 PR 03	0.8557X	-0.0279	0.0279
11 GR 01	0.8158X	-0.0883	0.0883
12 GR 02	0.7070X	0.1866	-0.1866
13 GR 03	0.8345X	0.2169	-0.2169
14 GR 04	0.7994X	-0.3673	0.3673X
15 GR 05	0.7154X	0.2781	-0.2781
16 IC 05	0.8704X	0.1986	-0.1986
17 IC 04	0.8263X	0.0815	-0.0815
18 IC 03	0.8421X	-0.2211	0.2211
19 IC 02	0.8361X	-0.2335	0.2335
20 IC 01	0.7750X	0.0045	-0.0045
% expl.Var.	59	6	6

Factor Scores with Corresponding Ranks

Statement/Factors	No.	1	2	3
The gospel is that Christ died to deliver us from poverty and disease.	1	-0.88 27	-1.22 30	0.00 17
I am a true Christian because I am indwelt by the Holy Spirit.	2	1.00 9	0.23 15	0.80 11
Christ calls all Christians to engage in evangelism and discipleship.	3	1.26 6	1.10 8	0.51 14
Not paying my tithes and offerings is robbing God.	4	0.33 15	1.22 5	-0.25 18
Pentecostal-Charismatic sermons accurately interpret the Bible.	5	-0.22 19	0.67 11	-1.01 29
Praying aloud in tongues is Spirit-inspired prayer.	6	-0.89 28	-1.20 29	-0.55 24
Healing the sick is evidence of an anointed man of God.	7	-0.44 20	0.54 12	-0.27 20
The gospel is that Christ died to make us rich and successful.	8	-1.40 34	-1.43 33	-0.50 21
I am a Christian because I speak in tongues.	9	-1.58 35	-1.53 34	-1.31 33
My active participation in church proves I am a serious Christian.	10	-0.93 29	0.21 18	-0.51 23
I must pay my tithes to properly prepare for Christ's second coming.	11	-1.39 33	-0.55 24	-1.79 35
Paying my tithes and offerings affirms my Christian faith.	12	-0.72 23	-1.31 31	-0.99 28
As a Christian, suffering should not be my portion in life.	13	-1.39 32	-0.33 22	-1.56 34
My faith in Christ's death and resurrection makes me a Christian.	14	1.26 5	-0.88 27	1.81 1
The fruit of the Holy Spirit demonstrates my Christian maturity.	15	1.31 4	1.53 2	0.25 15
Church leaders must demonstrate humility and self-sacrifice.	16	0.89 11	-0.00 20	1.26 6
The Holy Spirit guides us to pray according to God's will.	17	1.39 2	1.65 1	1.30 4
A mega church is evidence of the anointing of the man of God.	18	-0.98 30	-1.32 32	-0.51 23

Statement	#			
Discipleship is teaching Christians to faithfully follow Jesus.	19	1.02 8	1.10 8	1.01 9
Sound biblical doctrine results from disciplined Bible study.	20	0.71 12	0.77 10	0.80 11
A Bible text's meaning intended by the original author applies to me.	21	-0.09 17	1.31 4	-0.78 26
Pentecostal-Charismatic pastors must exemplify personal success.	22	-0.73 24	-0.00 20	-1.28 32
Praying in tongues is more effective than praying silently.	23	-0.82 26	-0.67 26	-1.03 31
The church's mandate is to make disciples of all nations.	24	1.56 1	1.32 3	1.52 2
Pentecostal-Charismatic pastors must practice servant leadership.	25	0.67 14	-0.67 26	1.03 8
Looking forward to Christ's second coming keeps Christians faithful.	26	0.70 13	0.33 14	1.03 8
As a Christian, I can, by faith, name and claim prosperity.	27	-0.49 22	1.20 6	-0.80 27
The gospel is that Christ died and rose again for our salvation.	28	1.36 3	0.77 10	1.31 3
Spiritual transformation prepares me for Christ's second coming.	29	0.22 16	0.33 14	0.00 17
The mission of the church is to end poverty in the lives of Christians.	30	-1.25 31	-1.87 35	-1.03 31
Discipleship is teaching Christians to be loyal church members.	31	-0.81 25	-0.55 24	-0.27 20
Not paying my tithes and offerings is forfeiting my blessings.	32	-0.19 18	-0.10 21	1.28 5
The second coming of Christ is the church's blessed hope.	33	0.98 10	0.22 17	0.51 14
Evangelism and discipleship demonstrate Christian mercy.	34	-0.49 21	-1.10 28	-0.74 25
Christians must eagerly anticipate Christ's second coming.	35	1.05 7	0.22 17	0.76 12

Correlations between Factor Scores

	1	2	3
1	1.0000	0.6734	0.8578
2	0.6734	1.0000	0.3953
3	0.8578	0.3953	1.0000

Factor Scores for Factor 1

Statement	No.	Z-SCORES
The church's mandate is to make disciples of all nations.	24	1.559
The Holy Spirit guides us to pray according to God's will.	17	1.387
The gospel is that Christ died and rose again for our salvation.	28	1.361
The fruit of the Holy Spirit demonstrates my Christian maturity.	15	1.311
My faith in Christ's death and resurrection makes me a Christian.	14	1.257
Christ calls all Christians to engage in evangelism and discipleship.	3	1.256
Christians must eagerly anticipate Christ's second coming.	35	1.047
Discipleship is teaching Christians to faithfully follow Jesus.	19	1.021
I am a true Christian because I am indwelt by the Holy Spirit.	2	0.996
The second coming of Christ is the church's blessed hope.	33	0.982
Church leaders must demonstrate humility and self-sacrifice.	16	0.895
Sound biblical doctrine results from disciplined Bible study.	20	0.710
Looking forward to Christ's second coming keeps Christians faithful.	26	0.697
Pentecostal-Charismatic pastors must practice servant leadership.	25	0.667
Not paying my tithes and offerings is robbing God.	4	0.334
Spiritual transformation prepares me for Christ's second coming.	29	0.217
A Bible text's meaning intended by the original author applies to me.	21	-0.089
Not paying my tithes and offerings is forfeiting my blessings.	32	-0.193

Statement	No.	Z-SCORES
Pentecostal-Charismatic sermons accurately interpret the Bible.	5	-0.224
Healing the sick is evidence of an anointed man of God.	7	-0.443
Evangelism and discipleship demonstrate Christian mercy.	34	-0.489
As a Christian, I can, by faith, name and claim prosperity.	27	-0.492
Paying my tithes and offerings affirms my Christian faith.	12	-0.721
Pentecostal-Charismatic pastors must exemplify personal success.	22	-0.725
Discipleship is teaching Christians to be loyal church members.	31	-0.812
Praying in tongues is more effective than praying silently.	23	-0.823
The gospel is that Christ died to deliver us from poverty and disease.	1	-0.878
Praying aloud in tongues is Spirit-inspired prayer.	6	-0.888
My active participation in church proves I am a serious Christian.	10	-0.928
A mega church is evidence of the anointing of the man of God.	18	-0.978
The mission of the church is to end poverty in the lives of Christians.	30	-1.253
As a Christian, suffering should not be my portion in life.	13	-1.388
I must pay my tithes to properly prepare for Christ's second coming.	11	-1.390
The gospel is that Christ died to make us rich and successful.	8	-1.400
I am a Christian because I speak in tongues.	9	-1.584

Factor Scores for Factor 2

Statement	No.	Z-SCORES
The Holy Spirit guides us to pray according to God's will.	17	1.647
The fruit of the Holy Spirit demonstrates my Christian maturity.	15	1.530
The church's mandate is to make disciples of all nations.	24	1.320
A Bible text's meaning intended by the original author applies to me.	21	1.308
Not paying my tithes and offerings is robbing God.	4	1.215
As a Christian, I can, by faith, name and claim prosperity.	27	1.203
Christ calls all Christians to engage in evangelism and discipleship.	3	1.098
Discipleship is teaching Christians to faithfully follow Jesus.	19	1.098
Sound biblical doctrine results from disciplined Bible study.	20	0.771
The gospel is that Christ died and rose again for our salvation.	28	0.771
Pentecostal-Charismatic sermons accurately interpret the Bible.	5	0.666
Healing the sick is evidence of an anointed man of God.	7	0.537
Looking forward to Christ's second coming keeps Christians faithful.	26	0.327
Spiritual transformation prepares me for Christ's second coming.	29	0.327
I am a true Christian because I am indwelt by the Holy Spirit.	2	0.234
The second coming of Christ is the church's blessed hope.	33	0.222
Christians must eagerly anticipate Christ's second coming.	35	0.222
My active participation in church proves I am a serious Christian.	10	0.210
Church leaders must demonstrate humility and self-sacrifice.	16	-0.000

Statement	No.	Z-SCORES
Pentecostal-Charismatic pastors must exemplify personal success.	22	-0.000
Not paying my tithes and offerings is forfeiting my blessings.	32	-0.105
As a Christian, suffering should not be my portion in life.	13	-0.327
I must pay my tithes to properly prepare for Christ's second coming.	11	-0.549
Discipleship is teaching Christians to be loyal church members.	31	-0.549
Praying in tongues is more effective than praying silently.	23	-0.666
Pentecostal-Charismatic pastors must practice servant leadership.	25	-0.666
My faith in Christ's death and resurrection makes me a Christian.	14	-0.876
Evangelism and discipleship demonstrate Christian mercy.	34	-1.098
Praying aloud in tongues is Spirit-inspired prayer.	6	-1.203
The gospel is that Christ died to deliver us from poverty and disease.	1	-1.215
Paying my tithes and offerings affirms my Christian faith.	12	-1.308
A mega church is evidence of the anointing of the man of God.	18	-1.320
The gospel is that Christ died to make us rich and successful.	8	-1.425
I am a Christian because I speak in tongues.	9	-1.530
The mission of the church is to end poverty in the lives of Christians.	30	-1.869

Factor Scores for Factor 3

Statement	No.	Z-SCORES
My faith in Christ's death and resurrection makes me a Christian.	14	1.809
The church's mandate is to make disciples of all nations.	24	1.524
The gospel is that Christ died and rose again for our salvation.	28	1.314
The Holy Spirit guides us to pray according to God's will.	17	1.295
Not paying my tithes and offerings is forfeiting my blessings.	32	1.276
Church leaders must demonstrate humility and self-sacrifice.	16	1.258
Pentecostal-Charismatic pastors must practice servant leadership.	25	1.029
Looking forward to Christ's second coming keeps Christians faithful.	26	1.029
Discipleship is teaching Christians to faithfully follow Jesus.	19	1.010
I am a true Christian because I am indwelt by the Holy Spirit.	2	0.800
Sound biblical doctrine results from disciplined Bible study.	20	0.800
Christians must eagerly anticipate Christ's second coming.	35	0.762
Christ calls all Christians to engage in evangelism and discipleship.	3	0.514
The second coming of Christ is the church's blessed hope.	33	0.514
The fruit of the Holy Spirit demonstrates my Christian maturity.	15	0.248
The gospel is that Christ died to deliver us from poverty and disease.	1	0.000
Spiritual transformation prepares me for Christ's second coming.	29	0.000
Not paying my tithes and offerings is robbing God.	4	-0.248
Healing the sick is evidence of an anointed man of God.	7	-0.267

Statement	No.	Z-SCORES
Discipleship is teaching Christians to be loyal church members.	31	-0.267
The gospel is that Christ died to make us rich and successful.	8	-0.496
My active participation in church proves I am a serious Christian.	10	-0.514
A mega church is evidence of the anointing of the man of God.	18	-0.514
Praying aloud in tongues is Spirit-inspired prayer.	6	-0.552
Evangelism and discipleship demonstrate Christian mercy.	34	-0.743
A Bible text's meaning intended by the original author applies to me.	21	-0.781
As a Christian, I can, by faith, name and claim prosperity.	27	-0.800
Paying my tithes and offerings affirms my Christian faith.	12	-0.991
Pentecostal-Charismatic sermons accurately interpret the Bible.	5	-1.010
Praying in tongues is more effective than praying silently.	23	-1.029
The mission of the church is to end poverty in the lives of Christians.	30	-1.029
Pentecostal-Charismatic pastors must exemplify personal success.	22	-1.276
I am a Christian because I speak in tongues.	9	-1.314
As a Christian, suffering should not be my portion in life.	13	-1.562
I must pay my tithes to properly prepare for Christ's second coming.	11	-1.791

Descending Array of Differences between Factors 1 and 2

Statement	No.	F 1	F 2	Difference
My faith in Christ's death and resurrection makes me a Christian.	14	1.257	-0.876	2.133
Pentecostal-Charismatic pastors must practice servant leadership.	25	0.667	-0.666	1.333
Church leaders must demonstrate humility and self-sacrifice.	16	0.895	-0.000	0.895
Christians must eagerly anticipate Christ's second coming.	35	1.047	0.222	0.825
I am a true Christian because I am indwelt by the Holy Spirit.	2	0.996	0.234	0.762
The second coming of Christ is the church's blessed hope.	33	0.982	0.222	0.760
The mission of the church is to end poverty in the lives of Christians.	30	-1.253	-1.869	0.617
Evangelism and discipleship demonstrate Christian mercy.	34	-0.489	-1.098	0.609
The gospel is that Christ died and rose again for our salvation.	28	1.361	0.771	0.590
Paying my tithes and offerings affirms my Christian faith.	12	-0.721	-1.308	0.587
Looking forward to Christ's second coming keeps Christians faithful.	26	0.697	0.327	0.370
A mega church is evidence of the anointing of the man of God.	18	-0.978	-1.320	0.342
The gospel is that Christ died to deliver us from poverty and disease.	1	-0.878	-1.215	0.337
Praying aloud in tongues is Spirit-inspired prayer.	6	-0.888	-1.203	0.315
The church's mandate is to make disciples of all nations.	24	1.559	1.320	0.239
Christ calls all Christians to engage in evangelism and discipleship.	3	1.256	1.098	0.158
The gospel is that Christ died to make us rich and successful.	8	-1.400	-1.425	0.025

Statement	No.	F 1	F 2	Difference
I am a Christian because I speak in tongues.	9	-1.584	-1.530	-0.054
Sound biblical doctrine results from disciplined Bible study.	20	0.710	0.771	-0.061
Discipleship is teaching Christians to faithfully follow Jesus.	19	1.021	1.098	-0.077
Not paying my tithes and offerings is forfeiting my blessings.	32	-0.193	-0.105	-0.088
Spiritual transformation prepares me for Christ's second coming.	29	0.217	0.327	-0.110
Praying in tongues is more effective than praying silently.	23	-0.823	-0.666	-0.157
The fruit of the Holy Spirit demonstrates my Christian maturity.	15	1.311	1.530	-0.219
The Holy Spirit guides us to pray according to God's will.	17	1.387	1.647	-0.260
Discipleship is teaching Christians to be loyal church members.	31	-0.812	-0.549	-0.263
Pentecostal-Charismatic pastors must exemplify personal success.	22	-0.725	-0.000	-0.725
I must pay my tithes to properly prepare for Christ's second coming.	11	-1.390	-0.549	-0.841
Not paying my tithes and offerings is robbing God.	4	0.334	1.215	-0.881
Pentecostal-Charismatic sermons accurately interpret the Bible.	5	-0.224	0.666	-0.890
Healing the sick is evidence of an anointed man of God.	7	-0.443	0.537	-0.980
As a Christian, suffering should not be my portion in life.	13	-1.388	-0.327	-1.061
My active participation in church proves I am a serious Christian.	10	-0.928	0.210	-1.138
A Bible text's meaning intended by the original author applies to me.	21	-0.089	1.308	-1.397
As a Christian, I can, by faith, name and claim prosperity.	27	-0.492	1.203	-1.695

Descending Array of Differences between Factors 1 and 3

Statement	No.	F 1	F 3	Difference
The fruit of the Holy Spirit demonstrates my Christian maturity.	15	1.311	0.248	1.063
Pentecostal-Charismatic sermons accurately interpret the Bible.	5	-0.224	-1.010	0.786
Christ calls all Christians to engage in evangelism and discipleship.	3	1.256	0.514	0.742
A Bible text's meaning intended by the original author applies to me.	21	-0.089	-0.781	0.692
Not paying my tithes and offerings is robbing God.	4	0.334	-0.248	0.582
Pentecostal-Charismatic pastors must exemplify personal success.	22	-0.725	-1.276	0.551
The second coming of Christ is the church's blessed hope.	33	0.982	0.514	0.468
I must pay my tithes to properly prepare for Christ's second coming.	11	-1.390	-1.791	0.401
As a Christian, I can, by faith, name and claim prosperity.	27	-0.492	-0.800	0.308
Christians must eagerly anticipate Christ's second coming.	35	1.047	0.762	0.285
Paying my tithes and offerings affirms my Christian faith.	12	-0.721	-0.991	0.270
Evangelism and discipleship demonstrate Christian mercy.	34	-0.489	-0.743	0.254
Spiritual transformation prepares me for Christ's second coming.	29	0.217	0.000	0.217
Praying in tongues is more effective than praying silently.	23	-0.823	-1.029	0.205
I am a true Christian because I am indwelt by the Holy Spirit.	2	0.996	0.800	0.197
As a Christian, suffering should not be my portion in life.	13	-1.388	-1.562	0.174
The Holy Spirit guides us to pray according to God's will.	17	1.387	1.295	0.092

Statement	No.	F 1	F 3	Difference
The gospel is that Christ died and rose again for our salvation.	28	1.361	1.314	0.048
The church's mandate is to make disciples of all nations.	24	1.559	1.524	0.035
Discipleship is teaching Christians to faithfully follow Jesus.	19	1.021	1.010	0.011
Sound biblical doctrine results from disciplined Bible Study.	20	0.710	0.800	-0.090
Healing the sick is evidence of an anointed man of God.	7	-0.443	-0.267	-0.176
The mission of the church is to end poverty in the lives of Christians.	30	-1.253	-1.029	-0.224
I am a Christian because I speak in tongues.	9	-1.584	-1.314	-0.270
Looking forward to Christ's second coming keeps Christians faithful.	26	0.697	1.029	-0.332
Praying aloud in tongues is Spirit-inspired prayer.	6	-0.888	-0.552	-0.336
Pentecostal-Charismatic pastors must practice servant leadership.	25	0.667	1.029	-0.362
Church leaders must demonstrate humility and self-sacrifice.	16	0.895	1.258	-0.363
My active participation in church proves I am a serious Christian.	10	-0.928	-0.514	-0.414
A mega church is evidence of the anointing of the man of God.	18	-0.978	-0.514	-0.464
Discipleship is teaching Christians to be loyal church members.	31	-0.812	-0.267	-0.546
My faith in Christ's death and resurrection makes me a Christian.	14	1.257	1.809	-0.552
The gospel is that Christ died to deliver us from poverty and disease.	1	-0.878	0.000	-0.878
The gospel is that Christ died to make us rich and successful.	8	-1.400	-0.496	-0.904
Not paying my tithes and offerings is forfeiting my blessings.	32	-0.193	1.276	-1.470

Descending Array of Differences between Factors 2 and 3

Statement	No.	F 2	F 3	Difference
A Bible text's meaning intended by the original author applies to me.	21	1.308	-0.781	2.089
As a Christian, I can, by faith, name and claim prosperity.	27	1.203	-0.800	2.003
Pentecostal-Charismatic sermons accurately interpret the Bible.	5	0.666	-1.010	1.676
Not paying my tithes and offerings is robbing God.	4	1.215	-0.248	1.463
The fruit of the Holy Spirit demonstrates my Christian maturity.	15	1.530	0.248	1.282
Pentecostal-Charismatic pastors must exemplify personal success.	22	-0.000	-1.276	1.276
I must pay my tithes to properly prepare for Christ's second coming.	11	-0.549	-1.791	1.242
As a Christian, suffering should not be my portion in life.	13	-0.327	-1.562	1.235
Healing the sick is evidence of an anointed man of God.	7	0.537	-0.267	0.804
My active participation in church proves I am a serious Christian.	10	0.210	-0.514	0.724
Christ calls all Christians to engage in evangelism and discipleship.	3	1.098	0.514	0.584
Praying in tongues is more effective than praying silently.	23	-0.666	-1.029	0.363
The Holy Spirit guides us to pray according to God's will.	17	1.647	1.295	0.352
Spiritual transformation prepares me for Christ's second coming.	29	0.327	0.000	0.327
Discipleship is teaching Christians to faithfully follow Jesus.	19	1.098	1.010	0.088
Sound biblical doctrine results from disciplined Bible study.	20	0.771	0.800	-0.029
The church's mandate is to make disciples of all nations.	24	1.320	1.524	-0.204

Statement	No.	F 2	F 3	Difference
I am a Christian because I speak in tongues.	9	-1.530	-1.314	-0.216
Discipleship is teaching Christians to be loyal church members.	31	-0.549	-0.267	-0.283
The second coming of Christ is the church's blessed hope.	33	0.222	0.514	-0.292
Paying my tithes and offerings affirms my Christian faith.	12	-1.308	-0.991	-0.317
Evangelism and discipleship demonstrate Christian mercy.	34	-1.098	-0.743	-0.355
Christians must eagerly anticipate Christ's second coming.	35	0.222	0.762	-0.540
The gospel is that Christ died and rose again for our salvation.	28	0.771	1.314	-0.543
I am a true Christian because I am indwelt by the Holy Spirit.	2	0.234	0.800	-0.566
Praying aloud in tongues is Spirit-inspired prayer.	6	-1.203	-0.552	-0.651
Looking forward to Christ's second coming keeps Christians faithful.	26	0.327	1.029	-0.702
A mega church is evidence of the anointing of the man of God.	18	-1.320	-0.514	-0.806
The mission of the church is to end poverty in the lives of Christians.	30	-1.869	-1.029	-0.841
The gospel is that Christ died to make us rich and successful.	8	-1.425	-0.496	-0.930
The gospel is that Christ died to deliver us from poverty and disease.	1	-1.215	0.000	-1.215
Church leaders must demonstrate humility and self-sacrifice.	16	-0.000	1.258	-1.258
Not paying my tithes and offerings is forfeiting my blessings.	32	-0.105	1.276	-1.381
Pentecostal-Charismatic pastors must practice servant leadership.	25	-0.666	1.029	-1.695
My faith in Christ's death and resurrection makes me a Christian.	14	-0.876	1.809	-2.685

Factor Q-Sort Values for Each Statement

Statement	No.	F 1	F 2	F 3
The gospel is that Christ died to deliver us from poverty and disease.	1	-2	-2	0
I am a true Christian because I am indwelt by the Holy Spirit.	2	2	0	1
Christ calls all Christians to engage in evangelism and discipleship.	3	2	2	1
Not paying my tithes and offerings is robbing God.	4	0	3	0
Pentecostal Charismatic sermons accurately interpret the Bible.	5	0	1	-2
Praying aloud in tongues is Spirit-inspired prayer.	6	-2	-2	-1
Healing the sick is evidence of an anointed man of God.	7	0	1	0
The gospel is that Christ died to make us rich and successful.	8	-4	-3	0
I am a Christian because I speak in tongues.	9	-4	-4	-3
My active participation in church proves I am a serious Christian.	10	-2	0	-1
I must pay my tithes to properly prepare for Christ's second coming.	11	-3	-1	-4
Paying my tithes and offerings affirms my Christian faith.	12	-1	-3	-2
As a Christian, suffering should not be my portion in life.	13	-3	-1	-4
My faith in Christ's death and resurrection makes me a Christian.	14	3	-2	4
The fruit of the Holy Spirit demonstrates my Christian maturity.	15	3	4	0
Church leaders must demonstrate humility and self-sacrifice.	16	1	0	2
The Holy Spirit guides us to pray according to God's will.	17	4	4	3
A mega church is evidence of the anointing of the man of God.	18	-2	-3	-1

Statement	No.	F 1	F 2	F 3
Discipleship is teaching Christians to faithfully follow Jesus.	19	2	2	2
Sound biblical doctrine results from disciplined Bible study.	20	1	1	1
A Bible text's meaning intended by the original author applies to me.	21	0	3	-1
Pentecostal-Charismatic pastors must exemplify personal success.	22	-1	0	-3
Praying in tongues is more effective than praying silently.	23	-1	-1	-3
The church's mandate is to make disciples of all nations.	24	4	3	4
Pentecostal-Charismatic pastors must practice servant leadership.	25	1	-1	2
Looking forward to Christ's second coming keeps Christians faithful.	26	1	1	2
As a Christian, I can, by faith, name and claim prosperity.	27	-1	2	-2
The gospel is that Christ died and rose again for our salvation.	28	3	1	3
Spiritual transformation prepares me for Christ's second coming.	29	0	1	0
The mission of the church is to end poverty in the lives of Christians.	30	-3	-4	-3
Discipleship is teaching Christians to be loyal church members.	31	-1	-1	0
Not paying my tithes and offerings is forfeiting my blessings.	32	0	0	3
The second coming of Christ is the church's blessed hope.	33	1	0	1
Evangelism and discipleship demonstrate Christian mercy.	34	0	-2	-1
Christians must eagerly anticipate Christ's second coming.	35	2	0	1
Variance = 4.571 St. Dev. = 2.138				

Factor Q-Sort Values for Statements Sorted by Consensus vs. Disagreement (Variance across Factor Z-Scores)

Statement	No.	F 1	F 2	F 3
The gospel is that Christ died to deliver us from poverty and disease.	1	-2	-2	0
I am a true Christian because I am indwelt by the Holy Spirit.	2	2	0	1
Christ calls all Christians to engage in evangelism and discipleship.	3	2	2	1
Not paying my tithes and offerings is robbing God.	4	0	3	0
Pentecostal-Charismatic sermons accurately interpret the Bible.	5	0	1	-2
Praying aloud in tongues is Spirit-inspired prayer.	6	-2	-2	-1
Healing the sick is evidence of an anointed man of God.	7	0	1	0
The gospel is that Christ died to make us rich and successful.	8	-4	-3	0
I am a Christian because I speak in tongues.	9	-4	-4	-3
My active participation in church proves I am a serious Christian.	10	-2	0	-1
I must pay my tithes to properly prepare for Christ's second coming.	11	-3	-1	-4
Paying my tithes and offerings affirms my Christian faith.	12	-1	-3	-2
As a Christian, suffering should not be my portion in life.	13	-3	-1	-4
My faith in Christ's death and resurrection makes me a Christian.	14	3	-2	4
The fruit of the Holy Spirit demonstrates my Christian maturity.	15	3	4	0
Church leaders must demonstrate humility and self-sacrifice.	16	1	0	2
The Holy Spirit guides us to pray according to God's will.	17	4	4	3
A mega church is evidence of the anointing of the man of God.	18	-2	-3	-1

Statement	No.	F 1	F 2	F 3
Discipleship is teaching Christians to faithfully follow Jesus.	19	2	2	2
Sound biblical doctrine results from disciplined Bible study.	20	1	1	1
A Bible text's meaning intended by the original author applies to me.	21	0	3	-1
Pentecostal-Charismatic pastors must exemplify personal success.	22	-1	0	-3
Praying in tongues is more effective than praying silently.	23	-1	-1	-3
The church's mandate is to make disciples of all nations.	24	4	3	4
Pentecostal-Charismatic pastors must practice servant leadership.	25	1	-1	2
Looking forward to Christ's second coming keeps Christians faithful.	26	1	1	2
As a Christian, I can, by faith, name and claim prosperity.	27	-1	2	-2
The gospel is that Christ died and rose again for our salvation.	28	3	1	3
Spiritual transformation prepares me for Christ's second coming.	29	0	1	0
The mission of the church is to end poverty in the lives of Christians.	30	-3	-4	-3
Discipleship is teaching Christians to be loyal church members.	31	-1	-1	0
Not paying my tithes and offerings is forfeiting my blessings.	32	0	0	3
The second coming of Christ is the church's blessed hope.	33	1	0	1
Evangelism and discipleship demonstrate Christian mercy.	34	0	-2	-1
Christians must eagerly anticipate Christ's second coming.	35	2	0	1

Factor Characteristics

	Factors		
	1	2	3
No. of Defining Variables	20	2	2
Average Rel. Coef.	0.800	0.800	0.800
Composite Reliability	0.988	0.889	0.889
S. E. of Factor Z-Scores	0.111	0.333	0.333

Standard Errors for Differences in Factor Z-Scores
(Diagonal Entries Are S. E. Within Factors)

Factors	1	2	3
1	0.157	0.351	0.351
2	0.351	0.471	0.471
3	0.351	0.471	0.471

Distinguishing Statements for Factor 1

($P < .05$; Asterisk (*) indicates significance at $P < .01$)
Both the Factor Q-Sort Value (Q-SV) and the Z-Score (Z-SCR) are shown.

		Factors					
		1		2		3	
Statement	No.	Q-SV	Z-SCR	Q-SV	Z-SCR	Q-SV	Z-SCR
A Bible text's meaning intended by the original author applies to me.	21	0	-0.09	3	1.31	-1	-0.78
Pentecostal-Charismatic sermons accurately interpret the Bible.	5	0	-0.22	1	0.67	-2	-1.01

Distinguishing Statements for Factor 2

(P <.05; Asterisk (*) indicates significance at P <.01)
Both the Factor Q-Sort Value (Q-SV) and the Z-Score (Z-SCR) are shown.

		Factors				
		1		2		3	
Statement	No.	Q-SV	Z-SCR	Q-SV	Z-SCR	Q-SV	Z-SCR
A Bible text's meaning intended by the original author applies to me.	21	0	-0.09	3	1.31*	-1	-0.78
Not paying my tithes and offerings is robbing God.	4	0	0.33	3	1.22	0	-0.25
As a Christian, I can, by faith, name and claim prosperity.	27	-1	-0.49	2	1.20*	-2	-0.80
Pentecostal-Charismatic sermons accurately interpret the Bible.	5	0	-0.22	1	0.67	-2	-1.01
Pentecostal-Charismatic pastors must exemplify personal success.	22	-1	-0.73	0	-0.00	-3	-1.28
Church leaders must demonstrate humility and self-sacrifice.	16	1	0.89	0	-0.00	2	1.26
As a Christian, suffering should not be my portion in life.	13	-3	-1.39	-1	-0.33*	-4	-1.56
I must pay my tithes to properly prepare for Christ's second coming.	11	-3	-1.39	-1	-0.55	-4	-1.79
Pentecostal-Charismatic pastors must practice servant leadership.	25	1	0.67	-1	-0.67*	2	1.03
My faith in Christ's death and resurrection makes me a Christian.	14	3	1.26	-2	-0.88*	4	1.81

Distinguishing Statements for Factor 3

(P <.05; Asterisk (*) indicates significance at P <.01)
Both the Factor Q-Sort Value (Q-SV) and the Z-Score (Z-SCR) are shown.

		Factors					
		1		2		3	
Statement	No.	Q-SV	Z-SCR	Q-SV	Z-SCR	Q-SV	Z-SCR
Not paying my tithes and offerings is forfeiting my blessings.	32	0	-0.19	0	-0.10	3	1.28*
The fruit of the Holy Spirit demonstrates my Christian maturity.	15	3	1.31	4	1.53	0	0.25*
The gospel is that Christ died to deliver us from poverty and disease.	1	-2	-0.88	-2	-1.22	0	0.00
The gospel is that Christ died to make us rich and successful.	8	-4	-1.40	-3	-1.43	0	-0.50
A Bible text's meaning intended by the original author applies to me.	21	0	-0.09	3	1.31	-1	-0.78
Pentecostal-Charismatic sermons accurately interpret the Bible.	5	0	-0.22	1	0.67	-2	-1.01

Consensus Statements:
Those that Do Not Distinguish between ANY Pair of Factors

All listed statements are non-significant at P>.01, and those flagged with an * are also non-significant at P>.05.

		Factors					
		1		2		3	
Statement	No.	Q-SV	Z-SCR	Q-SV	Z-SCR	Q-SV	Z-SCR
The gospel is that Christ died to deliver us from poverty and disease.	1	-2	-0.88	-2	-1.22	0	0.00
I am a true Christian because I am indwelt by the Holy Spirit.	2	2	1.00	0	0.23	1	0.80
Christ calls all Christians to engage in evangelism and discipleship.	3	2	1.26	2	1.10	1	0.51
Not paying my tithes and offerings is robbing God.	6	-2	-0.89	-2	-1.20	-1	-0.55
Pentecostal Charismatic sermons accurately interpret the Bible.	8	-4	-1.40	-3	-1.43	0	-0.50
Praying aloud in tongues is Spirit-inspired prayer.	9	-4	-1.58	-4	-1.53	-3	-1.31
Healing the sick is evidence of an anointed man of God.	12	-1	-0.72	-3	-1.31	-2	-0.99
The gospel is that Christ died to make us rich and successful.	17	4	1.39	4	1.65	3	1.30
I am a Christian because I speak in tongues.	18	-2	-0.98	-3	-1.32	-1	-0.51
My active participation in church proves I am a serious Christian.	19	2	1.02	2	1.10	2	1.01
I must pay my tithes to properly prepare for Christ's second coming.	20	1	0.71	1	0.77	1	0.80

Conclusions and Recommendations

		Factors					
		1		2		3	
Statement	No.	Q-SV	Z-SCR	Q-SV	Z-SCR	Q-SV	Z-SCR
Paying my tithes and offerings affirms my Christian faith.	23	-1	-0.82	-1	-0.67	-3	-1.03
As a Christian, suffering should not be my portion in life.	24	4	1.56	3	1.32	4	1.52
My faith in Christ's death and resurrection makes me a Christian.	26	1	0.70	1	0.33	2	1.03
The fruit of the Holy Spirit demonstrates my Christian maturity.	28	3	1.36	1	0.77	3	1.31
Church leaders must demonstrate humility and self-sacrifice.	29	0	0.22	1	0.33	0	0.00
The Holy Spirit guides us to pray according to God's will.	30	-3	-1.25	-4	-1.87	-3	-1.03
A mega church is evidence of the anointing of the man of God.	31	-1	-0.81	-1	-0.55	0	-0.27
Discipleship is teaching Christians to faithfully follow Jesus.	33	1	0.98	0	0.22	1	0.51
Sound biblical doctrine results from disciplined Bible Study.	34	0	-0.49	-2	-1.10	-1	-0.74
A Bible text's meaning intended by the original author applies to me.	35	2	1.05	0	0.22	1	0.76

APPENDIX B

Q Methodology Data of the Jude Sort

Correlation Matrix between Sorts

SORTS	1	2	3	4	5	6	7	8	9	10	11	12	13	14	15	16	17	18	19	20	21
1 LC 01	100	65	40	42	54	50	54	57	57	73	52	42	56	62	51	69	64	56	56	57	51
2 LC 02	65	100	39	29	49	29	42	49	35	47	51	51	56	41	54	62	59	35	51	61	39
3 LC 04	40	39	100	19	31	35	39	44	36	45	42	49	57	18	47	57	47	39	19	32	25
4 AC 03	42	29	19	100	51	46	32	41	42	48	37	30	54	36	41	39	41	41	51	30	51
5 AC 02	54	49	31	51	100	44	44	52	46	69	56	61	61	55	41	61	65	66	60	64	65
6 AC 01	50	29	35	46	44	100	58	62	68	57	63	37	47	61	49	52	65	71	64	49	57
7 AC 04	54	42	39	32	44	58	100	71	59	66	69	45	69	68	61	74	53	63	68	51	59
8 PR 01	57	49	44	41	52	62	71	100	68	64	76	61	68	73	54	69	67	69	74	69	59
9 PR 02	57	35	36	42	46	68	59	68	100	77	62	52	61	73	50	56	54	71	65	64	68
10 PR 03	73	47	45	48	69	57	66	64	77	100	60	69	69	67	59	70	61	76	66	62	65
11 GR 01	52	51	42	37	56	63	69	76	62	60	100	51	69	70	55	65	70	70	65	56	61
12 GR 02	42	51	49	30	61	37	45	61	52	69	51	100	59	56	44	57	47	57	52	64	48
13 GR 03	56	56	57	54	61	47	69	68	61	69	69	59	100	57	69	77	63	68	62	54	69
14 GR 04	62	41	18	36	55	61	68	73	73	67	70	56	57	100	38	68	64	71	70	58	59
15 GR 05	51	54	47	41	41	49	61	54	50	59	55	44	69	38	100	64	63	51	61	47	51
16 IC 05	69	62	57	39	61	52	74	69	56	70	65	57	77	68	64	100	76	74	65	62	61
17 IC 04	64	59	47	41	65	65	53	67	54	61	70	47	63	64	63	76	100	65	72	63	59
18 IC 03	56	35	39	41	66	71	63	69	71	76	70	57	68	71	51	74	65	100	68	64	69
19 IC 02	56	51	19	51	60	64	68	74	65	66	65	52	62	70	61	71	72	68	100	71	69
20 IC 01	57	61	32	30	64	49	51	69	64	62	56	64	54	58	47	62	63	64	71	100	62
21 Jude	51	39	25	51	65	57	59	59	68	65	61	48	69	59	51	61	59	69	69	62	100

Conclusions and Recommendations

Unrotated Factor Matrix

SORTS \ Factors	1	2	3	4	5	6	7	8
1 LC 01	0.7521	0.1458	0.1509	0.0006	-0.2176	0.4626	-0.2401	-0.1073
2 LC 02	0.6427	0.4765	0.3142	-0.0842	-0.3468	0.0114	-0.0549	0.1040
3 LC 04	0.5229	0.6120	-0.3564	0.0494	0.3332	0.1714	0.1635	0.0142
4 AC 03	0.5522	-0.1750	0.2200	0.6841	0.0770	0.0335	-0.0270	0.0499
5 AC 02	0.7439	-0.0111	0.4466	0.0723	0.1926	-0.0410	0.1996	-0.2522
6 AC 01	0.7291	-0.3147	-0.2790	0.1081	-0.0412	0.2591	0.2731	0.1676
7 AC 04	0.7822	-0.0547	-0.3381	-0.0527	-0.1349	-0.2118	-0.2667	-0.1363
8 PR 01	0.8439	-0.0588	-0.1442	-0.1739	-0.0402	-0.1197	0.0687	0.0940
9 PR 02	0.7914	-0.2813	-0.1263	-0.0843	0.1647	0.1824	-0.1780	0.2629
10 PR 03	0.8552	-0.0192	0.0714	0.0038	0.2356	0.1877	-0.2643	-0.0040
11 GR 01	0.8148	-0.0568	-0.1988	-0.0879	-0.0987	-0.1323	0.1862	-0.1270
12 GR 02	0.7028	0.1986	0.1971	-0.2638	0.4263	-0.1499	-0.0347	0.1440
13 GR 03	0.8377	0.1993	-0.0890	0.2195	0.1207	-0.2290	-0.1132	-0.1260
14 GR 04	0.7984	-0.3217	-0.0193	-0.2740	-0.0786	0.0604	-0.1213	-0.1790
15 GR 05	0.7124	0.2815	-0.1914	0.2837	-0.1779	-0.1560	-0.0956	0.2656
16 IC 05	0.8661	0.2211	-0.0654	-0.0342	-0.0984	-0.0208	-0.0361	-0.2408
17 IC 04	0.8230	0.1022	0.0175	0.0368	-0.2375	0.1189	0.3584	-0.0656
18 IC 03	0.8449	-0.2054	-0.0861	-0.0630	0.1850	0.0554	0.1047	-0.1448
19 IC 02	0.8393	-0.2251	0.0926	0.0179	-0.2329	-0.1748	0.0274	0.1289
20 IC 01	0.7769	0.0080	0.3029	-0.2948	-0.0171	-0.0518	0.1131	0.2726
21 Jude	0.7823	-0.2471	0.1244	0.1598	0.0850	-0.1683	-0.0194	-0.0083
Eigenvalues	12.3897	1.3171	0.9815	0.9349	0.8318	0.6408	0.6071	0.5428
% expl.Var.	59	6	5	4	4	3	3	3

Cumulative Communalities Matrix

SORTS \ Factors	1	2	3	4	5	6	7	8
1 LC 01	0.5657	0.5870	0.6098	0.6098	0.6571	0.8711	0.9288	0.9403
2 LC 02	0.4131	0.6402	0.7389	0.7460	0.8663	0.8664	0.8694	0.8802
3 LC 04	0.2735	0.6481	0.7750	0.7775	0.8885	0.9179	0.9446	0.9448
4 AC 03	0.3050	0.3356	0.3840	0.8520	0.8580	0.8591	0.8598	0.8623
5 AC 02	0.5534	0.5535	0.7530	0.7582	0.7953	0.7970	0.8368	0.9004
6 AC 01	0.5316	0.6306	0.7084	0.7201	0.7218	0.7889	0.8635	0.8916
7 AC 04	0.6118	0.6148	0.7291	0.7318	0.7501	0.7949	0.8660	0.8846
8 PR 01	0.7122	0.7157	0.7365	0.7667	0.7683	0.7826	0.7874	0.7962
9 PR 02	0.6263	0.7055	0.7214	0.7285	0.7556	0.7889	0.8206	0.8897
10 PR 03	0.7314	0.7318	0.7369	0.7369	0.7924	0.8277	0.8976	0.8976
11 GR 01	0.6639	0.6671	0.7066	0.7144	0.7241	0.7416	0.7763	0.7924
12 GR 02	0.4939	0.5333	0.5722	0.6417	0.8235	0.8460	0.8472	0.8679
13 GR 03	0.7018	0.7415	0.7494	0.7976	0.8122	0.8646	0.8775	0.8933
14 GR 04	0.6374	0.7409	0.7413	0.8163	0.8225	0.8261	0.8409	0.8729
15 GR 05	0.5075	0.5867	0.6233	0.7038	0.7355	0.7598	0.7689	0.8395
16 IC 05	0.7501	0.7989	0.8032	0.8044	0.8141	0.8145	0.8158	0.8738
17 IC 04	0.6774	0.6878	0.6881	0.6895	0.7459	0.7600	0.8885	0.8928
18 IC 03	0.7139	0.7561	0.7635	0.7675	0.8017	0.8048	0.8158	0.8367
19 IC 02	0.7044	0.7551	0.7637	0.7640	0.8182	0.8488	0.8495	0.8661
20 IC 01	0.6035	0.6036	0.6953	0.7822	0.7825	0.7852	0.7980	0.8723
21 Jude	0.6120	0.6731	0.6886	0.7141	0.7213	0.7497	0.7500	0.7501
cum% expl.Var.	59	65	70	74	78	81	84	87

Factor Matrix with an X Indicating a Defining Sort

	Loadings		
QSORT	1	2	3
1 LC 01	0.7521X	0.1458	-0.1458
2 LC 02	0.6427X	0.4765X	-0.4765
3 LC 04	0.5229X	0.6120X	-0.6120
4 AC 03	0.5522X	-0.1750	0.1750
5 AC 02	0.7439X	-0.0111	0.0111
6 AC 01	0.7291X	-0.3147	0.3147X
7 AC 04	0.7822X	-0.0547	0.0547
8 PR 01	0.8439X	-0.0588	0.0588
9 PR 02	0.7914X	-0.2813	0.2813
10 PR 03	0.8552X	-0.0192	0.0192
11 GR 01	0.8148X	-0.0568	0.0568
12 GR 02	0.7028X	0.1986	-0.1986
13 GR 03	0.8377X	0.1993	-0.1993
14 GR 04	0.7984X	-0.3217	0.3217X
15 GR 05	0.7124X	0.2815	-0.2815
16 IC 05	0.8661X	0.2211	-0.2211
17 IC 04	0.8230X	0.1022	-0.1022
18 IC 03	0.8449X	-0.2054	0.2054
19 IC 02	0.8393X	-0.2251	0.2251
20 IC 01	0.7769X	0.0080	-0.0080
21 Jude	0.7823X	-0.2471	0.2471
% expl.Var.	59	6	6

Factor Scores with Corresponding Ranks

		Factors		
Statement	No.	1	2	3
The gospel is that Christ died to deliver us from poverty and disease.	1	-0.94 28	-1.18 29	0.00 17
I am a true Christian because I am indwelt by the Holy Spirit.	2	0.98 9	0.17 18	0.78 11
Christ calls all Christians to engage in evangelism and discipleship.	3	1.22 6	1.09 8	0.51 14
Not paying my tithes and offerings is robbing God.	4	0.29 16	1.18 6	-0.25 18
Pentecostal-Charismatic sermons accurately interpret the Bible.	5	-0.27 19	0.63 11	-1.02 29
Praying aloud in tongues is Spirit-inspired prayer.	6	-0.84 27	-1.22 30	-0.53 24
Healing the sick is evidence of an anointed man of God.	7	-0.46 21	0.58 12	-0.26 20
The gospel is that Christ died to make us rich and successful.	8	-1.45 34	-1.43 33	-0.51 21
I am a Christian because I speak in tongues.	9	-1.51 35	-1.55 34	-1.30 33
My active participation in church proves I am a serious Christian.	10	-0.94 29	0.25 15	-0.51 23
I must pay my tithes to properly prepare for Christ's second coming.	11	-1.35 32	-0.55 24	-1.80 35
Paying my tithes and offerings affirms my Christian faith.	12	-0.69 23	-1.34 32	-1.01 28
As a Christian, suffering should not be my portion in life.	13	-1.41 33	-0.34 22	-1.55 34
My faith in Christ's death and resurrection makes me a Christian.	14	1.28 4	-0.88 27	1.80 1
The fruit of the Holy Spirit demonstrates my Christian maturity.	15	1.24 5	1.55 2	0.25 15
Church leaders must demonstrate humility and self-sacrifice.	16	0.91 11	0.00 20	1.28 6
The Holy Spirit guides us to pray according to God's will.	17	1.38 3	1.64 1	1.29 4

A mega church is evidence of the anointing of the man of God.	18	-0.96 30	-1.31 31	-0.51 23
Discipleship is teaching Christians to faithfully follow Jesus.	19	1.08 7	1.09 8	1.02 9
Sound biblical doctrine results from disciplined Bible study.	20	0.67 13	0.76 10	0.78 11
A Bible text's meaning intended by the original author applies to me.	21	-0.06 17	1.34 3	-0.78 26
Pentecostal-Charismatic pastors must exemplify personal success.	22	-0.75 24	0.00 20	-1.28 32
Praying in tongues is more effective than praying silently.	23	-0.78 25	-0.63 26	-1.03 31
The church's mandate is to make disciples of all nations.	24	1.58 1	1.31 4	1.54 2
Pentecostal-Charismatic pastors must practice servant leadership.	25	0.70 12	-0.63 26	1.03 8
Looking forward to Christ's second coming keeps Christians faithful.	26	0.67 14	0.34 14	1.03 8
As a Christian, I can, by faith, name and claim prosperity.	27	-0.55 22	1.22 5	-0.78 27
The gospel is that Christ died and rose again for our salvation.	28	1.41 2	0.76 10	1.30 3
Spiritual transformation prepares me for Christ's second coming.	29	0.29 15	0.34 14	0.00 17
The mission of the church is to end poverty in the lives of Christians.	30	-1.27 31	-1.85 35	-1.03 31
Discipleship is teaching Christians to be loyal church members.	31	-0.83 26	-0.55 24	-0.26 20
Not paying my tithes and offerings is forfeiting my blessings.	32	-0.21 18	-0.12 21	1.28 5
The second coming of Christ is the church's blessed hope.	33	0.97 10	0.21 17	0.51 14
Evangelism and discipleship demonstrate Christian mercy.	34	-0.44 20	-1.09 28	-0.76 25
Christians must eagerly anticipate Christ's second coming.	35	1.06 8	0.21 17	0.77 12

Factor Scores For Factor 1

Statement	No.	Z-SCORES
The church's mandate is to make disciples of all nations.	24	1.575
The gospel is that Christ died and rose again for our salvation.	28	1.406
The Holy Spirit guides us to pray according to God's will.	17	1.376
My faith in Christ's death and resurrection makes me a Christian.	14	1.282
The fruit of the Holy Spirit demonstrates my Christian maturity.	15	1.243
Christ calls all Christians to engage in evangelism and discipleship.	3	1.224
Discipleship is teaching Christians to faithfully follow Jesus.	19	1.081
Christians must eagerly anticipate Christ's second coming.	35	1.060
I am a true Christian because I am indwelt by the Holy Spirit.	2	0.976
The second coming of Christ is the church's blessed hope.	33	0.968
Church leaders must demonstrate humility and self-sacrifice.	16	0.914
Pentecostal-Charismatic pastors must practice servant leadership.	25	0.695
Sound biblical doctrine results from disciplined Bible study.	20	0.674
Looking forward to Christ's second coming keeps Christians faithful.	26	0.671
Spiritual transformation prepares me for Christ's second coming.	29	0.289
Not paying my tithes and offerings is robbing God.	4	0.287
A Bible text's meaning intended by the original author applies to me.	21	-0.059
Not paying my tithes and offerings is forfeiting my blessings.	32	-0.214

Pentecostal-Charismatic sermons accurately interpret the Bible.	5	-0.270
Evangelism and discipleship demonstrate Christian mercy.	34	-0.437
Healing the sick is evidence of an anointed man of God.	7	-0.456
As a Christian, I can, by faith, name and claim prosperity.	27	-0.554
Paying my tithes and offerings affirms my Christian faith.	12	-0.689
Pentecostal-Charismatic pastors must exemplify personal success.	22	-0.748
Praying in tongues is more effective than praying silently.	23	-0.782
Discipleship is teaching Christians to be loyal church members.	31	-0.830
Praying aloud in tongues is Spirit-inspired prayer.	6	-0.843
The gospel is that Christ died to deliver us from poverty and disease.	1	-0.943
My active participation in church proves I am a serious Christian.	10	-0.945
A mega church is evidence of the anointing of the man of God.	18	-0.958
The mission of the church is to end poverty in the lives of Christians.	30	-1.273
I must pay my tithes to properly prepare for Christ's second coming.	11	-1.351
As a Christian, suffering should not be my portion in life.	13	-1.413
The gospel is that Christ died to make us rich and successful.	8	-1.446
I am a Christian because I speak in tongues.	9	-1.511

Factor Scores For Factor 2

Statement	No.	Z-SCORES
The Holy Spirit guides us to pray according to God's will.	17	1.642
The fruit of the Holy Spirit demonstrates my Christian maturity.	15	1.554
A Bible text's meaning intended by the original author applies to me.	21	1.343
The church's mandate is to make disciples of all nations.	24	1.306
As a Christian, I can, by faith, name and claim prosperity.	27	1.219
Not paying my tithes and offerings is robbing God.	4	1.182
Christ calls all Christians to engage in evangelism and discipleship.	3	1.095
Discipleship is teaching Christians to faithfully follow Jesus.	19	1.095
Sound biblical doctrine results from disciplined Bible study.	20	0.759
The gospel is that Christ died and rose again for our salvation.	28	0.759
Pentecostal-Charismatic sermons accurately interpret the Bible.	5	0.635
Healing the sick is evidence of an anointed man of God.	7	0.584
Looking forward to Christ's second coming keeps Christians faithful.	26	0.336
Spiritual transformation prepares me for Christ's second coming.	29	0.336
My active participation in church proves I am a serious Christian.	10	0.248
The second coming of Christ is the church's blessed hope.	33	0.212
Christians must eagerly anticipate Christ's second coming.	35	0.212
I am a true Christian because I am indwelt by the Holy Spirit.	2	0.175
Church leaders must demonstrate humility and self-sacrifice.	16	0.000

Pentecostal-Charismatic pastors must exemplify personal success.	22	0.000
Not paying my tithes and offerings is forfeiting my blessings.	32	-0.124
As a Christian, suffering should not be my portion in life.	13	-0.336
I must pay my tithes to properly prepare for Christ's second coming.	11	-0.547
Discipleship is teaching Christians to be loyal church members.	31	-0.547
Praying in tongues is more effective than praying silently.	23	-0.635
Pentecostal-Charismatic pastors must practice servant leadership.	25	-0.635
My faith in Christ's death and resurrection makes me a Christian.	14	-0.883
Evangelism and discipleship demonstrate Christian mercy.	34	-1.095
The gospel is that Christ died to deliver us from poverty and disease.	1	-1.182
Praying aloud in tongues is Spirit-inspired prayer.	6	-1.219
A mega church is evidence of the anointing of the man of God.	18	-1.306
Paying my tithes and offerings affirms my Christian faith.	12	-1.343
The gospel is that Christ died to make us rich and successful.	8	-1.430
I am a Christian because I speak in tongues.	9	-1.554
The mission of the church is to end poverty in the lives of Christians.	30	-1.853

Factor Scores For Factor 3

Statement	No.	Z-SCORES
My faith in Christ's death and resurrection makes me a Christian.	14	1.804
The church's mandate is to make disciples of all nations.	24	1.536
The gospel is that Christ died and rose again for our salvation.	28	1.296
The Holy Spirit guides us to pray according to God's will.	17	1.289
Not paying my tithes and offerings is forfeiting my blessings.	32	1.282
Church leaders must demonstrate humility and self-sacrifice.	16	1.275
Pentecostal-Charismatic pastors must practice servant leadership.	25	1.029
Looking forward to Christ's second coming keeps Christians faithful.	26	1.029
Discipleship is teaching Christians to faithfully follow Jesus.	19	1.022
I am a true Christian because I am indwelt by the Holy Spirit.	2	0.782
Sound biblical doctrine results from disciplined Bible study.	20	0.782
Christians must eagerly anticipate Christ's second coming.	35	0.768
Christ calls all Christians to engage in evangelism and discipleship.	3	0.514
The second coming of Christ is the church's blessed hope.	33	0.514
The fruit of the Holy Spirit demonstrates my Christian maturity.	15	0.254
The gospel is that Christ died to deliver us from poverty and disease.	1	0.000
Spiritual transformation prepares me for Christ's second coming.	29	0.000
Not paying my tithes and offerings is robbing God.	4	-0.254
Healing the sick is evidence of an anointed man of God.	7	-0.261

Discipleship is teaching Christians to be loyal church members.	31	-0.261
The gospel is that Christ died to make us rich and successful.	8	-0.507
My active participation in church proves I am a serious Christian.	10	-0.514
A mega church is evidence of the anointing of the man of God.	18	-0.514
Praying aloud in tongues is Spirit-inspired prayer.	6	-0.528
Evangelism and discipleship demonstrate Christian mercy.	34	-0.761
A Bible text's meaning intended by the original author applies to me.	21	-0.775
As a Christian, I can, by faith, name and claim prosperity.	27	-0.782
Paying my tithes and offerings affirms my Christian faith.	12	-1.015
Pentecostal-Charismatic sermons accurately interpret the Bible.	5	-1.022
Praying in tongues is more effective than praying silently.	23	-1.029
The mission of the church is to end poverty in the lives of Christians.	30	-1.029
Pentecostal-Charismatic pastors must exemplify personal success.	22	-1.282
I am a Christian because I speak in tongues.	9	-1.296
As a Christian, suffering should not be my portion in life.	13	-1.550
I must pay my tithes to properly prepare for Christ's second coming.	11	-1.797

Descending Array of Differences between Factors 1 and 2

Statement	No.	F 1	F 2	Difference
My faith in Christ's death and resurrection makes me a Christian.	14	1.282	-0.883	2.165
Pentecostal-Charismatic pastors must practice servant leadership.	25	0.695	-0.635	1.330
Church leaders must demonstrate humility and self-sacrifice.	16	0.914	0.000	0.914
Christians must eagerly anticipate Christ's second coming.	35	1.060	0.212	0.849
I am a true Christian because I am indwelt by the Holy Spirit.	2	0.976	0.175	0.801
The second coming of Christ is the church's blessed hope.	33	0.968	0.212	0.756
Evangelism and discipleship demonstrate Christian mercy.	34	-0.437	-1.095	0.658
Paying my tithes and offerings affirms my Christian faith.	12	-0.689	-1.343	0.654
The gospel is that Christ died and rose again for our salvation.	28	1.406	0.759	0.648
The mission of the church is to end poverty in the lives of Christians.	30	-1.273	-1.853	0.581
Praying aloud in tongues is Spirit-inspired prayer.	6	-0.843	-1.219	0.376
A mega church is evidence of the anointing of the man of God.	18	-0.958	-1.306	0.348
Looking forward to Christ's second coming keeps Christians faithful.	26	0.671	0.336	0.335
The church's mandate is to make disciples of all nations.	24	1.575	1.306	0.269
The gospel is that Christ died to deliver us from poverty and disease.	1	-0.943	-1.182	0.239
Christ calls all Christians to engage in evangelism and discipleship.	3	1.224	1.095	0.129
I am a Christian because I speak in tongues.	9	-1.511	-1.554	0.043

Discipleship is teaching Christians to faithfully follow Jesus.	19	1.081	1.095	-0.013
The gospel is that Christ died to make us rich and successful.	8	-1.446	-1.430	-0.016
Spiritual transformation prepares me for Christ's second coming.	29	0.289	0.336	-0.047
Sound biblical doctrine results from disciplined Bible study.	20	0.674	0.759	-0.085
Not paying my tithes and offerings is forfeiting my blessings.	32	-0.214	-0.124	-0.089
Praying in tongues is more effective than praying silently.	23	-0.782	-0.635	-0.147
The Holy Spirit guides us to pray according to God's will.	17	1.376	1.642	-0.266
Discipleship is teaching Christians to be loyal church members.	31	-0.830	-0.547	-0.283
The fruit of the Holy Spirit demonstrates my Christian maturity.	15	1.243	1.554	-0.312
Pentecostal-Charismatic pastors must exemplify personal success.	22	-0.748	0.000	-0.748
I must pay my tithes to properly prepare for Christ's second coming.	11	-1.351	-0.547	-0.804
Not paying my tithes and offerings is robbing God.	4	0.287	1.182	-0.895
Pentecostal-Charismatic sermons accurately interpret the Bible.	5	-0.270	0.635	-0.904
Healing the sick is evidence of an anointed man of God.	7	-0.456	0.584	-1.040
As a Christian, suffering should not be my portion in life.	13	-1.413	-0.336	-1.078
My active participation in church proves I am a serious Christian.	10	-0.945	0.248	-1.193
A Bible text's meaning intended by the original author applies to me.	21	-0.059	1.343	-1.402
As a Christian, I can, by faith, name and claim prosperity.	27	-0.554	1.219	-1.773

Descending Array of Differences between Factors 1 and 3

Statement	No.	F 1	F 3	Difference
The fruit of the Holy Spirit demonstrates my Christian maturity.	15	1.243	0.254	0.989
Pentecostal-Charismatic sermons accurately interpret the Bible.	5	-0.270	-1.022	0.752
A Bible text's meaning intended by the original author applies to me.	21	-0.059	-0.775	0.716
Christ calls all Christians to engage in evangelism and discipleship.	3	1.224	0.514	0.710
Not paying my tithes and offerings is robbing God.	4	0.287	-0.254	0.541
Pentecostal-Charismatic pastors must exemplify personal success.	22	-0.748	-1.282	0.535
The second coming of Christ is the church's blessed hope.	33	0.968	0.514	0.453
I must pay my tithes to properly prepare for Christ's second coming.	11	-1.351	-1.797	0.446
Paying my tithes and offerings affirms my Christian faith.	12	-0.689	-1.015	0.326
Evangelism and discipleship demonstrate Christian mercy.	34	-0.437	-0.761	0.324
Christians must eagerly anticipate Christ's second coming.	35	1.060	0.768	0.292
Spiritual transformation prepares me for Christ's second coming.	29	0.289	0.000	0.289
Praying in tongues is more effective than praying silently.	23	-0.782	-1.029	0.247
As a Christian, I can, by faith, name and claim prosperity.	27	-0.554	-0.782	0.228
I am a true Christian because I am indwelt by the Holy Spirit.	2	0.976	0.782	0.194
As a Christian suffering should not be my portion in life.	13	-1.413	-1.550	0.137
The gospel is that Christ died and rose again for our salvation.	28	1.406	1.296	0.110

Statement				
The Holy Spirit guides us to pray according to God's will.	17	1.376	1.289	0.086
Discipleship is teaching Christians to faithfully follow Jesus.	19	1.081	1.022	0.060
The church's mandate is to make disciples of all nations.	24	1.575	1.536	0.039
Sound biblical doctrine results from disciplined Bible study.	20	0.674	0.782	-0.108
Healing the sick is evidence of an anointed man of God.	7	-0.456	-0.261	-0.195
I am a Christian because I speak in tongues.	9	-1.511	-1.296	-0.215
The mission of the church is to end poverty in the lives of Christians.	30	-1.273	-1.029	-0.244
Praying aloud in tongues is Spirit-inspired prayer.	6	-0.843	-0.528	-0.315
Pentecostal-Charismatic pastors must practice servant leadership.	25	0.695	1.029	-0.333
Looking forward to Christ's second coming keeps Christians faithful.	26	0.671	1.029	-0.358
Church leaders must demonstrate humility and self-sacrifice.	16	0.914	1.275	-0.362
My active participation in church proves I am a serious Christian.	10	-0.945	-0.514	-0.431
A mega church is evidence of the anointing of the man of God.	18	-0.958	-0.514	-0.443
My faith in Christ's death and resurrection makes me a Christian.	14	1.282	1.804	-0.522
Discipleship is teaching Christians to be loyal church members.	31	-0.830	-0.261	-0.569
The gospel is that Christ died to make us rich and successful.	8	-1.446	-0.507	-0.939
The gospel is that Christ died to deliver us from poverty and disease.	1	-0.943	0.000	-0.943
Not paying my tithes and offerings is forfeiting my blessings.	32	-0.214	1.282	-1.496

Descending Array of Differences between Factors 2 and 3

Statement	No.	F 2	F 3	Difference
A Bible text's meaning intended by the original author applies to me.	21	1.343	-0.775	2.118
As a Christian, I can, by faith, name and claim prosperity.	27	1.219	-0.782	2.001
Pentecostal-Charismatic sermons accurately interpret the Bible.	5	0.635	-1.022	1.656
Not paying my tithes and offerings is robbing God.	4	1.182	-0.254	1.435
The fruit of the Holy Spirit demonstrates my Christian maturity.	15	1.554	0.254	1.301
Pentecostal-Charismatic pastors must exemplify personal success.	22	0.000	-1.282	1.282
I must pay my tithes to properly prepare for Christ's second coming.	11	-0.547	-1.797	1.250
As a Christian, suffering should not be my portion in life.	13	-0.336	-1.550	1.214
Healing the sick is evidence of an anointed man of God.	7	0.584	-0.261	0.845
My active participation in church proves I am a serious Christian.	10	0.248	-0.514	0.763
Christ calls all Christians to engage in evangelism and discipleship.	3	1.095	0.514	0.580
Praying in tongues is more effective than praying silently.	23	-0.635	-1.029	0.394
The Holy Spirit guides us to pray according to God's will.	17	1.642	1.289	0.352
Spiritual transformation prepares me for Christ's second coming.	29	0.336	0.000	0.336
Discipleship is teaching Christians to faithfully follow Jesus.	19	1.095	1.022	0.073
Sound biblical doctrine results from disciplined Bible study.	20	0.759	0.782	-0.023
The church's mandate is to make disciples of all nations.	24	1.306	1.536	-0.230

I am a Christian because I speak in tongues.	9	-1.554	-1.296	-0.258
Discipleship is teaching Christians to be loyal church members.	31	-0.547	-0.261	-0.287
The second coming of Christ is the church's blessed hope.	33	0.212	0.514	-0.303
Paying my tithes and offerings affirms my Christian faith.	12	-1.343	-1.015	-0.328
Evangelism and discipleship demonstrate Christian mercy.	34	-1.095	-0.761	-0.333
The gospel is that Christ died and rose again for our salvation.	28	0.759	1.296	-0.538
Christians must eagerly anticipate Christ's second coming.	35	0.212	0.768	-0.557
I am a true Christian because I am indwelt by the Holy Spirit.	2	0.175	0.782	-0.608
Praying aloud in tongues is Spirit-inspired prayer.	6	-1.219	-0.528	-0.690
Looking forward to Christ's second coming keeps Christians faithful.	26	0.336	1.029	-0.693
A mega church is evidence of the anointing of the man of God.	18	-1.306	-0.514	-0.792
The gospel is that Christ died to make us rich and successful.	8	-1.430	-0.507	-0.923
The mission of the church is to end poverty in the lives of Christians.	30	-1.853	-0.825	-1.029
The gospel is that Christ died to deliver us from poverty and disease.	1	-1.182	0.000	-1.182
Church leaders must demonstrate humility and self-sacrifice.	16	0.000	1.275	-1.275
Not paying my tithes and offerings is forfeiting my blessings.	32	-0.124	1.282	-1.407
Pentecostal-Charismatic pastors must practice servant leadership.	25	-0.635	1.029	-1.663
My faith in Christ's death and resurrection makes me a Christian.	14	-0.883	1.804	-2.687

Factor Q-Sort Values for Each Statement

Statement	No.	Factor Arrays			
		1	2	3	Jude
The gospel is that Christ died to deliver us from poverty and disease.	1	-2	-2	0	-4*
I am a true Christian because I am indwelt by the Holy Spirit.	2	2	0	1	1
Christ calls all Christians to engage in evangelism and discipleship.	3	2	2	1	1
Not paying my tithes and offerings is robbing God.	4	0	2	0	-1*
Pentecostal-Charismatic sermons accurately interpret the Bible.	5	0	1	-2	-2*
Praying aloud in tongues is Spirit-inspired prayer.	6	-2	-2	-1	0
Healing the sick is evidence of an anointed man of God.	7	0	1	0	-1
The gospel is that Christ died to make us rich and successful.	8	-4	-3	0	-4*
I am a Christian because I speak in tongues.	9	-4	-4	-3	0*
My active participation in church proves I am a serious Christian.	10	-2	0	-1	-2
I must pay my tithes to properly prepare for Christ's second coming.	11	-3	-1	-4	-1*
Paying my tithes and offerings affirms my Christian faith.	12	-1	-3	-2	0*
As a Christian, suffering should not be my portion in life.	13	-3	-1	-4	-3
My faith in Christ's death and resurrection makes me a Christian.	14	3	-2	4	3*
The fruit of the Holy Spirit demonstrates my Christian maturity.	15	3	4	0	0*
Church leaders must demonstrate humility and self-sacrifice.	16	1	0	2	2
The Holy Spirit guides us to pray according to God's will.	17	3	4	3	2

Conclusions and Recommendations

A mega church is evidence of the anointing of the man of God.	18	-2	-3	-1	-1
Discipleship is teaching Christians to faithfully follow Jesus.	19	2	2	2	4
Sound biblical doctrine results from disciplined Bible study.	20	1	1	1	0
A Bible text's meaning intended by the original author applies to me.	21	0	3	-1	1
Pentecostal-Charismatic pastors must exemplify personal success.	22	-1	0	-3	-2
Praying in tongues is more effective than praying silently.	23	-1	-1	-3	0*
The church's mandate is to make disciples of all nations.	24	4	3	4	3
Pentecostal-Charismatic pastors must practice servant leadership.	25	1	-1	2	2*
Looking forward to Christ's second coming keeps Christians faithful.	26	1	1	2	0
As a Christian, I can, by faith, name and claim prosperity.	27	-1	3	-2	-3*
The gospel is that Christ died and rose again for our salvation.	28	4	1	3	4*
Spiritual transformation prepares me for Christ's second coming.	29	0	1	0	3*
The mission of the church is to end poverty in the lives of Christians.	30	-3	-4	-3	-3
Discipleship is teaching Christians to be loyal church members.	31	-1	-1	0	-2
Not paying my tithes and offerings is forfeiting my blessings.	32	0	0	3	-1*
The second coming of Christ is the church's blessed hope.	33	1	0	1	1
Evangelism and discipleship demonstrate Christian mercy.	34	0	-2	-1	1*
Christians must eagerly anticipate Christ's second coming.	35	2	0	1	2
Variance = 4.571 St. Dev. = 2.138					

Factor Q-Sort Values for Statements Sorted by Consensus vs. Disagreement (Variance across Factor Z-Scores)

Statement	Factor Arrays			
	No.	1	2	3
The gospel is that Christ died to deliver us from poverty and disease.	1	-2	-2	0
I am a true Christian because I am indwelt by the Holy Spirit.	2	2	0	1
Christ calls all Christians to engage in evangelism and discipleship.	3	2	2	1
Not paying my tithes and offerings is robbing God.	4	0	2	0
Pentecostal-Charismatic sermons accurately interpret the Bible.	5	0	1	-2
Praying aloud in tongues is Spirit-inspired prayer.	6	-2	-2	-1
Healing the sick is evidence of an anointed man of God.	7	0	1	0
The gospel is that Christ died to make us rich and successful.	8	-4	-3	0
I am a Christian because I speak in tongues.	9	-4	-4	-3
My active participation in church proves I am a serious Christian.	10	-2	0	-1
I must pay my tithes to properly prepare for Christ's second coming.	11	-3	-1	-4
Paying my tithes and offerings affirms my Christian faith.	12	-1	-3	-2
As a Christian, suffering should not be my portion in life.	13	-3	-1	-4
My faith in Christ's death and resurrection makes me a Christian.	14	3	-2	4
The fruit of the Holy Spirit demonstrates my Christian maturity.	15	3	4	0
Church leaders must demonstrate humility and self-sacrifice.	16	1	0	2
The Holy Spirit guides us to pray according to God's will.	17	3	4	3
A mega church is evidence of the anointing of the man of God.	18	-2	-3	-1
Discipleship is teaching Christians to faithfully follow Jesus.	19	2	2	2

Sound biblical doctrine results from disciplined Bible study.	20	1	1	1
A Bible text's meaning intended by the original author applies to me.	21	0	3	-1
Pentecostal-Charismatic pastors must exemplify personal success.	22	-1	0	-3
Praying in tongues is more effective than praying silently.	23	-1	-1	-3
The church's mandate is to make disciples of all nations.	24	4	3	4
Pentecostal-Charismatic pastors must practice servant leadership.	25	1	-1	2
Looking forward to Christ's second coming keeps Christians faithful.	26	1	1	2
As a Christian, I can, by faith, name and claim prosperity.	27	-1	3	-2
The gospel is that Christ died and rose again for our salvation.	28	4	1	3
Spiritual transformation prepares me for Christ's second coming.	29	0	1	0
The mission of the church is to end poverty in the lives of Christians.	30	-3	-4	-3
Discipleship is teaching Christians to be loyal church members.	31	-1	-1	0
Not paying my tithes and offerings is forfeiting my blessings.	32	0	0	3
The second coming of Christ is the church's blessed hope.	33	1	0	1
Evangelism and discipleship demonstrate Christian mercy.	34	0	-2	-1
Christians must eagerly anticipate Christ's second coming.	35	2	0	1

Distinguishing Statements for Factor 1

(P < .05; Asterisk (*) indicates significance at P < .01)
Both the Factor Q-Sort Value (Q-SV) and the Z-Score (Z-SCR) are shown.

Statement		Factors				
		1		2		3	
	No.	Q-SV	Z-SCR	Q-SV	Z-SCR	Q-SV	Z-SCR
A Bible text's meaning intended by the original author applies to me.	21	0	-0.06	3	1.34	-1	-0.78
Pentecostal-Charismatic sermons accurately interpret the Bible.	5	0	-0.27	1	0.63	-2	-1.02

Distinguishing Statements for Factor 2

(P <.05; Asterisk (*) indicates significance at P < .01)
Both the Factor Q-Sort Value (Q-SV) and the Z-Score (Z-SCR) are shown.

Statement		Factors					
		1		2		3	
	No.	Q-SV	Z-SCR	Q-SV	Z-SCR	Q-SV	Z-SCR
A Bible text's meaning intended by the original author applies to me.	21	0	-0.06	3	1.34*	-1	-0.78
Pentecostal-Charismatic sermons accurately interpret the Bible.	27	-1	-0.27	3	1.22*	-2	-0.78
Not paying my tithes and offerings is robbing God.	4	0	0.29	2	1.18	0	-0.25
Pentecostal-Charismatic sermons accurately interpret the Bible.	5	0	-0.27	1	0.63	-2	-1.02
Pentecostal-Charismatic pastors must exemplify personal success.	22	-1	-0.75	0	0.00	-3	-1.28
Church leaders must demonstrate humility and self-sacrifice.	16	1	0.91	0	0.00*	2	1.28
As a Christian, suffering should not be my portion in life.	13	-3	-1.41	-1	-0.34	-4	-1.55
I must pay my tithes to properly prepare for Christ's second coming.	11	-3	-1.35	-1	-0.55	-4	-1.80
Pentecostal-Charismatic pastors must practice servant leadership.	25	1	0.70	-1	-0.63*	2	1.03
My faith in Christ's death and resurrection makes me a Christian.	14	3	1.28	-2	-0.88*	4	1.80

Distinguishing Statements for Factor 3

(P <.05; Asterisk (*) indicates significance at P < .01)
Both the Factor Q-Sort Value (Q-SV) and the Z-Score (Z-SCR) are shown.

Statement		Factors					
		1		2		3	
	No.	Q-SV	Z-SCR	Q-SV	Z-SCR	Q-SV	Z-SCR
Not paying my tithes and offerings is forfeiting my blessing.	32	0	-0.21	0	-0.12	3	1.28*
The fruit of the Holy Spirit demonstrates my Christian maturity.	15	3	1.24	4	1.55	0	0.25*
The gospel is that Christ died to deliver us from poverty and disease.	1	-2	-0.94	-2	-1.18	0	0.00
A Bible text's meaning intended by the original author applies to me.	21	0	-0.06	3	1.34	-1	-0.78
Pentecostal-Charismatic sermons accurately interpret the Bible.	5	0	-0.27	1	0.63	-2	-1.02

Consensus Statements: Those that Do Not Distinguish between ANY Pair of Factors

All listed statements are non-significant at P>.01, and those flagged with an * are also non-significant at P>.05.

Statement		Factors					
		1		2		3	
	No.	Q-SV	Z-SCR	Q-SV	Z-SCR	Q-SV	Z-SCR
I am a true Christian because I am indwelt by the Holy Spirit.	2	2	0.98	0	0.17	1	0.78
Christ calls all Christians to engage in evangelism and discipleship.	3	2	1.22	2	1.09	1	0.51
Praying aloud in tongues is Spirit-inspired prayer.	6*	-2	-0.84	-2	-1.22	-1	-0.53
I am a Christian because I speak in tongues.	9*	-4	-1.51	-4	-1.55	-3	-1.30
Paying my tithes and offerings affirms my Christian faith.	12*	-1	-0.69	-3	-1.34	-2	-1.01
The Holy Spirit guides us to pray according to God's will.	17*	3	1.38	4	1.64	3	1.29
A mega church is evidence of the anointing of the man of God.	18*	-2	-0.96	-3	-1.31	-1	-0.51
Discipleship is teaching Christians to faithfully follow Jesus.	19*	2	1.08	2	1.09	2	1.02
Sound biblical doctrine results from disciplined Bible study.	20*	1	0.67	1	0.76	1	0.78
Praying in tongues is more effective than praying silently.	23*	-1	-0.78	-1	-0.63	-3	-1.03

The church's mandate is to make disciples of all nations.	24*	4	1.58	3	1.31	4	1.54
Looking forward to Christ's second coming keeps Christians faithful.	26*	1	0.67	1	0.34	2	1.03
The gospel is that Christ died and rose again for our salvation.	28*	4	1.41	1	0.76	3	1.30
Spiritual transformation prepares me for Christ's second coming.	29*	0	0.29	1	0.34	0	0.00
The mission of the church is to end poverty in the lives of Christians.	30*	-3	-1.27	-4	-1.85	-3	-1.03
Discipleship is teaching Christians to be loyal church members.	31*	-1	-0.83	-1	-0.55	0	-0.26
The second coming of Christ is the church's blessed hope.	33	1	0.97	0	0.21	1	0.51
Evangelism and discipleship demonstrates Christian mercy.	34*	0	-0.44	-2	-1.09	-1	-0.76
Christians must eagerly anticipate Christ's second coming.	35	2	1.06	0	0.21	1	0.77

Bibliography

Action Faith Ministries International, Prayer Cathedral. http://actionchapel. net/?page_id=3187. (accessed March 2, 2017).

Adeleye, Femi. *Preachers of a Different Gospel: A Pilgrim's Reflections on Contemporary Trends in Christianity*. Carlisle: HippoBooks, 2011.

Adeyemo, Tokunboh. "Jude." Pages 1539–42 in *Africa Bible Commentary*. Nairobi: WordAlive Publishers, 2006.

Akrong, Abraham. "The 'Born Again' Concept in the Charismatic Movement in Ghana." *Evangelical Review of Theology* 35, no. 1 (2011): 31–40.

Aland, Barbara, Kurt Aland, Johannes Karavidopoulos, Carlo Martini M., and Bruce M. Metzger. "The Epistle of Jude." In *The Greek New Testament*, 4th ed. New York: United Bible Societies in co-operation with the Institute for New Testament Textual Research, 1983.

Amanor, Jones Darkwa. "Pentecostalism in Ghana: An African Reformation." *Cyberjournal For Pentecostal-Charismatic Research* 13, no. 1 (2008). www.pctii.org/cyberj/cyberj13/amanor.html.

Amanor, Kwabena J. D. "Pentecostal and Charismatic Churches in Ghana and the African Culture: Confrontation or Compromise?" *Journal of Pentecostal Theology* 18, no. 1 (2009): 123–40.

Amenumey, D. E. K. *Ghana: A Concise History from Pre-Colonial Times to the 20th Century*. Accra: Woeli Publications, 2008.

Anderson, Allan Heaton. *To The Ends of the Earth: Pentecostalism and the Transformation of World Christianity*. Oxford: Oxford University Press, 2013.

Anderson, Gordon L. "Pentecostal Hermeneutics: Part 1." *Paraclete* 28, no. 1 (Winter 1994).

Annorbah-Sarpei, J. "The Rise of Prophetism: A Socio-Political Explanation." In *The Rise of Independent Churches in Ghana*. Accra: Asempa Publishers, 1990.

Michael J. Anthony, ed. *Introducing Christian Education: Foundations for the Twenty-First Century*. Grand Rapids: Baker Academic, 2001.

Antwi, D. J. "A Sense of Community: An African Perspective of the Church as Koinonia." *Trinity Journal of Church and Theology* 6 (1996): 65–71.

Arndt, William, Frederick W. Danker, and Walter Bauer. *A Greek-English Lexicon of the New Testament and Other Early Christian Literature*. Chicago: University of Chicago Press, 2000.

Asamoa, E. A. "The Christian Church and African Heritage." *International Review of Missions* 44, no. 175 (July 1955): 292–301.

Asamoah-Gyadu, J. Kwabena. *African Charismatics: Current Developments within Indigenous Pentecostalism in Ghana*. Achimota: Africa Christian Press, 2005.

———. *Contemporary Pentecostal Christianity: Interpretations from an African Context*. Regnum Studies in Global Christianity. Oxford: Regnum Books International, 2013.

———. "'Go Near and Join Thyself to This Chariot . . .': African Pneumatic Movements and Transformational Discipleship." *International Review of Missions*, 2017, 336–55.

———. *Sighs and Signs of the Spirit: Ghanaian Perspectives on Pentecostalism and Renewal in Africa*. Oxford: Regnum Africa, 2015.

———. "Witchcraft Accusations and Christianity in Africa." *International Bulletin of Missionary Research* 39, no. 1 (2015): 23–27.

Asante, Emmanuel. "The Gospel in Context." *Interpretation: A Journal of Bible and Theology* 55, no. 4 (2001): 355–66.

Atta-Baffoe, Victor. "Ministerial Formation and Theological Education in Ghana: Prospects and Challenges." *Journal of Anglican Studies* 6 (2008): 41–48.

Baeta, C. G. *Prophetism in Ghana: A Study of Some Spiritual Churches*. Achimota: Africa Christian Press, 2004.

William Barclay, ed. *The Letters of John and Jude*. 3rd ed. Louisville: Westminster John Knox Press, 2002.

Barker, Kenneth L., and John R. Kohlenberger. *Expositor's Bible Commentary: New Testament*. Grand Rapids: Zondervan, 1994.

Barker, Peter, and Samuel Boadi-Siaw. *Changed by the Word: The Story of Scripture Union in Ghana*. Accra: Scripture Union Ghana, 2003.

Bauckham, Richard. *Jude–2 Peter*. Vol. 50 of *Word Biblical Commentary*. Edited by David A. Hubbard, Glenn W. Barker, and Ralph P. Martin. Grand Rapids: Zondervan, 1983.

Bevans, Stephen B., and Roger P. Schroeder. *Constants in Context*. Maryknoll: Orbis Books, 2004.

Bigg, Charles. *A Critical and Exegetical Commentary on the Epistles of St. Peter and St. Jude*. Forgotten Books, 2012.

Boa, Kenneth. *Conformed to His Image: Biblical and Practical Approaches to Spiritual Formation*. Grand Rapids: Zondervan, 2001.

———. "Q Methodology." In *Missiological Research: Social Science Draft Version*. Edited by Marvin Gilbert and Alan Johnson. Springfield: Assemblies of God Theological Seminary, 2011.

Braswell, Robert D. "Passing Down Pentecost." *Paraclete: A Journal of Pentecostal Studies* 28, no. 3 (1994): 1–11.

Brown, Steven R. "Q Methodology." *The Sage Encyclopedia of Qualitative Research Methods* 2:699–702. Thousand Oaks: Sage Publications, Inc., 2008.

———. "Q Methodology and Qualitative Research." *Qualitative Health Research* 6, no. 4 (November 1996): 561–67.

Burgess, S. M. "Neo-Charismatics," in *The New International Dictionary of Pentecostal and Charismatic Movements*, ed. by S. M. Burgess. Grand Rapids: Zondervan, 2003.

Church, J. E. *Quest for the Highest: A Diary of the East African Revival*. Exeter: Paternoster, 1981.

Coder, Maxwell S. *Jude: The Acts of the Apostates*. Chicago: Moody Press, 1958.

Debrunner, Hans. *A History of Christianity in Ghana*. Accra: Waterville Publishing House, 1967.

———. *Witchcraft in Ghana: A Study on the Belief in Destructive Witches and Its Effect on the Akan Tribes*. Accra: Presbyterian Book Depot, 1959.

Denscombe, Martyn. *The Good Research Guide*. 4th ed. Maidenhead: Open University Press, 2010.

Dijk, Rijk Van. "Time and Transcultural Technologies of the Self in the Ghanaian Pentecostal Diaspora." In *Between Babel and Pentecost*, eds. Andre Cortan and Ruth Marshall-Fratani. Bloomington: Indiana University Press, 2001.

Dilley, Andrea Palpant. "The Surprising Discovery About Those Colonialist, Proselytizing Missionaries." *Christianity Today*, February 2014.

Douglas, J. D., and Merrill C. Tenney. *New International Bible Dictionary*. Grand Rapids: Zondervan, 1987.

Dunn, James D. G. *Jesus and the Spirit*. London: SCM, 1975.

Edwards, Jeffrey L. "The Literary Structure of Jude and How It Affects the Interpretation of 'The Faith' in Jude 3." Dissertation, Baptist Bible Seminary, 2012.

Ekem, John D. K. "Wesleyan Methodism and Bible Translation in the Gold Coast." In *Christianity, Missions and Ecumenism in Ghana*, ed. J. Kwabena Asamoah-Gyadu. Accra: Asempa Publishers, 2009.

Elliott, John M. "Leadership Development in the Early Church: Jewish and Greco-Roman Background." In *Designing and Implementing Effective Theological Training Models: Supplemental Reader*. Lome: Pan-Africa Theological Seminary, 2010.

Elliston, Edgar J. *Home Grown Leaders*. Pasadena: William Carey Library, 1992.

———. *Introduction to Missiological Research Design*. Pasadena: William Carey Library, 2011.

Ericson, Norman R. "The Theology of Jude." *Baker's Evangelical Dictionary of Biblical Theology*. Grand Rapids: Baker Book House Company, 1996.

Essamuah, Casely. *Genuinely Ghanaian: A History of the Methodist Church Ghana: 1961–2000.* Trenton: Africa World Press, Inc., 2010.
Fee, Gordon D. "1 Corinthians 7:1 in the NIV." *Journal of the Evangelical Theological Society* 23, no. 4 (December 1980): 307–14.
———. *The Disease of the Health and Wealth Gospels.* Vancouver: Regent College Publishing, 2006.
———. *New Testament Exegesis.* 3rd ed. Louisville: Westminster John Knox, 2002.
Fee, Gordon D., and Douglas K. Stuart. *How to Read the Bible Book by Book: A Guided Tour.* Grand Rapids: Zondervan, 2002.
Fee, Gordon D., and Douglas K. Stuart. *How to Read the Bible for All Its Worth.* 3rd ed. Grand Rapids: Zondervan, 2003.
Fee, Gordon D., and Douglas K. Stuart. *How To Read The Bible For All Its Worth.* 4th ed. Grand Rapids: Zondervan, 2014.
Ferdinando, Keith. *The Battle Is God's: Reflecting on Spiritual Warfare for African Believers.* Nairobi: African Christian Textbooks, 2012.
Foli, Richard. *Christianity in Ghana: A Comparative Church Growth Study.* Accra: Trust Publications, 2006.
Gehman, Richard J. *African Traditional Religion in Biblical Perspective.* Kijabe: Kijabe Printing Press, 1993.
———. *Learning to Lead: The Making of a Christian Leader in Africa.* Wheaton: Oasis International, 2008.
Joshua Project. "Ghana." https://joshuaproject.net/countries/GH.
"Ghana: A Profile." http://www.ghana.gov.gh/.
Gifford, Paul. "A View of Ghana's New Christianity." Pages 81–96 in *The Changing Face of Christianity: Africa, the West, and the World.* New York: Oxford University Press, 2005.
———. *African Christianity: Its Public Role.* Bloomington: Indiana University Press, 1998.
———. *Christianity, Development and Modernity in Africa.* London: C. Hurst and Company, 2015.
———. *Christianity, Politics and Public Life in Kenya.* London: Hurst and Company, 2009.
———. "Ghana's Charismatic Churches." *Journal of Religion in Africa* 24, no. 3 (August 1994): 241–65.
———. *Ghana's New Christianity: Pentecostalism in a Globalising African Economy.* London: Hurst and Company, 2004.
Gilbert, Marvin. "Integrative Critical Analysis," n.d. Unpublished Manuscript.
Gilbert, Marvin, and Alan Johnson. "Interdisciplinary Research: An Epistemological Framework in Missiological Research: Social Science Draft Version." Capetown: Published privately, 2011.

Gilbert, Marvin et al. *Research Methods and Proposal Development: Doctoral Study Guide*. Lome: Pan-Africa Theological Seminary, 2014.

Gingrich, F. Wilbur et al. *Shorter Lexicon of the Greek New Testament*. 2nd ed. Chicago: University of Chicago Press, 1983.

Githae, Wanjohi. "Tough Laws to Now Tame Rogue Clergy." *Sunday Nation*. January 3, 2016.

Global Revival Ministries. "History." http://globalrevivalministries.com

Green, Michael. *The Second Epistle of Peter and the General Epistle of Jude: An Introduction and Commentary*. Grand Rapids: Eerdmans, 1975.

Hackett, Rosalind. "Charismatic/Pentecostal Appropriation of Media Technologies in Ghana and Nigeria." *Journal of Religion in Africa* 28, no. 3 (1998): 1–19.

Hanson, Kobena T. "Landscapes of Survival and Escape: Social Networking and Urban Livelihoods in Ghana." *Environment and Planning* 37 (2005): 1291–310.

Harrington, Daniel J. "Jude and 2 Peter." In *Sacra Pagina: 1 Peter, Jude and 2 Peter*. Collegeville: The Liturgical Press, 2003.

Harvey, Robert, and Philip H. Towner. *2 Peter and Jude*. The IVP New Testament Commentary Series. Downers Grove: IVP Academic, 2009.

Hastings, Adrian. *A History of African Christianity, 1950–1975*. African Studies Series 26. Cambridge: Cambridge University Press, 1979.

———. *The Church in Africa: 1450–1950*. Oxford: Oxford University Press, 1996.

Heibert, D. Edmond. "Selected Studies from Jude Part 1: An Exposition of Jude 3–4." *Bibliotheca Sacra* BSAC 142:566 (April 1985).

Hiebert, Paul G., and Eloise Hiebert Meneses. *Incarnational Ministry: Planting Churches in Band, Tribal, Peasant, and Urban Societies*. Grand Rapids: Baker, 1995.

Hiebert, Paul G., R. Daniel Shaw, and Tite Tienou. "Responding to Split-Level Christianity and Folk Religion." *International Journal of Frontier Missions* 16, no. 4 (October 1999).

Hillyer, Norman. *1 & 2 Peter, Jude*. Grand Rapids: Baker, 1992.

Holtum, Colin, and Fey Holtum. *The Cell Church Experience*. Nairobi: SIM Kenya, 2010.

Hughes, Selwyn. *Revival: Times of Refreshing*. Farnham: CWR, 2004.

Hummel, Charles E. *The Prosperity Gospel: Health and Wealth and the Faith Movement*. Downers Grove: InterVarsity Press, 1991.

International Central Gospel Church. http://www.centralgospel.com/?root=about.

Janvier, George E. *Understanding Leadership: An African Christian Model*. Jos: African Christian Textbooks, 1997.

Jenkins, Philip. *The Next Christendom: The Coming of Global Christianity*. Rev. and enl. ed. Oxford: Oxford University Press, 2007.

Johnson, Alan R. *Strategies for Reaching Unreached People Groups: Doctoral Study Guide*. Lome: Pan-Africa Theological Seminary, 2010.

Kalu, Ogbu. *African Pentecostalism: An Introduction*. Oxford: Oxford University Press, 2008.

Kato, Byang H. *Biblical Christianity in Africa: A Collection of Papers and Addresses*. Theological Perspectives in Africa, no. 2. Achimota: Africa Christian Press, 1985.

Keener, Craig S. *Biblical Interpretation: Studying God's Word with Understanding*. Nairobi: SIM Kenya, 2006.

Kelly, J. N. D. *A Commentary on the Epistles of Peter and Jude*. Grand Rapids: Baker, 1981.

Kirby, Jon. "Toward a Christian Response to Witchcraft in Northern Ghana." *International Bulletin of Missionary Research* 39, no. 1 (January 2015): 19–22.

Klein, William W., Craig Blomberg, and Robert L. Hubbard. *Introduction to Biblical Interpretation*. Nashville: Thomas Nelson, 2004.

Koduah, Alfred. *Christianity in Ghana Today*. Accra: Advocate Publishing Ltd, 2004.

Kraft, Charles H. "Culture, Worldview and Contextualization." In *Perspectives on the World Christian Movement*. Edited by Ralph D. Winter and Steven C. Hawthorne, 4th ed. Pasadena: William Carey Library, 2009.

———. "The Development of Contextualization Theory in Euroamerican Missiology." In *Appropriate Christianity*. Edited by Charles H. Kraft. Pasadena: William Carey Library, 2005.

Kraft, Charles H., and Dean S. Gilliland, eds. *Appropriate Christianity*. Pasadena: William Carey Library, 2005.

Krodel, Gerhard. *The General Letters: Hebrews, James, 1–2 Peter, Jude, 1–3 John*. Minneapolis: Fortress, 1995.

Larbi, Emmanuel Kingsley. *Pentecostalism: The Eddies of Ghanaian Christianity*. Studies in African Pentecostal Christianity 1. Dansoman: CPCS, 2001.

———. "The Nature of Continuity and Discontinuity of Ghanaian Pentecostal Concept of Salvation in African Cosmology." *Cyberjournal for Pentecostal-Charismatic Research* 10, no. 1 (2001). http://www.pctii.org/cyberj/cyberj10/larbi.html.

Lawrenz, Mel. *The Dynamics of Spiritual Formation*. Grand Rapids: Baker, 2000.

Lighthouse Chapel International. https://www.churchesdenominationstoday.org/church/index.php/denominations-today/35-lighthouse-chapel-international.

Lowenberg, Douglas P. *Current Issues in New Testament Interpretation*. Lome: Pan-Africa Theological Seminary, 2013.

———. *Reading the Bible with Help from African Pentecostals*. J. Phillip Hogan World Missions Series Monograph No. VI. Springfield: Assemblies of God Theological Seminary, 2012.

Lucas, Dick, and Christopher Green. *The Message of 2 Peter and Jude*. Leicester: Inter-Varsity Press, 1995.
Malcolm, Matthew R. "Premature Triumphalism in Corinth." *The Expository Times* 128, no. 3 (December 1, 2016): 115–25.
Mason, Jim. *God's Challenge in Ghana*. Belleville, Canada: Guardian Books, 2013.
Mayor, Joseph R. *The Epistle of St. John and the Second Epistle of St. Peter*. Grand Rapids: Baker, 1965.
Mbugua, Kenneth et al. *Prosperity? Seeking the True Gospel*. Nairobi: African Christian Textbooks, 2015.
Metzger, Bruce M. *A Textual Commentary on the Greek New Testament*. 2nd ed. New York: United Bible Societies, 2012.
Meyer, Birgit. "Delivered from the Powers of Darkness: Confessions of Satanic Riches in Christian Ghana." *Africa* 65, no. 2 (1995): 236–55.
———. "Pentecostalism and Neo-Liberal Capitalism: Faith, Prosperity and Vision in African-Charismatic Churches." *Journal for the Study of Religion* 20, no. 2 (2007): 5–28.
———. "Praise the Lord: Popular Cinema and Pentecostalite Style in Ghana's New Public Sphere." *American Ethnologist* 31, no. 1 (2004): 92–110.
———. *Translating the Devil: Religion and Modernity Among the Ewe in Ghana*. Edinburgh: Edinburgh University Press, 1999.
Mills, Dag Heward. www.daghewardmills.org.
Moo, Douglas J. *The NIV Application Commentary: 2 Peter and Jude*. Grand Rapids: Zondervan, 1996.
Mounce, William D. *Basics of Biblical Greek Grammar*. 3rd ed. Grand Rapids: Zondervan, 2009.
Musyimi, John. *A Counterfeit Gospel*. Nairobi: Publish4All, 2016.
Neyrey, Jerome H., ed. *2 Peter, Jude: A New Translation with Introduction and Commentary*. The Anchor Bible, v. 37C. New York: Doubleday, 1993.
O'Donovan, Wilbur. *Biblical Christianity in Modern Africa*. Carlisle: Paternoster, 2000.
Omenyo, Cephas. *Pentecost Outside Pentecostalism: A Study of the Development of Charismatic Renewal in the Mainline Churches in Ghana*. Zoetermeer: Boekencentrum Publishing House, 2006.
Oosthuizen, Gerhardus. *The Healer-Prophet in Afro-Christian Churches*. Leiden: Brill, 1992.
Opoku Onyinah. "Deliverance as a Way of Confronting Witchcraft in Modern Africa: Ghana as a Case History." *Cyberjournal For Pentecostal-Charismatic Research*, 2001. http://www.pctii.org/cyberj/cyberj10/onyinah.html.
Osei-Mensah, Gottfried. *Wanted: Servant-leaders: The Challenge of Christian Leadership in Africa Today*. Achimota: Africa Christian Press, 1990.
Packer, J. I. *A Passion For Holiness*. Nottingham: Crossway, 1992.

———. *Keep in Step with the Spirit: Finding Fullness in Our Walk with God*. Grand Rapids: Baker, 2005.
Perez Chapel International. "Founders." https://perezchapel.org/.
Platt, David. *Follow Me*. Carol Stream: Tyndale House, 2013.
Punch, Keith. *Introduction to Research Methods in Education*. Los Angeles: Sage, 2009.
Quayesi-Amakye, Joseph. *Prophetism in Ghana Today: A Study in Ghanaian Pentecostal Prophetism*. Accra: Joseph Quayesi-Amakye, 2013.
Reed, Colin. *Walking in the Light: Reflections on the East African Revival and Its Link to Australia*. Brunswick East: Acorn Press, 2007.
Reinhardt, Bruno. "A Christian Plane of Immanence: Contrapuntal Reflections on Deleuze and Pentecostal Spirituality." *Hau: Journal of Ethnographic Theory* no. 5 (2015): 405–36.
Robbins, Joel. "The Globalization of Pentecostal and Charismatic Christianity." *Annual Review of Anthropology* 33, no. 1 (2004): 117–43.
Robinson, Haddon W. *Biblical Preaching: The Development and Delivery of Expository Messages*. 3rd ed. Grand Rapids: Baker Academic, 2014.
Sanneh, Lamin O. *Disciples of All Nations: Pillars of World Christianity*. New York: Oxford University Press, 2008.
———. *Translating the Message: The Missionary Impact on Culture*. Rev. and enl. ed. American Society of Missiology Series, no. 42. Maryknoll: Orbis Books, 2009.
———. *West African Christianity: The Religious Impact*. Maryknoll: Orbis Books, 1983.
———. *Whose Religion Is Christianity? The Gospel Beyond the West*. Grand Rapids: Eerdmans, 2003.
Schmolck, Peter. "PQMethod," 2014. http://schmolck.userweb.mwn.de/qmethod/pqmanual.htm.
Shaw, Mark R. *Global Awakening: How 20th-Century Revivals Triggered a Christian Revolution*. Downers Grove: IVP Academic, 2010.
———. *The Kingdom of God in Africa: A Short History of African Christianity*. Grand Rapids: Baker, 1998.
Sinclair, Daniel. *A Vision of the Possible: Pioneer Church Planting in Teams*. Downers Grove: InterVarsity Press, 2005.
Smeeton, Donald. *The Church: From Pentecost to the Reformation*. Springfield: Global University, 1999.
Steer, Roger. *George Müller: Delighted in God*. Wheaton: Harold Shaw, 1981.
Stein, Robert H. *A Basic Guide to Interpreting the Bible: Playing by the Rules*. 2nd ed. Grand Rapids: Baker, 2011.
Stevens, Gerald L. *New Testament Greek Intermediate: From Morphology to Translation*. Eugene: Cascade Books, 2008.

Stott, John R. W. *Christian Mission in the Modern World.* London: Falcon Books, 1975.

Swinton, John, and Harriet Mowat. *Practical Theology and Qualitative Research.* London: SCM, 2006.

"The Legislation Providing for the Grant of Independence to Ghana." *Journal of African Law* 1 (Summer 1957): 99–112.

Thiselton, A. C. "Realized Eschatology at Corinth." *New Testament Studies* 24, no. 4 (1978): 510–24.

Turaki, Yusufu. *Foundations of African Traditional Religion and Worldview.* Nairobi: WordAlive Publishers, 2006.

Turner, Harold W. *Religious Innovation in Africa: Collected Essays on New Religious Movements.* Boston: Hall, 1994.

Vander Pol, Mark. "An Over-Realized What?" *Gig Harbor Reformed* (blog), September 30, 2009. https://gigharborreformed.wordpress.com/2009/09/30/an-over-realized-what.

Vyhmeister, Nancy J. *Quality Research Papers for Students of Religion and Theology.* 2nd ed. Grand Rapids: Zondervan, 2008.

Walls, Andrew F. "The Evangelical Revival: The Missionary Movement in Africa." In *Evangelicalism: Comparative Studies of Popular Protestantism in North America, The British Isles, and Beyond, 1700–1990 (Religion in America)*, edited by Mark A. Noll, David Bebbington and George A. Rawlyk. London: Oxford University Press, 1994.

Waltner, Erland, and J. Daryl Charles. *Believers Church Bible Commentary: 1–2 Peter, Jude.* Scottdale: Herald Press, 1999.

Ward, Kevin, and Emma Wild-Wood. *The East African Revival: History and Legacies.* Farnham: Ashgate Publishing Ltd, 2012.

Watson, Daniel F. *Invention, Arrangement and Style: Rhetoric Criticism of Jude and II Peter.* Atlanta: Scholars Press, 1988.

Watts, Simon, and Paul Stenner. "Doing Q Methodology: Theory, Method and Interpretation." *Qualitative Research in Psychology* 2 (2005): 67–91.

Whittaker, Colin C. *Great Revivals.* Springfield: Gospel Publishing House, 1984.

Witte, Marleen De. "Spirit Media: Charismatics, Traditionalists, and Mediation Practices in Ghana." PhD Thesis, University of Amsterdam, 2008.

———. "The Spectacular and the Spirits: Charismatics and Neo-Traditionalists on Ghanaian Television." *Material Religion* 1, no. 3: 314–35.

Woodberry, Robert D. "The Missionary Roots of Liberal Democracy." *American Political Science Review* 106, no. 2 (May 2012): 244–74.

Worthge, Carolyn. "Praying for Prosperity: Pentecostal Christianity and Community Identity in Ghana's Globalizing Economy." Thesis submitted in partial fulfillment of a Bachelor of Arts degree in Sociology/Anthropology, Lewis & Clark College, 2011.

Wright, Christopher J. H. *The Mission of God: Unlocking the Bible's Grand Narrative*. Downers Grove. IVP Academic, 2006.

Wright, Walter. *Relational Leadership*. Carlisle: Paternoster, 2006.

York, John V., and Chip Block. MIS 9253: Leadership and Training Issues in the Context of Global Mission: Doctoral Study Guide. Lome: Pan-Africa Theological Seminary, 2016.

Langham Literature, with its publishing work, is a ministry of Langham Partnership.

Langham Partnership is a global fellowship working in pursuit of the vision God entrusted to its founder John Stott –

to facilitate the growth of the church in maturity and Christ-likeness through raising the standards of biblical preaching and teaching.

Our vision is to see churches in the Majority World equipped for mission and growing to maturity in Christ through the ministry of pastors and leaders who believe, teach and live by the word of God.

Our mission is to strengthen the ministry of the word of God through:
- nurturing national movements for biblical preaching
- fostering the creation and distribution of evangelical literature
- enhancing evangelical theological education

especially in countries where churches are under-resourced.

Our ministry

Langham Preaching partners with national leaders to nurture indigenous biblical preaching movements for pastors and lay preachers all around the world. With the support of a team of trainers from many countries, a multi-level programme of seminars provides practical training, and is followed by a programme for training local facilitators. Local preachers' groups and national and regional networks ensure continuity and ongoing development, seeking to build vigorous movements committed to Bible exposition.

Langham Literature provides Majority World preachers, scholars and seminary libraries with evangelical books and electronic resources through publishing and distribution, grants and discounts. The programme also fosters the creation of indigenous evangelical books in many languages, through writer's grants, strengthening local evangelical publishing houses, and investment in major regional literature projects, such as one volume Bible commentaries like the *Africa Bible Commentary* and the *South Asia Bible Commentary*.

Langham Scholars provides financial support for evangelical doctoral students from the Majority World so that, when they return home, they may train pastors and other Christian leaders with sound, biblical and theological teaching. This programme equips those who equip others. Langham Scholars also works in partnership with Majority World seminaries in strengthening evangelical theological education. A growing number of Langham Scholars study in high quality doctoral programmes in the Majority World itself. As well as teaching the next generation of pastors, graduated Langham Scholars exercise significant influence through their writing and leadership.

To learn more about Langham Partnership and the work we do visit **langham.org**

www.ingramcontent.com/pod-product-compliance
Lightning Source LLC
Chambersburg PA
CBHW070315240426
43661CB00057B/2651